D0896667

ScreenPlay
cinema/videogames/interfaces

ScreenPlay
cinema/videogames/interfaces

edited by geoff king & tanya krzywinska

WALLFLOWER PRESS
LONDON AND NEW YORK

First published in Great Britain in 2002 by
Wallflower Press
5 Pond Street, London NW3 2PN
www.wallflowerpress.co.uk

Copyright © Geoff King & Tanya Krzywinska 2002

The moral right of Geoff King & Tanya Krzywinska to be identified as the editors
of this work has been asserted in accordance with the Copyright, Designs and
Patents Act of 1988

All rights reserved. No part of this publication may be reproduced, stored in
a retrieval system, or transported in any form or by any means, electronic,
mechanical, photocopying, recording or otherwise, without the prior permission
of both the copyright owners and the above publisher of this book.

A catalogue for this book is available from the British Library

ISBN 1-903364-23-X (pbk)
ISBN 1-903364-54-X (hbk)

Printed in Great Britain by Antony Rowe Ltd., Chippenham, Wiltshire

Contents

Notes on Contributors

Dave Bessell is a graduate in composition from the Royal College of Music and is currently studying for a PhD at Kingston University on the relationship between electronic and orchestral music. He has written on technical aspects of music production for popular music magazine *Melody Maker*. His pieces have been performed at the South Bank and in the USA. Notable works include *Grimoire* for orchestra and electronics and *Transmutation* for mixed chamber ensemble.

Jo Bryce is a Lecturer in Psychology at the University of Central Lancashire. Her research interests include technological development and changing leisure practice, gender and leisure, and the social and psychological aspects of computer gaming. With Jason Rutter, she is currently working on the Digiplay Initiative (www.digiplay.org.uk), a broad-ranging investigation of computer gaming as a contemporary leisure activity from the perspective of the individual, the community and the computer games industry.

Derek A. Burrill recently completed his PhD in Contemporary Performance and Culture at the University of California, Davis. He is currently a lecturer at both U.C. Davis and San Jose State University.

Diane Carr is a researcher at the Institute of Education, University of London, where she is analysing aspects of textuality, play and narrative in computer games. Her background is in visual arts practice, womens' studies and film theory. Research interests include gendered pleasures and identity politics, acquired deafness and spatial cognition, and science fiction movies. Diane is currently playing *Baldur's Gate* and *Shenmue*.

Margit Grieb is a PhD candidate in German Studies at the University of Florida. She is currently completing her dissertation titled 'New Media and Established Systems of Representation'. She has written and presented papers on Wim Wenders' feature films, Valie Export's multimedia projects, and the Internet as a medium for foreign language teaching.

Sacha A. Howells has written for and about videogames since 1995, working on games such as *MechWarrior2: Ghost Bear's Legacy, Apocalypse,* and *Heavy Gear,* and covering the game industry for the online commer-zine *CheckOut.com.* He continues to write about technology, entertainment, and freedom of speech issues.

Leon Hunt is a Senior Lecturer in Film and TV Studies at Brunel University, London. He is the author of *British Low Culture: From Safari Suits to Sexploitation* (Routledge, 1998), and has published work on martial arts films, Italian horror, and action TV. He is currently writing a book about kung fu movies for Wallflower Press.

Stephen Keane is a Lecturer in Film and Media at Bretton Hall, University of Leeds. He is the author of *Disaster Movies: The Cinema of Catastrophe* (Wallflower Press, 2001) and is currently working on a book on Cyberculture for Polity Press.

Geoff King is Course Director in Film and TV Studies at Brunel University, London. He is the author of *Spectacular Narratives: Hollywood in the Age of the Blockbuster* (I.B. Tauris, 2000), *New Hollywood Cinema: An Introduction* (I.B. Tauris, 2002), *Film Comedy* (Wallflower Press, 2002) and, jointly with Tanya Krzywinska, *Science Fiction Cinema: From Outerspace to Cyberspace* (Wallflower Press, 2000).

Tanya Krzywinska is a Senior Lecturer in Film and TV Studies at Brunel University, London. She is the author of *A Skin for Dancing In: Possession, Voodoo and Witchcraft in Film* (Flicks Books, 2000), co-author, with Geoff King, of *Science Fiction Cinema* (Wallflower Press, 2000), has had articles on pornography, *Buffy the Vampire Slayer,* melodrama and the horror genre published, and is currently working on a book-length project entitled *Sex in the Cinema* for Wallflower Press.

Andrew Mactavish is Assistant Professor of Multimedia in the School of the Arts at McMaster University, Ontario, Canada, where he teaches courses in the theory and practice of multimedia. His research interests include digitally interactive art and entertainment, computer game culture, hypertext theory, humanities computing, and streaming media. He is a research member of IRIS (Infrastructure for Research on Internet Streaming), a project funded by the Canada Foundation for Innovation. One of his current projects is a book-length study of technological pleasure and interactive digital culture.

Sue Morris is a PhD candidate in Media and Cultural Studies at the University of Queensland, Brisbane, Australia, researching online multiplayer computer game culture. Her other research interests include identity and interaction within virtual environments, gender and computer games, and moral panics concerning computer games and new media. She co-edited the 'game' issue of *M/C — A Journal of Media and Culture* (www.media-culture.org.au/archive.html#game) and publishes the *Game Culture* webpage (www.game-culture.com). She is a dedicated gamer and founder of Australia's first all-female *Quake II* clan.

Jason Rutter is a Research Fellow at the ESRC-funded Centre for Research on Innovation and Competition at the University of Manchester. His research interests include social aspects of e-commerce, computer gaming, sociability in online communities and humour research. With Jo Bryce he is currently working on the Digiplay Initiative (www.digiplay.org.uk), a broad-ranging investigation of computer gaming as a contemporary leisure activity from the perspective of the individual, the community and the computer games industry.

Marcus Cheng Chye Tan is currently pursuing an Accelerated Master of Arts (English Literature) by research following his Bachelor of Arts degree with Honours in English Literature (National University of Singapore). His dissertation deals with the interaction of music in the semiology of performance with specific regard to Shakespeare. Although his main interest lies in Shakespearean studies, other research interests include medieval literature, psychoanalysis, and popular culture.

Paul Ward lectures in Film and Television Studies at Brunel University, London. He is also completing doctoral research into animation, film studies and higher education at the Institute of Education, University of London. He is the author of *Defining 'animation': the animated film and the emergence of the film bill* (*Scope: An Online Journal of Film Studies*, 2000) and is currently working on a book on documentary for Wallflower Press.

Wee Liang Tong graduated with Honours in English Literature and is currently pursing a Master of Arts (English Literature) by research at the National University of Singapore. His dissertation is on Language Poetry and Critical Theory. The study of popular culture, including film and computer games, is among his other research interests.

Tomb Raider (2001), the big-screen debut of the most famous icon of the contemporary gaming world. Synergies between film and game production are regular occurrences. Most, if not all, Hollywood studios have at some point diversified into the games market, while the software house Squaresoft recently generated a film production arm, Square Pictures (*Final Fantasy: The Spirits Within* (2001)). In some cases the two media operate in parallel in the process of exploiting a single franchise, as in the simultaneous international release of the film and multi-platform videogame versions of *Harry Potter and the Philosopher's Stone* (titled *Harry Potter and the Sorcerer's Stone* in the US) in November 2001. The interface between cinema and games extends well beyond the direct spin-off or industrial convergence, however. Many games draw on cinematic devices, tropes and associations in a more diffuse manner. Games have become a point of reference for some films and have contributed to the framing of some arguments about the state of contemporary Hollywood cinema, especially. Some similar issues have been explored in relation to both media forms. An overlap exists between the worlds of cinema and games, but there are also many important differences and distinctions. Games based on films, or games that draw more generally on particular cinematic devices, remain games rather than films; they have to be understood in their own right, according to their own logics, as well as in relation to other media. Likewise, films based on games or films that might appear to have been influenced by some aspects of game structure. The aim of this collection is to explore the relationship between cinema and videogames in the hope of increasing our understanding of points of both contact and divergence.

The principal focus of most of the contributors to this volume is on games-in-the-light-of-cinema, rather than vice-versa. One reason for this emphasis is the relative underdevelopment of videogames as a field for close formal or textual analysis, a situation that has only recently shown evidence of much change. Videogames have been in existence for more than four decades. They have been a significant commercial phenomenon since the early 1970s and increasingly so during the 1980s, 1990s, and early 2000s.[2] The majority of studies of games produced in previous decades have been from sociological or psychological perspectives, responding in many cases to broader social 'concern' about games and their potential 'effects', especially on children. Fuelled by the dramatic growth of games in the youth market, old anxieties about the 'harmful' effects of youth culture have been given a fresh airing. Academic and media interest in games have also tended to focus on issues of representation, particularly the intersection between games, gender and the kinds of values games are said to embody (on issues of gender, see essays in this volume by Derek Burrill and Diane Carr). Such approaches have in the past tended to pay relatively little attention to the specific qualities of games, including formal subtleties that shape or contextualise the experience of any given title. The study of videogames in their own right — as particular kinds of textual systems that operate in their own distinctive ways — has been less common, so much so that one prominent figure declared 2001 to be the 'Year One' of computer games studies as an emerging academic field (Aarseth, 'Computer Game Studies, Year One'). The emphasis of this collection is also the outcome of our specific interests, as editors, coming to games from the more established discipline of film studies with an interest in, and enthusiasm for, games as a relatively new and important entertainment medium. Three principal questions underlie the agenda set by the book:

- the extent to which some games can be understood in terms similar to those used in the analysis of film

- the extent to which such games also diverge from film, sometimes radically, in a manner important to our understanding of how games function distinctively as games (and, by implication, of how cinema functions distinctively as cinema)

- the extent to which the examination of games in the light of cinema might also encourage us to question some of the ways we understand cinema itself (a question addressed implicitly more than explicitly in this collection and to which more attention might be directed elsewhere)

Our choice of focus on the relationship between games and cinema is in no way designed to stake any grand claim on behalf of cinema, or film theory, as a privileged perspective on games. Cinema is an important point of reference for many games, we argue, as do most of our contributors. But the extent to which this is the case varies from one game to another. Many games, and many types of game, clearly have very little point of contact with cinema or the cinematic. Examples range from abstract or puzzle games such as *Pac-Man* (Midway, 1980) and *Tetris* (Pajitnov, 1989) to the innumerable driving or other sports-based simulation games, and many others, including multi-player online games. The focus of this collection is not on all games, but only those that might, in various ways, be understood to some extent with reference to cinema. Perspectives drawn from the study of film offer one set of tools with which to approach some videogames, we argue: no more than that. This is not designed to be an 'imperialist' enterprise, seeking to claim the relatively unsettled territory of games largely or exclusively for film-oriented approaches. Such an approach could be possible, following the previous tendency to apply literary theory to earlier generations of text-based games (for criticism of this process, see Aarseth 1997). With the movement of adventure-type games from text to pictures and subsequently to three-dimensional graphics, a process that started in the early 1980s, a displacement of literary theory by film theory might seem inevitable; one colonising set of paradigms being replaced by another that seems closer to the particular formal qualities of more recent generations of games. One of the concerns of this collection is to avoid any such tendency by carefully establishing the parameters within which it is appropriate or otherwise to examine the one medium in the light of the other. Contemporary cinema and videogames are both part of the same audio-visual media landscape, however, which might suggest some broader reasons for considering the nature of the specific relationship that exists between the two, among others. For Jay David Bolter and Richard Grusin (1999), for example, the points of contact between

3

cinema and games are typical of those found more generally between newer and more established media forms.

Digital media such as videogames, Bolter and Grusin suggest, tend to 'borrow avidly from each other as well as from their analog predecessors such as film, television, and photography' (1999: 9). Such borrowings, termed 'remediation' by Bolter and Grusin, can occur in both directions. Games remediate aspects of cinema (including certain forms of plotting or point-of-view structures), while cinema, in return, remediates aspects of games (especially in the use of digital graphics in special effects). The outcome of the process of remediation, in their account, is a dialectical exchange between 'immediacy' and 'hypermediacy', a process that helps to illuminate the relationship that sometimes exists between cinema and games. Immediacy is based on the creation of an impression of 'liveness' or 'presence'; hypermediacy on an awareness of active mediation, often through a consciousness of the process in which one medium draws on devices associated with another. The impression of immediacy created in some games 'is generated in large part by the player's expectations derived from the medium of film' (1999: 98). A sense of presence can be defined in terms of 'inhabiting' or exploring a digitally produced landscape that evokes some of the characteristics of cinema. The possibility of seeming to move 'inside' the fictional world on screen is sometimes seen as a defining characteristic of games, especially those based recognisably on individual films, franchises or film genres. The player can, at one remove, 'become' the central figure in a cinematic environment, following and extending the kinds of experiences offered in film. *Aliens vs. Predator 2* (Sierra/Fox Interactive, 2001),[3] for example, can be played as either marine, alien or predator. The world of the film is extended in terms of both interactivity and variation of perspective/allegiance. A novelty offered by the sequel is the ability to experience the world of the alien through its entire life-cycle; the opportunity to take on the first-person point-of-view of lowly forms such as the 'face-hugger' and the 'chest-burster', to inhabit the world of the alien franchise from a position very different from that available in the films.

A sense of immediacy, here, is closely tied up with the process of hypermediacy. The sense of presence exists at a second-order level: presence within another form of mediation, specifically, in this case, that of cinema. As Bolter and Grusin put it in an analysis of *Myst* (Cyan/Broderbund, 1993), that can be applied more widely, the game satisfies the viewer's desire for immediacy 'by seeming to put her in a film. Her sense of immediacy comes only through an awareness of mediation' (1999: 98). The cinematic dimension, in this case, is a substantial component of the specific experience offered by the game as a game, and not merely something imported externally as a weak form of comparison between one medium and another.

The latter is always a danger in the use of one medium as a point of reference in the study of another. A direct parallel can be suggested, again, between the use of film and literature-based approaches in relation to games, particularly as both tend to place emphasis on narrative. Terms relevant to film can easily be substituted for the references to literature in the following complaint by Espen Aarseth:

Figure 1 First-person clawer: taking on the perpective of the alien in *Aliens vs. Predator 2* (Sierra/Fox Interactive, 2001)

Two of the most common approaches to adventure games seem to be apologetics and trivialization. Both generally fail to grasp the intrinsic qualities of the genre, because they both privilege the aesthetic ideals of another genre, that of narrative literature, typically the novel. For the apologists, adventure games may one day — when their Cervantes or Dickens comes along — reach their true potential, produce works of literary value that rival the current narrative masterpieces, and claim their place in the canon. For the trivialists, this will never happen; adventure games are games — they cannot possibly be taken seriously as literature nor attain the level of sophistication of a good novel. Although the trivialists are right — adventure games will never become good novels — they are also making an irrelevant point, because adventure games are not novels at all. The adventure game is an artistic genre of its own, a unique aesthetic field of possibilities, which must be judged on its own terms. And while the apologists are certainly wrong, in that the games will never be considered good novels, they are right in insisting that the genre may improve and eventually turn out something rich and wonderful. This may or may not happen, so the only way to understand the genre is to study the various works that already exist and how they are played. (1997: 106–7)

To judge or appraise games in terms of their 'cinematic' qualities, shortcomings or potentials, is, as Aarseth suggests, often to miss the point: that they are

5

games, first and foremost, rather than attempts to be something else. And games are very different entities from media such as books or films, an issue to which we return in more detail below. Games have goals and rules that involve the player in a form of challenge, the outcome of which varies from one playing-experience to another. Existing games should be studied in their own terms, the criteria for which might diverge considerably from those relevant to cinema. In some cases, however — in particular games, types of game, or particular aspects of some games — reference to the cinematic is clearly part of the repertoire of the game itself. A major novelty selling point of the third-person action-adventure game *Max Payne* (Remedy/GodGames, 2001), for example, is the use of slow-motion 'bullet-time' and 'bullet-dodge' modes that enable shoot-out action to be slowed down to a point at which the player can dodge bullets, a direct lift from the John Woo style of Hong Kong action cinema and, more specifically, the use of the device in Hollywood in *The Matrix*.

Max Payne is also sold on the basis of providing fast-paced, story-driven gameplay with cinematic cut-frame sequences more tightly integrated into the experience than has been usual in the genre. Each of these selling points is predicated on the assumption that, in a case such as this, 'more cinematic' equals 'better' and more distinctive gameplay, a judgement accepted by many reviewers.[4] What is required on our part here is a sense of balance: reference to the cinematic where it is appropriate, combined with sensitivity to aspects

Figure 2 Balletic death in slo-mo, John Woo style: *Max Payne* (Remedy/GodGames, 2001)

of games that obey different or competing logics. One of the benefits of examining games in the light of cinema, if done in a non-imperialist manner, is the opportunity any such comparison offers to highlight differences as well as similarities. It is when compared in close detail with cinema — or any other medium — that some of the most distinctive characteristics of games might come to light, just as some of the characteristics of cinema might also be underlined through comparison with games.

If some games remediate aspects of cinema, they also draw on features from a range of other media not considered in detail in this collection. Three-dimensional graphics draw, ultimately, on traditions of 'realistic' perspective painting (see Bolter & Grusin 1999: 94), a precedent that underlies the generation and visual style of 3D gaming environments facilitated by developments in graphics card technology. Television is another obvious point of reference in many games, often more so than cinema (for more on this see Bolter & Grusin 1999: 93). *The Sims* (EA, 2000), for example, draws on formats such as soap opera; the various *Who Wants to be a Millionaire?* games are based more directly on the game show of the same name. If cinema is the remediated form to which attention is most often drawn, by the industry as well as by commentators such as those gathered in this collection, the reason is probably the greater cultural prestige possessed by both cinema (as an institution) and film (as a medium of expression). Or, if not prestige — to which painting might seem to have larger claim — then at least a form of contemporary cachet, of 'coolness' or 'sexiness', to the likely target audience (relatively youthful and probably of greater than average contemporary media-literacy). The 'cinematic', in general, enjoys a standing higher in our dominant cultural hierarchies than the 'televisual' or the qualities associated with videogames, a factor that adds to its potential appeal to the games industry.

The positive benefits of such associations are far from guaranteed, however. Many gamers and game reviewers are, not unreasonably, suspicious of directly movie-linked games, many of which are viewed as transparent attempts to cash in on successful movie franchises with products that lack much in the way of compelling gameplay of their own. *Evil Dead: Hail to the King* (Heavylron/THQ, 2001) is a recent example that generated a high level of interest yet was roundly received as disappointingly repetitive, un-engaging and unable to reflect the innovation, pace and humour of the *Evil Dead* films. Highly rated direct movie tie-in games are relatively few and far between, notable exceptions including the James Bond title *GoldenEye* (Rare/Nintendo, 1997), the subject of an essay in this collection by Derek Burrill.

At the level of industry more generally, the linking together of cinema and games is far from arbitrary in an environment in which some of the key producers and distributors of both forms of entertainment are located within the same media corporations and in which game spin-offs offer substantial additional revenues to the Hollywood studios. At the larger, corporate level, the Sony Corporation is the most obvious example, home to both Sony Pictures and the PlayStation games platforms. In the year ending March 2000, sales and operating revenue accounted for $4.6 billion from pictures and $5.9 billion from games (Sony, Annual

Report, 2000). On a smaller, more independent corporate scale, companies that form part of the empire of George Lucas, the creator of the lucrative Star Wars franchise, include the original Lucasfilm and LucasArts Entertainment, a major developer of game software for a variety of platforms. Universal Studios signed a five-year licensing agreement with the games developers Konami to produce film spin-off games including *The Mummy* (2000), *The Grinch* (2000), *The Thing* (2002) and *Jurassic Park 3* (2003) (P2, 2000a). Whether licensing deals for film tie-ins are negotiated in-house or with outside developers, games represent a significant source of profits for the studios. The numerous Star Wars games developed by LucasArts generated revenues of more than $450 million during the 1990s (these and the following details are from Donahue & Swanson 2000: 9, 74). James Bond games developed by Electronic Arts, in conjunction with the studio MGM/UA and the production house Danjaq, achieved sales of $250 million in the three years to December 2000. Studio owners of the rights to titles usually take from 10 to 20 per cent of the profits earned by spin-off games, in addition to licensing fees paid in advance.

In addition to such earnings, tie-in games are also valued by Hollywood as a way of attracting new audiences for major properties such as the Bond franchise, particularly via the youth market. Exit polling conducted during screenings of *The World Is Not Enough* (1999) suggested that games had helped to broaden the audience 'to include a whole new generation of Bond collectors', according to David Bishop of the MGM home entertainment group (quoted by Donahue & Swanson 2000: 74). The development and production process required by games has also come to take on some of the characteristics, and scale, of the film business. Very much on the model of contemporary Hollywood, the games industry has become a strongly hit-driven business. The bulk of profits are earned by a small number of increasingly expensive top-selling titles. Fewer than 5 per cent of some 6,000 games released each year make money, according to the *Financial Times* (14 August 2001), a commercial dynamic that tends not to encourage innovation (for more on this see interviews with game designers Chris Crawford and Jordan Mechner in Rouse 2001: 270–1, 369–70). Game design and programming has moved from a small-scale enterprise to an effort requiring many separate skills, development typically over a period of about two years and Hollywood-style budgets running up to tens of millions of dollars (see Poole 2000: 86). The games industry also shares with Hollywood the continued use of individual 'author' names, in some cases, to sell products within the more anonymous corporate context. Some programmers have gained high-profile status within the gaming community – individuals such as John Carmack, creator of the game engines *Quake* (1996) and *Doom III* (forthcoming), built by id Software. A figure such as Carmack might be seen as the games equivalent of a high-status 'auteur' in the film business, working collectively with many others but with his name carrying a marketable cachet, signifying a certain level of quality in any individual product to which it is attached. Other examples include the addition of possessive 'auteur' credits to the titles of games such as *American McGee's Alice* (Rogue/Electronic Arts, 2001), sold on the name of the designer, and *Clive Barker's Undying* (Electronic Arts, 2001), sold on the basis of associations with the author-figure's work in the same genre (horror) in other media.

Films based on games are less common, for reasons considered below. They have not tended to achieve the greatest commercial or critical success. Most of the leading adaptations in the 1990s — with the exception of *Mortal Kombat* (1995) which grossed $100 million — were considered to be underachievers at the box office, titles including *Super Mario Brothers* (1993), *Street Fighter* (1994) and *Wing Commander* (1999) (Hazelton 2000: 1). *Lara Croft: Tomb Raider* had an impressive opening weekend ($47.7 million), grossing $130 million in the US by the end of the summer of 2001, a healthy if far from blockbuster performance on a budget of $80 million. *Final Fantasy: The Spirits Within* fared much less well, costing some $137 million and taking only $11.4 million in its opening weekend in America (figures from the Internet Movie DataBase). Crossing over into film can still be a source of substantial licensing revenue for games producers, however, as well as providing an opportunity to give games the higher-profile and higher-prestige media coverage usually gained by cinema releases.

The regulation of films and games is often separate, on the basis of assumptions about their distinct nature as forms of popular entertainment, although similar principles often apply at the industrial level. The regulation of videogames is covered in Britain by the joint efforts of the Video Standards Council (VSC) and European Leisure Software Publishers Association (ELSPA). The VSC, an independent body set up by government, was instrumental in establishing a rating system designating the age groups for which individual games are deemed to be suitable. This is intended to 'protect' potential gamers from allegedly harmful effects, but also to insulate the industry from both damaging publicity and any stronger forms of outside regulation; very much the same kind of dynamic as that found in the certification of films and videos. Collaboration between the two bodies is also intended to preserve the exemption of games from the provisions of the 1984 Video Recordings Act, which require all films and videos to be submitted to either the British Board of Film Classification (BBFC) or the VSC for rating.

So far, the regulatory framework has recognised a clear distinction between games and films or videos, on the basis of their status as less 'realistic' forms of representation. This could come under threat, however, with the development of high-specification graphics technologies. Games would lose their exemption if they depicted 'realistic scenes of gross violence or sexual activity', according to advisory comments by ELSPA on its code of practice. How this issue will be negotiated remains to be seen, but it is in the interest of the games industry to seek to maintain the status quo. Individual games have in the past lost their exception without jeopardising the situation more generally. Some violent games have been submitted voluntarily for rating by the BBFC, which might demand cuts or other changes in order to grant a title a particular classification. The same criteria are used by the BBFC for games as for films or videos. The *Doom, Resident Evil* and *Quake* series were all voluntarily submitted to the BBFC and, with the exception of *Resident Evil*, which was rated 18, gained 15 certificates. BBFC classification is not required for games to be released, however. *Carmageddon* (SCI, 1997), for example, was voluntarily submitted in 1997 and refused certification in its original form because, in the BBFC's opinion, 'the pleasures on offer were killing for kicks'. It was still released in Britain, having been deemed acceptable by the VSC and with ELSPA claiming the exemption under the Video Recordings Act.

In the US videogames are also subject to regulation at a voluntary level from within the industry by the Entertainment Software Rating Board (ESRB), established in 1994 by the Interactive Digital Software Association (IDSA). Violent games are usually assigned an Mi (Mature Interactive, 17+) or Ai (Adult interactive, over 18) classification, the restrictive categories being imposed on games judged to use 'realistic' violence that does not enhance the objectives of the game. The ESRB notes that 70 per cent of games submitted are rated as Ei for everyone. The effectiveness of the Board came under scrutiny (along with a number of other aspects of popular culture) in the wake of the Columbine High School massacre in 1999. President Clinton requested a report from the Federal Trade Commission to appraise the evidence of the 'effects' of violent video games. Here, as in Britain and the rest of Europe, self-regulation is used to protect the industry from the effects of changes in government and local policy; a strategy that has its origins in the system used to regulate cinema from the late 1920s. More direct state regulation is found in some contexts, as in Australia, where all games are rated by the Office of Film and Literature Classification (OFLC), which is directly answerable to the government. In 1995 it was agreed at government level that games should be treated more strictly than films, with no 'adults-only' rating permitted. This has not had the impact on availability that might be expected, however, because the ratings themselves are more liberal, with games currently rated as 18 in Britain gaining an M15+ certificate under the Australian system.

What, though, are the broad points of contact, and departure, between cinema and games at the aesthetic, formal or textual level, or in the kinds of experiences offered to viewer/player? The following is an initial sketch of some key issues, most of which are taken up in more detail in the essays that follow.

Associations with cinema or the cinematic, beyond the immediate film adaptation, can be found in games at a variety of different levels. These range from broad categories, types or genres to minor detail or the use of more specific formal devices. Genre is an obvious point of contact, with many of the more film-oriented games occupying territory familiar from the generic categories of cinema — and often drawing on devices specific to these genres in the cinema, rather than elsewhere — prominent examples being action-adventure, horror, science fiction and war. If some games are direct spin-offs, such as the James Bond titles, others occupy similar generic territory, an example being the Bond-like *No One Lives Forever* (Monolith/Fox Interactive, 2000), examined in the essay in this collection by Wee Liang Tong and Marcus Cheng Chye Tan. The process at work here — between games and films and between games and other games — is much the same as that found in Hollywood, in which successful formats, sometimes related to particular franchises owned by an individual studio, are copied by others; a process in which the specific, copyright-protected brand item becomes the basis for a wider genre or sub-genre to which all producers have access (for more on this in relation to film, see Altman 1999). The horror genre, similarly, contains many games that draw generally on the qualities and atmospherics of the horror film, or a particular sub-genre, as well as on specific films (see essay by Tanya Krzywinska). The action-movie format is another frequent point of reference for games (see essay by Geoff King), especially given its suitability for the specifically gamic ability to position the player in a pro-active relation to events.

Action-adventure-type games tend to draw on a restricted number of familiar milieux, 'a few basic templates', as Steven Poole puts it, that are sometimes rooted in the production designs of individual films:

> There is the blasted, neon-lit *Blade Runner* cityscape; the dank metal corridors with exposed piping, steam vents and unpredictable lighting are straight from *Alien*; steel catwalks and pools of orange molten metal ring the *Terminator* bell. Cute, unthreatening worlds in primary colours come straight from animated cartoons. (Poole 2000: 224)

The appeal of such environments is partly their cinematic association but also, as Poole suggests, the more prosaic fact that stylised landscapes, such as those of tech-noir, science fiction and horror, lend themselves to the limited and particular representational capacities of games (especially where priority in the use of processing resources is given to gameplay rather than the detailed quality of backgrounds). In the case of the *Blade Runner* look:

> The night-time setting meant the processor had less to draw, could fill large areas of the scene with black; neon lighting is gaudy and luminous in a way that computer graphics can easily imitate; and the absence of vegetation freed the machine from the very processor-hungry task of creating a convincing tree with hundreds of leaves and different shades of green. (Poole 2000: 88–9)

Design decisions driven by the need to be economic in the use of graphics processing resources can result directly in the creation of effective gameplay, as in the use of fog to save on the reproduction of background detail but also to establish the characteristic atmospherics and tension of *Silent Hill* (Konami, 1999). Developments in real-time image-processing have increased considerably the ability of games to recreate organic shapes, dynamic real-time lighting effects and more complex textures, although a limited repertoire of settings (often involving sparse industrial interiors littered with boxes) is still found in many titles.

The most obvious links between games and cinema are the 'cut-scenes' found in many games: short, 'pre-rendered' audio-visual sequences in which the player usually performs the role of more detached observer than is the case in the more active periods of gameplay. Many games use cut-scenes to establish the initial setting and background storyline. Most are entirely animated, although

Figure 3 Gameplay screen, *Halo* (Bungie/Microsoft, 2002)

some use live action characters married with animation, as in *Emperor: Battle for Dune* (Westwood Studios/Electronic Arts, 2001).

Opening cut-scenes frequently employ the same expository devices as cinema, using a combination of long shots, mid-shots and close-ups to provide orientation for the player. Cut-scenes are also used at varying intervals throughout many games, to forward the storyline and to reward players with sequences of spectacular action and/or dialogue. They may be used to provide clues or to establish enigmas that have a bearing on the trajectory of the game. Lengthy cut-scenes often feature at the end of a game, as in the *Tomb Raider* series (Core/Eidos, 1996–2000) and *Max Payne*. Critics of the use of cinema as a reference point for games often suggest that cut-scenes provide the only formal connection between the two because they are freer than interactive sequences to use the particular kinds of framing, editing or music associated with film (on the use of music, see the essay by David Bessell; on cut-scenes more generally see Sacha Howells, Krzywinska, Wee and Tan). There has, to date, usually been a clearly visible gap between the higher quality of graphics found in cut-scenes and the lower-quality images that characterise more interactive periods of gameplay. This gap is being reduced, however, with the introduction of more powerful graphics processors, as in *Halo* (Bungie/Microsoft, 2002), one of the games used to launch Microsoft's X-Box console, in which the difference between image quality of cut-scenes and gameplay is negligible (see figures 3 and 4).

Cinematic devices can also be used as a reference point for a number of other formal qualities found in games, whether in terms of similarity or difference. Issues of point-of-view are central to both media. Pre-rendered camera angles are used during gameplay in some third-person shooter games, including *Dino*

Figure 4 Cut-scene, *Halo* (Bungie/Microsoft, 2002)

Crisis (Capcom, 1999), the *Resident Evil* games (Capcom, 1997, 1998, 1999) and, to a lesser extent, the *Tomb Raider* series. Predetermined framing of this kind acts like that of a film, to some extent, directing the attention of the player and creating visual diversity through shifts of perspective, although at the expense of player freedom (see Krzywinska essay for more on this in relation to *Resident Evil 3: Nemesis*). Such devices are not found in first-person shooters or games designed to be playable in multi-player mode (such as *Quake* and *Half-Life* (Valve/Sierra, 1998)). The resonances of framing in 'stand-alone' first and third-person shooters are perhaps more 'cinematic' than those found in most other types of game, although important differences remain. The first-person perspective is a rarity in film in other than brief sequences (the major exception being the 1946 film noir *The Lady in the Lake*), a point highlighted by the limited extent to which it is used even in the combat sequences of *Wing Commander*, a direct adaptation from the game. A game-like perspective is offered, first-person, through the cockpit window of a fighter spacecraft, complete with on-screen targeting reticule and information displays, but only for very brief periods in sequences that obey the usual regime of Hollywood-style construction, combining the first-person with a range of other perspectives on the action. The same is true of *Strange Days* (1995), in which a first-person view is used in virtual reality 'play-back' sequences that account for only a small proportion of the running time (see Krzywinska 2000: 55—64). Third-person cinema, meanwhile, usually involves a much greater and more fluid range of orientations between camera, protagonist and viewer than is found in games. The fixed views offered by games such as *Resident Evil* and *Dino Crisis* have a rigidity that creates a very different, sometimes frustratingly limited, perspective on the action.

Role-playing games (RPGs) and 'God' games such as *Sim City* (Maxis, 1989), in its various incarnations, and *Black and White* (Lionhead/Electronic Arts, 2001) – in which the player creates a world or presides over a society – are among examples of formats that have fewer cinematic associations in terms of formal strategies. Most real-time strategy (RTS) games and RPGs such as the *Final Fantasy* series (Squaresoft, 1990–), *Baldur's Gate* (Bioware/Interplay, 1998) and the campaign mode in *Emperor: The Battle for Dune* display the field of battle or action in aerial shot. The priority is the pragmatic value of the omniscient view to the player as opposed to potentially more cinematic qualities of the restrictive tracking, point-of-view and eye-level shots used in first and third-person shooters, although some RPGs offer a more fluid range of possibilities (see Tan and Wee on *Ground Control* (Sierra/Massive, 2000)).

Different devices of visual orientation operate in games, even if they have some cinematic resonances, because of the different relationships established between players and the space-time coordinates of game worlds. Mainstream cinema has developed well-established systems of spatial orientation, especially the continuity editing system, to avoid confusing the viewer during shifts from one camera position to another. Many first or third-person games permit the player to look and move throughout 360 degrees (as far as obstacles permit). This is possible with less disorientation than would usually be expected in a cinematic context because the player/avatar moves through a particular virtual space in real time with the camera-view often seamlessly anchored to a single viewpoint. This is not an absolute distinction – the camera can break the 180 degree 'rule' in cinema, for example, particularly in first-person 'subjective' sequences, and the exploration of 360-degree space in games can become disorienting, especially when done under pressure or in a rush – but it does help to explain why particular devices are generally more suited to one medium than the other. Games are far less likely than films to use ellipses to eliminate 'dead' time. Time in games may be spent exploring (without always getting anywhere) or interacting with objects that do not have any significant bearing on the main tasks. Most films only give screen time to what is deemed to be essential to storyline, spectacle or the building of character or mood. Action-adventure-type games operate mainly in something closer to real time with ellipses occurring primarily at the end of chapters and levels. This creates a significant difference between the pace (and length) of games and that of films. Despite the shared use of some aspects of framing, *mise-en-scène*, dialogue and music, the handling of time and space are quite different (points of divergence explored by a number of contributors to this volume).

An assortment of other forms of reference to cinema are found in games, implicit and explicit. The climactic ending of many action-adventure games is reminiscent of their big-screen equivalents, including credits that roll once the explosive climax is completed in *Max Payne*. Car chase scenes borrowed from the 1969 film provide the main substance of the game version of *The Italian Job* (SCI, 2001), while some other driving games also draw on cinematic car-chase resonances, including *Grand Theft Auto III* (Rockstar, 2002), in which the player can watch movie-like slow-motion perspectives on the action. *Max Payne* is filled with citations of aspects of popular culture including film genres, comics and Payne's own reference to himself as both Jackie Chan and Sam Spade (and, in one hallucinatory sequence, reference to himself as a character in a computer game!). If the slow-motion 'bullet-dodge' mode is a reference to *The Matrix*, this is made even more overt in its availability for use in an early sequence set in a subway station, the location of one of the key stylised slow-motion action sequences of the movie. Another more general cinematic convention found at one point in the game is the use of a fish-eye distorted-lens perspective to signify Payne's experience under the influence of the drug Valkyr. One mission in the PC first-person-shooter *Medal of Honour: Allied Assault* (2015/Electronic Arts, 2002) seeks to recreate the immersive-authenticity impact of the D-Day landing scenes of the film *Saving Private Ryan* (1998). The game reproduces very closely the opening moments of the film, as the player's avatar joins troops disembarking from landing craft and making their way up Omaha Beach under punishingly heavy fire.

The director of the film, Steven Spielberg, was involved in the development of the original *Medal of Honour* PlayStation game (DreamWorks/Electronic Arts, 1999). If parts of the game mimic the film, the transition is smoothed considerably in this case by the similarity between some qualities of the latter and those associated more generally with the first-person-shooter format. Much of the beach-landing sequence in *Saving Private Ryan* is shot in an unsteady-cam 'subjective' mode, utilising long, often jerky mobile takes to create an impression of documentary-style 'immersion' in the action, a form relatively close to that of

Figure 5 *Medal of Honour: Allied Assault* (2015/Electronic Arts, 2002)

the first-person shooter. The conventions used to create a sense of presence are similar, in some respects, in each case.

Identifying game-like qualities in films is generally a more difficult business. The principal flow of influence appears to be in the other direction, for reasons that have already been suggested, including the fact that cinema has been in existence for longer, as an established and culturally-recognised medium, and tends to have greater cultural prestige as a result. The attribution of film-like qualities to games is usually seen as a form of praise; the term 'cinematic' is a favourite, often over-used, in reviews and publicity blurbs. The opposite tends to be the case when films are described in terms of games. Some critics of contemporary Hollywood cinema cite games, along with other formats such as film-based theme-park rides, as a potentially deleterious influence on films, contributing to a process in which narrative, particularly, is said to be undermined in favour of the production of spectacle and sensation. There are numerous problems with this argument. The extent to which narrative is under threat in even the most clumsy and sensational Hollywood blockbuster has often been overstated, while plenty of factors other than the influence of games can be cited to explain the particular qualities exhibited by such films (for more on these issues see King 2000, 2002). The fact that some films might be produced with more than one eye on their potential for conversion into games is not, in itself, sufficient to suggest that the films themselves are shaped differently as a result. Games, or extrapolations of games to something closer to virtual reality, have been embraced by a number of films as part of their subject matter, from *Tron* (1982) to *eXistenZ* (1999) (see essay in this collection by Stephen Keane), but that is a different matter.

Films that clearly exhibit formal qualities drawn specifically from the aesthetics of games are few and far between. Films based directly on games have not usually had much, fundamentally, in common with games, despite the tendency of critics loosely to associate the weakness of many examples with their point of origin. This has often been a case of guilt-by-association: if a film is bad, and is based on a game, then, given the low cultural standing of games, it is bad because it is based on a game, rather than just a weak film in its own right. A film such as *Street Fighter*, for example, may not be very impressive, even within the confines of the fighting-action genre, but its characteristics (or its weaknesses) are cinematic rather than rooted in the successful games of the same name. Games in general do not lend themselves particularly well to cinematic adaptation, however, as Henry Jenkins (2001) suggests, because their core characteristics tend not to emphasise narrative and character, dimensions that remain important — even if not developed with any great subtlety — to films, even those that put the emphasis on qualities such as action, adventure and spectacle. Films provide ready-made character and narrative resonances that can carry over and play into the experience of a spin-off game, even where the dimensions of character and narrative are not greatly elaborated within the game itself. This is an effect that is generally much harder to achieve in reverse. The ability vicariously to explore and interact with a world akin to that found in screen fictions — generally or specifically — is a potential source of additional pleasure for the film viewer who plays games. Audio-visual qualities of games are lower, but compensation for this is likely to be found in the extra dimension of engagement that is permitted. Moving from game to big screen offers higher audio-visual quality but, for the viewer accustomed to the specific pleasures of interactivity, the trade-off might be less effective; the dominant sense more negative, one of 'loss' rather than gain.

Moments of apparent similarity serve often to emphasise the real difference. Watched on a non-widescreen pre-recorded videotape, for example, the opening of *Street Fighter* bears a superficial resemblance to that of many action-adventure games. The basic narrative scenario is established via television news reports of the kind that might be used in the initial cut-scenes of a game. The opening sequence, which includes the titles, is presented in the original widescreen format, 'letterboxed' across the middle of the screen. This, and the subsequent move to a televisual ratio, creates a dynamic rather like that of the opening of a game: the move into gameplay from cut-scenes that are typically presented in a letterbox format to create a 'cinematic' effect (in the past this was also a more practical necessity, conserving processing resources during the use of higher-resolution graphics; recent developments have made this less important, but the device is still employed in some games, notably *Halo*, with its reduced gap between gameplay and cut-scene graphics, to indicate the non-interactive status of the cut-scene). In the case of the *Street Fighter* video, the change in aspect ratio marks a movement from introductory exposition to the development of the specific narrative events to be depicted in the film. Unlike the move from cut-scene to game-proper, however, it does not mark any substantial change in the role of the viewer. The similarity remains superficial, as in a scene later in the film in which the evil villain cries 'game over!' after using a television monitor screen and remotely-activated weapons to destroy a boat carrying his nemesis; a gesture to the film's game origins rather than an embrace by the film of specifically game-related qualities.

Much the same can be said of most, if not all, films that have antecedents in the world of games. The film version of the role-playing game *Dungeons and Dragons* (2001), for example, includes devices familiar from the game in its electronic and earlier card-and-dice based incarnations. These include: references to the group or guild action that characterises many RPGs; the collection of items such as a sword, scroll and jewel by the hero, to facilitate his access to a dungeon and to allow the villain to be defeated; the performance by the hero of *Tomb Raider*-style tasks such as traversing a maze full of hazards, including belching flames and swinging pendulums, and jumping across a floor covered with symbols, only some of which can be stepped on in safety. Games have become one of the sources from which films such as this draw, especially those clearly targeted at least in part at the game-playing audience. This does not make the film itself like a game, however, in other than a superficial sense.

A more substantial adoption of 'video game logic' is identified by Warren Buckland in *The Fifth Element* (1997), although the extent to which this is the case is also debatable. Buckland identifies a number of similarities between the structure and events of the film and videogames, but it is far from clear that these can be traced to games as a point of origin or influence, anything more than just a degree of similarity or overlap. Qualities that Buckland associates with games, and identifies in the film, include serialised repetition of actions, multiple levels of adventure, space-time warps, magical transformations and disguises, and immediate rewards and punishments that act as feedback loops (2000: 160). The problem is that these qualities are either not realised in anything like the same form in the film – especially serialised repetition – or very hard to identify so strongly with games, as opposed to plenty of other films operating in the same kind of broadly generic territory. If a central plot action is repeated in *The Fifth Element* – principally the capture of a case of stones crucial to the narrative premise, which has to be achieved more than once – what does not happen is the actual repetition of exactly the same action, in anything like the form of serial attempts/repetition that is basic to many experiences of gameplay. The fact that broadly similar events or confrontations are repeated, in different locations and often at an accelerating pace, does not seem greatly to distinguish *The Fifth Element* from plenty of other action-adventure or science-fiction-fantasy movies. Neither do events such as magical transformations or an emphasis not on character development but on survival; the latter is precisely the kind of ground on which Hollywood action movies are regularly castigated.

A rare example of a film that owes a more substantial debt to the structure of games, radically departing from the mainstream cinematic norm, is *Run Lola Run* (1998), the subject of Margit Grieb's contribution to this volume. Game-like qualities include a structure of repetition-with-difference, as various options are worked on the basic race-against-time narrative scenario, and a climactic time-out device at the end of each sequence almost identical to that used in some games, in which a clock ticks down the final seconds to deadline in a strip that emerges along the lower edge of the frame. *The Matrix* offers implausible acrobatics that have something in common with the style of fighting games, but the genealogy here is more complex than that might suggest, as is often the case, the initial inspiration for both coming from Hong Kong action cinema (see essay by Leon Hunt). *Lara Croft: Tomb Raider* is another case in which patterns of game/cinema influence are mixed. The film is, obviously, a spin-off from the game, but the game franchise itself draws to a significant extent on cinematic precedents, particularly the Indiana Jones series. *Lara Croft* has as much or more in common with its cinematic roots – a combination, in some respects, of Indiana Jones, James Bond and some other major action franchises – as it does with the *Tomb Raider* games. The film-of-the-game misses out on potential opportunities to incorporate aspects of game-logic, as Kate Stables suggests:

> The movie doesn't have the wit to be mockingly self-referential about Lara's pre-existence as a game character, to underscore it with a repeating sequence, in the manner of *Groundhog Day* (1993) or *Run Lola Run* (1998), which would capitalize on the similarly repetitive strand in *Tomb Raider* gameplay. Instead, it opts to make its protagonist superhuman, without even the slips, falls and heart-in-mouth fragility of

the virtual Lara, who fails repeatedly at challenges because the player fails. (2001: 19)

How much more interesting and innovative the film would be if Lara was seen to die, even if only on one occasion, and then to be able to restart a sequence, game-style, for another attempt. That the producers of even a feature so overtly based on a game are reluctant to embrace any such departure from the norms of Hollywood-style action cinema says much about the gulf that divides some of the key features of the two media (central action heroes are permitted to suffer painful setbacks, as part of the narrative dynamic designed to emphasise eventual triumph, but not death, unless in an act of willed heroic and usually climactic self-sacrifice). A few minor references to the game-world are inserted into the film, including a 'game over' screen on a CCTV image and the attempts of the techno-geek character to guide a 'blind' Lara through a series of armed obstacles, mirroring to some extent the relationship between the gamer and the virtual Lara. These are insubstantial nods to players of the games, however, rather than anything central to the structure or form of the film. The film has had an influence on the game, meanwhile, the forthcoming installment *Tomb Raider: Angel of Darkness* (Core/Eidos, 2002) featuring a figure of Lara Croft remodelled somewhat to resemble her cinematic manifestation, in the shape of Angelina Jolie.

The experience offered by games is likely to have become a factor in the design of some films, given the extent of overlap between the target audiences of the two media. Hollywood has a magpie-like tendency more generally to draw stylistically on devices from rival/contemporary media products where these are seen as offering an element of innovation that can be contained within its broader aesthetic norms. Specific points of contact are not easy to pin down, however, and it is easy to slip into rather loose generalisations about similarities when points of difference are often more easily identifiable. The situation is complicated by the fact that viewers might bring associations from games to films that might not be traceable to any clear-cut influences between one medium and the other, as might be the case for a player of *Gran Turismo 3* (Polyphony Digital/SCEA, 2001), for example, attracted to a film such as *The Fast and the Furious* (2001), with its hyper-fast-driving action scenes. A number of sequences in *The Matrix* contain in-joke references to the gaming world, including an exaggeratedly semi-parodic shoot-out action sequence in which the principals are given access to an enormous range of firepower, as if they have implemented a 'get all weapons' cheat code.[5] The extent to which resonances from one media product are or are not likely to be carried across to another, in terms of the ongoing experience of the viewer/player, is extremely difficult to ascertain in anything other than a subjective or speculative fashion.

The fact that new standards of 'realism' in computer-generated graphics are offered as one selling point of both games and animated films creates another point of cross-over between the two media. This is especially the case in a film such as *Final Fantasy: The Spirits Within*, based on the successful *Final Fantasy* games series. The cross-over between more overtly 'fantastic' digital special effects in live-action cinema and those used in games, such as the transformational morphing effects in *American McGee's Alice*, is another prominent point of contact. The same animation software is used by both cinema and games in some cases, most notably Alias/Wavefront's 3D and character animating tool, Maya. Widely used in animation and effects for cinema, Maya has been adopted by major games studios including Electronic Arts, Infogrames, Rare and Core Design, to create both cut-scenes and in-game material (*Edge*, 2002: 10). Similar representational capacities are drawn upon by the two media, a fact of significance to the repertoires of images, image-textures and devices available to each. The availability of particular kinds of effects might in some cases encourage particular types of production. Horror and fantasy, for example, lend themselves especially well to the spectacular display of morphing effects in both films and games (although it is an exaggeration in either case to suggest that the availability of such capacities is the driving force in the development of anything like a majority of products, as is sometimes implied in the case of contemporary Hollywood cinema).

Important differences remain, however, even when such fundamentally similar building blocks are involved. The standard of surface 'realism' attained in the film version of *Final Fantasy* is much higher than that found in any game at the time of writing, for example — even those at the cutting edge played on machines using the most advanced graphics cards — partly because priorities other than graphical realism have an important call on the resources of games processing (for more on issues of animation/realism, from film to game, see the essay in this collection by Paul Ward). The same goes for the morphing effects in *American McGee's Alice* as compared with their equivalent on film. A similar kind of transformation might be presented in some films and games, creating similar potential for the development of particular narrative-type developments or spectacular effects. But the quality of resolution — and, arguably, the importance of this factor among others — remains different. This has various implications for effects produced in the name of both 'realism' and spectacular-attraction-for-its-own-sake. The relative scales at which all of these qualities are produced vary greatly from one medium to the other, because they are driven by substantially different agendas and priorities.

Future developments in graphics cards might close the gap, however, a promise that figures largely in advance publicity claims for forthcoming products such as the new generation of games designed to take advantage of the capabilities of the nVidia GeForce3. According to Gabe Newell, managing director of the games developer Valve: 'The GeForce3 pixel and vertex shaders allow us to create characters and environments that rival those previously reserved for the big screen and multi-million dollar Hollywood production budgets' (quoted by Evans 2001). nVidia itself has discussed its intentions in terms of the achievement of 'photorealistic' images such as those produced in *Final Fantasy: The Spirits Within*. The potential to realise such an ambition was suggested in a joint demonstration by nVidia and Squaresoft at the SIGGRAPH computer conference in Los Angeles in August 2001. Scenes from the film were generated in real-time (as required in ongoing gameplay) using nVidia's latest workstation graphics technology 'to overcome the technical challenges presented in creating realistic skin, hair, clothing and other organic attributes' (nVidia Corporation).

A standard complaint aimed at film adaptations from games — especially the high-profile game titles that made the cross-over in the 1990s — is that the weakness of the films is the direct result of one of the key differences between films and games: the relative importance of narrative structure or narrative development. A more concrete pattern of game-to-film influence is charted here than the general diagnosis cited above, in which games are sometimes 'blamed', among other things, for contributing towards the attenuation of narrative in contemporary Hollywood. The status of games in relation to narrative has been one of the most prevalent issues in recent writing on the subject (including a number of contributors to this book), to the annoyance of some games theorists, for whom this is another imperialist attempt to set an agenda from elsewhere that is unfitting to the qualities offered by many types of game (see, for example, Eskelinen 2001). Narrative is a culturally-sanctioned, entrenched and 'respectable' quality, against which both games and some kinds of cinema are often measured and found wanting. Henry Jenkins (Fuller & Jenkins 1995), for example, has played a leading part in establishing some of the specific ways in which narrative structure is built into many games, particularly at the level of 'embedded' narratives; that is to say, pre-set narrative structures realised by the gamer through the act of playing, often through the exploration of space. At the same time, however, he has called for games to embody more substantial, respectable and responsible dimensions, rooted primarily in narrative qualities (to make violence 'meaningful', for example, through its location in relation to character, narrative consequences and to be 'about something' (Jenkins 2001)). Significantly, Jenkins offers a comparison between games and cinema that locates the current state of development of games at a stage equivalent to that occupied by cinema at 1905 or 1910, when it was 'locked into the chase film' rather than exploring its greater potential. Games, for Jenkins, are at a similar threshold point, destined either to remain in a ghetto location (the fate of comics, for example) or to develop into a more mature form.

The trouble with such a formulation — a shift from analysis to a more evangelical approach [6] — is its inbuilt teleological assumptions: that games should 'develop', to fulfil some more culturally acceptable/respectable destiny, rather than being taken for what they are, at present, and are likely to remain to a large extent in the immediate future. This tendency, against which Aarseth also warns, is rife in the analysis of new media technologies, largely as a result of the process of demonisation and scapegoating they often undergo. A similar insistence of the potential for 'improvement', defined in terms of greater narrative development, is found in the work of Janet Murray. Speculation on this issue is often linked to the prospect of 'imminent' or future technological developments that promise a greater capacity for games to embrace more complex dimensions of experience. This is a discourse that also operates in the industrial arena and in consideration of the likely suitability of future games for translation to the big screen:

> Producers and game companies are hoping that upcoming adaptations will have more going for them than their predecessors did. For one thing, sophisticated games for state-of-the-art personal computers and new consoles like Sony's PlayStation 2 and Microsoft's X-Box should provide more grist for the movie mill. (Hazelton 2000: 1)

That this is more than an idle hope was indicated by Microsoft Games Studio's investment in the expert services of the leading talent agency CAA as a route into Hollywood for its games franchises during the $500 million worldwide marketing campaign accompanying the release of the X-Box. Five members of the agency, with access to major Hollywood players, spent a day looking at thirty upcoming X-Box and PC games for potential sources of film or television adaptations (Gaudiosi 2002).

One of the most important points of difference between cinema and games lies in the much used – some would say, abused – notion of 'interactivity'. If games can offer something like a cinematic experience, in some respects, this is extended (and/or complicated, and maybe 'reduced') by the most obvious distinguishing characteristic of games: the fact that they are to be 'played', engaged with in a manner that is much more active and formative of the resulting experience than anything usually involved in the process of film viewing. An initial caution is required here. It is easy to set up an opposition between game-playing and film-viewing that falls into an overly simplistic distinction between 'interactivity' or 'activity', on the one hand (games), and 'passivity' on the other (cinema). There is a clear difference between the experiences offered by the two media, but it is not quite as simple as such a formulation suggests. Cinema-going, or film-viewing in other arenas, such as on videotape, is far from an entirely passive process. It involves a range of cognitive and other processes in the act of interpretation. Games, however, place a central emphasis on the act of doing that goes beyond the kinetic and emotional responses that might be produced in the cinema (responses such as laughter, tears, shock, physical startling, increased heart-rate, and so on, that might also be generated by games). To describe specific qualities such as these, the term 'interactive' is problematic, Aarseth suggests, 'as it connotes various vague ideas of computer screens, user freedom, and personalized media, while denoting nothing' (1997: 48). Taken literally, the term can be applied so widely as to have little value in distinguishing between the inter-actions that occur between users and texts of all kinds; it tends to imply a less 'interactive' point of negative reference, such as literature or cinema, with which games are compared. In its place, Aarseth proposes the term 'ergotic' (derived from the Greek ergon and hodos, meaning 'work' and 'path'), to identify forms in which 'nontrivial effort is required to allow the reader to traverse the text' (1997: 1), an effort greater than that involved in reading a novel, watching a film, or cognitively processing the material contained in such forms.

The videogame player has to respond to events in a manner that affects what happens on screen, something not usually demanded of readers of books or viewers of films. Success often depends on rapid responses, effective hand-eye coordination and learned moves or skills effected through devices such as joypads and keyboards, or puzzle-solving skills. A key difference between games and films, ignored at the peril of the games analyst, is that games 'raise the stakes of interpretation to those of intervention' (Aarseth 1997: 4). Games are, generally, much more demanding forms of audio-visual entertainment: popular, mainstream games require sustained work of a kind that is not usually associated with the experience of popular, mainstream cinema. It is possible to 'fail' games, or to be 'rejected' by them — to give up in frustration — if the player does not develop the skills demanded by a particular title, a fate that does not really have an equivalent in mainstream cinema. Despite the reservations expressed by Aarseth, the term 'interactive' is retained in this collection. Given a clear definition, in the specific context of games — and their relation with other media such as the cinema — it remains a useful term; it has also gained an ubiquity in the field that makes its avoidance near-impossible.

Games can have narrative structures and can share some structural traits with narrativity, as Jesper Juul suggests, in opposition to those (including his own earlier work) who argue that games and narratives are entirely unrelated (2001: 5, 17): 'Many computer games contain narrative elements, and in many cases the player may play to see a cut-scene or realise a narrative sequence' (2001: 17). But there are important differences between the two forms. Games and stories 'do not translate to each other the way that novels and movies do' (17). There is an inherent conflict, Juul argues

> between the now of the interaction and the past or 'prior' of the narrative. You can't have narration and interactivity at the same time; there is no such thing as a continuously interactive story. The relations between reader/story and player/game are completely different — the player inhabits a twilight zone where he/she is both an empirical subject outside the game and undertakes a role inside the game (17).

Narrative is pre-set, built into the fabric of the game, available to be discovered or realised, in whole or in part — or, in some cases, in one version or another, depending on the paths taken by the player. Narrative has happened, or been created, while 'playing' is always happening, a particular realisation of the potential offered by the game, the precise shape or outcome of which is indeterminate.

The ideal suggested by the game designer Richard Rouse is to achieve a balance between narrative as predetermined and structured into the game and the variable 'player's story' generated in each individual experience. The player's story, Rouse argues, 'is the most important story to be found in the game, since it is the story the player will be most involved with, and it is the story in which the player's decisions have the most impact' (2001: 216–17). Carefully predetermined narrative structure is necessary, however, to games in which dynamics such as variable pace, tension, the foreshadowing of events and building towards a climax are important or desirable. The extent to which narrative dimensions are experienced as separate from, or a part of, gameplay is also determined by the kinds of storytelling devices used by individual games. The sense that narrative is essentially separate from gameplay is encouraged by the prevalence of what Rouse terms 'out-of-game' narrative devices, such as cut-scenes, that break into gameplay. Strongly favoured by Rouse is the use of 'in-game' devices to provide story information during the course of gameplay: written material such as signs or notes in the game-world that can be read without switching out of the scene into a separate screen filled with text, dialogue with non-playing characters (NPCs), behaviour of NPCs and the design of level settings (Rouse 2001: 224–5). *Half-Life*, for example, is a first-person shooter with a narrative more complex than is usually found in the format, but does not resort to cut-scenes or information that has to be accessed by the player outside the main game-space. Instead, scenes that are important to the trajectory of the plot are fully interactive, allowing the player to move around, while basic information is relayed in-game by NPCs and other integrated devices. The effect is a sense of seamlessness closer to that usually experienced in the cinema. As Rouse puts it:

> If one stops for a moment to consider the nature of out-of-game devices for storytelling in games, one will be struck by what a strange concept it is to disrupt the interactive experience with a non-interactive one. For instance, when you go to a movie, do the theater workers ever stop the film, bring up the lights, and direct the audience to read a book that they handed out? Sometimes text is shown on the screen, but never in a way that requires the audience to read more than a few words at a time. Instead, films present a consistent media experience for the audience. Games, on the other hand, still mix media in seemingly unnatural ways, forcing users who may just want to play a game to have to read a bit of a book, watch a movie, and only then actually get to play. (2001: 223–4)

Moments of the most heightened and intensively interactive gameplay often entail features such as cause/effect relationships and linear progression (although the latter, in particular, is far from always guaranteed: it is quite possible to regress, to lose ground, during activities such as combat or the negotiation of difficult terrain). These are qualities often associated with narrative, as, for example, in David Bordwell's (1985) influential formulation of 'classical' Hollywood narrative. By themselves, however, at the local level, they are not sufficient to constitute narrative or story, unless these are to be defined at a very minimal level. Moment-by-moment developments gain narrative resonance through their position in a wider frame that is largely pre-established. 'Emergent' narratives, constructed in the mode of play itself, particularly the interactions of players in multiplayer games, are more likely in RPGs and 'God' games. But even here certain narrative developments and plot nodes are likely to be built into the parameters of gameplay.

A useful way of understanding the difference between the situation of narrative frameworks in cinema and games is suggested by Craig Lindley (2002). If cinematic narrative is often understood in terms of a three-act structure comprising a 'beginning' (establishment of conflict), 'middle' (playing out of implications of conflict) and 'end' (resolution of conflict), Lindley suggests, the same framework can be identified in many games, although in rather different proportions. The second act, in games, is massively extended and is the location of the 'core gameplay' experience, in which the higher levels of narrative have little impact (2002: 206). A similar breakdown into three-act structure is identified by Lindley in individual game levels and, within levels, in individual game tasks. In each case, the core gameplay experience occurs in the second act, framed by introductory or climactic material that does most of the narrative work, often through the use of devices such as cut-scenes. Gameplay and narrative are essentially at odds in this account: gameplay has 'little impact' on narrative form while 'the higher levels of narrative form could often be completely eliminated with very little impact upon the core gameplay experience' (2002: 206).

The precise nature of the relationship between narrative and gameplay remains a subject of much debate, however. For a commentator such as Markku Eskelinen, 'cinematic' or narrative-related aspects of games are strictly secondary, 'just uninteresting elements or gift-wrappings to games' (2001: 16). This, we would argue, is an overly polemical stance. It is understandable, perhaps, in an effort to encourage approaches focused on factors specific to games. But games, or even the most frenzied periods of gameplay, do not exist in a vacuum. It is important to pay due attention to the distinctive aspects of games, but these are unlikely to exist in a pure state. Intertextual resonances can certainly enrich the player's experience, but beyond this the industry has a strong economic investment in 'brand' or generic recognition achieved most easily through the use of cross-media franchises or formats. Many games are best understood as hybrids, often combining elements of narrative with more interactive or ergotic gameplay. Resonances such as those derived from narrative frameworks – from cinema or other sources, from particular films, genres or broader cultural archetypes – can play into the gameplay context, and this is likely to be one of the appeals of games. As Rune Klevjer puts it: 'Yes, we want to be free, to play, to master and to conquer, but we also want our actions to be meaningful within a mythical fictional universe. This is the paradox of make-believe, the contradiction between the given and the agency' (2002: 197). One of the major dynamics of many of the kinds of games considered above is the oscillation between these different modes of engagement, the rhythm of which often varies from one example to another.

Videogames, even at their most 'cinematic', are not a form of 'interactive cinema', as has sometimes been implied. Whether they might point in that direction, along with formats such as interactive movies on DVD, as one potential line of development among others, remains to be seen. We have sought to resist the temptation to speculate about such 'future potential' – a problem endemic in the consideration of new media forms generally – to focus instead on points of similarity and difference between cinema and games as they currently exist or are likely to be shaped in the immediate future. The specific qualities of both media will have to be taken into account, and some central contradictions overcome, for any such hybrid medium to become viable, but that is another story.

Before sketching the organisation of the book, a word is needed on the categorisation of games. The terms in which games are identified differ in important respects from those used in relation to film. This is the result of the distinctive nature of games as both particular kinds of audio-visual entertainment and as products of a particular industrial formulation. Games can be categorised on at least four levels: according to platform, genre, mode and milieu. The game platform is the type of hardware system on which a game is played: either personal computer (PC) of assorted configurations or various forms of console, such as the PlayStation, the PlayStation 2, the GameBoy, the Sega DreamCast, the Nintendo 64, Microsoft's X-Box and a range of arcade-based machines (and other non-specialist media such as cable/satellite television and mobile phones). Some games are designed with the capacities of a particular platform in mind. Some are licensed exclusively to one platform as part of the strategy of industrial competition existing between the principal hardware players in the market. The success or failure of some platforms, particularly consoles, depends on the range of software available, most living or dying on the basis of having a 'killer-app' (a software application) that sells the platform, such as the highly successful series of Pokemon games designed to promote Nintendo's GameBoy. This is a practice similar to that employed in the early years of the film industry, in which hardware and software producers — most notably Thomas Edison — claimed ownership of the rights to basic technologies and formats. Edison, for example, patented the 1.33:1 aspect ratio that was to become the industry standard, forcing some competitors to use other formats or risk legal action. 'Format wars' involving connections between particular systems and individual titles have also been a characteristic, initially, of succeeding generations of home-video technology. A drive for industry-wide technological compatibility has characterised the film business, however, to an extent that is far from being achieved in the games market, although many games have been adapted, or 'ported', to platforms other than those for which they were originally designed.

We use the term genre in much the same way as it is used in the wider gaming community — including industry, players, specialist magazines and web-sites — to mark some of the major distinctions between types of games. The nature of these distinctions is different from those found under the heading of genre in film, a reflection of some of the central differences between the two media. Genre is used in games to distinguish between broad categories such as 'action-adventure', 'driving', or 'strategy', to which few additions have been made in recent years. These can often be sub-divided or combined in various forms. Another level of distinction can be made according to the mode in which the game-world is experienced by the player. Action-adventure and driving games, for example, might be available in first-person or third-person mode, or a combination of the two; 'strategy' games can be 'real-time' or 'turn-based'; and so on. Modes can also be sub-divided. A first-person shooter, for example, might be played in single or multi-player options (and the latter might be differentiated according to whether played on the internet or through physical proximity to other players on a local area network (LAN)).

We suggest the term milieu to be used in relation to games in much the same way that genre is usually employed in film, to describe the types of worlds reproduced within games in terms such as location and atmospheric or stylistic conventions. This would include categories such as 'horror' and 'science fiction'. It might seem confusing to describe this as 'milieu' rather than 'genre', especially given the role already discussed of cinematic genre in helping to construct the texture of some games. The reason for adopting this terminology, however, is to avoid imposing a film-oriented framework upon games, from the outside, rather than working more closely with the dominant discourses surrounding games themselves. 'Genre' is a relatively privileged classificatory term, for both producers and consumers; it is unsurprising, therefore, that it should be used to designate different kinds of features that loom more largely in different kinds of media products (genre distinctions also become more complex the closer they are examined, as suggested by Altman and Neale in relation to film).

A movement can be traced between these terms, in the order presented here, from the more general to the more specific. A particular platform can be home to any genre (although some genres might be better suited to one platform than another), while different modes and milieux can be experienced within individual genres. Distinctions such as these are important — whatever terms are used — if we are to be clear precisely which aspects of games we are considering at any given moment and the nature of the relationships between one aspect and another.

Another factor that can be important in the consideration of the specific attributes of games — individually or collectively — is the role played by game engines, the elements of code that provide a game with its basic functionality. Game engines have different components that handle different aspects of games. The graphics engine takes care of visual components, determining the manner in which images are delivered to the screen. Working with the specific attributes of particular platforms and graphics cards, the graphics engine is responsible for qualities such as frame-rate, resolution, texture-mapping and is used to create effects including perspective, camera-angles, lighting and shadows (all key components of 3D games). The physics engine establishes the rules according to which characters or objects exist or move within the game, simulating qualities such as gravity or solidity. The sound engine is responsible for sound effects, while networking engines establish the specific capabilities needed for online gaming.

Some games developers create bespoke engines for particular games, a costly and lengthy business that creates potential for innovation. Others pay fees to license the use of existing engines, permitting shorter and less expensive development time and enabling the developer to benefit from the status of engines that have already earned a good reputation in the gaming community. This is also a way of ensuring that troublesome 'bugs' have already been eradicated. Engines created by id Software for the various *Quake* games have been licensed by third-party developers for their own innovative titles, examples including *Half-Life* (*Quake II* engine), *Star Trek: Voyager Elite Force* (Activision/Raven, 2000 (*Quake III Arena* engine, first person)) and *American McGee's Alice* (*Quake*

III Arena engine, third person).[7] The differences in perspective used by the latter two games demonstrate the built-in flexibility of the *Quake* engine. id Software's *Doom III* game engine, in development at the time of writing, is designed to make specific use of the features offered by the new generation of nVidia graphics cards, aiming to establish the basis for increased graphical realism. It is in the commercial interests of developers to offer innovations and differences of their own, however, even while using pre-existing and more standardised engines, in order to establish distinctive selling points in the market. Financial success in the licensing business depends on the capacity of game engines to offer a range of facilities sufficiently flexible to be used creatively by third parties.

Some argue that the practice of licensing game engines inhibits processes of 'evolution and innovation' within the gaming sector (Mike Kulas quoted in *P2*, 2001a: 10). There is no guarantee that bespoke engines bring such benefits, however. *Red Faction* (THQ/Volition, 2001) has its own engine but reviews suggested that this did not translate into offering anything very new to the existing repertoire of FPS games. First-person shooters such as *Quake III Arena* (id Software/Activision, 1999) and *Unreal Tournament* (Epic MegaGames & Digital Extremes/GT Interactive, 1999) have much in common at the level of gameplay, despite the fact that each uses its own engine. Both include 'capture the flag' and 'deathmatch' modes and many aspects of their in-game physics are similar. The main differences, giving each game its distinctive 'feel', are how the two engines handle graphics (especially lighting), in-game items such as weapons or tools and particular aspects of physics such as speed of movement. This is as much a matter of how the engine is used by the developer, however, as of the qualities of the engine itself.

The investment in 3D graphics engines that characterises many recent games is an important factor in other debates about the nature of games, including some of those addressed earlier in this Introduction. The production of a compelling game world, in three-dimensional graphics, often appears to be privileged over dimensions such as both narrative and gameplay. Games developers, designers and programmers often appear to devote more energy to the creation of spectacular, coherent and (in their own terms) believable worlds than to the quality or variety of gameplay itself. This may be because this dimension of game construction presents the kind of technological challenge to which they are often attracted. It may also be a commercial convenience: to redesign the texture of the explorable environment might be considerably less challenging than to seek substantial innovation in gameplay. As James Hague, a games developer and historian, puts it:

> Does the combination of game engine and editor reduce to a construction kit from which dozens of games can be created? If so, it is the job of the game designer to design such a construction kit rather than a finished game. By definition, this eliminates a large class of games that don't fit the construction kit model — consider such classic non-electronic games such as poker or baseball. If baseball were designed by a game development house, one inning would take place underground, the next

on a rock floating on a pool of lava and the next on Easter Island. [...] There are certain design considerations and rules that come into play once you start down the 'player in a world' path, and those considerations tend to conflict with games that don't fit that model. (2000: 6)

The appeal of being able to explore spectacular 3D virtual worlds in real time should not be underestimated, however (in relation to emphasis on narrative or other more game-specific factors). The specific abilities of particular game engines to create potentially immersive worlds is another factor that helps to account for the favouring of particular types of material such as fantasy and science fiction. Frank Herbert's *Dune* series (1965–85) is a good example of a highly developed imaginary world that has been adapted from novel to film, television and games. Similarly, Tolkein's *Lord of the Rings* (1954, 1955) has been 'remediated' by a number of games, including *Baldur's Gate* and *EverQuest* (UbiSoft/Sony, 2000) as well as becoming a substantial film franchise with its own tie-in games. The available repertoire of 3D engines may be flexible, providing a diverse range of gaming options. In a more general sense, however, their specific capabilities have a significant impact on the content, shape and form of games, marking out a substantial core point of difference between games and other audio-visual entertainment media.

The essays that make up this collection have been organised, approximately, to move from the more general in focus to the more specific; from broad issues of the formal qualities of games/cinema to examinations of individual genres or titles. There is much overlap, however, and to reflect this degree of fluidity we have not divided the material into separate sections. The first two chapters ('Technological Pleasure: The Performance and Narrative of Technology in *Half-Life* and other High-Tech Computer Games', by Andrew Mactavish, and 'Die Hard/ Try Harder: Narrative, Spectacle and Beyond, from Hollywood to Videogame', by Geoff King) include a central focus on the relationship in games between narrative and qualities such as spectacle, sensation and kinaesthesia. One of the main arguments made by Mactavish is that the pleasure of gameplay is not just one of 'immersion' in the virtual world — an experience emphasised by some other contributors — but also of conscious awareness and enjoyment of the quality of the technological spectacle itself. Issues of narrative and spectacle are also explored in the following chapter ('Spectacle of the Deathmatch: Character and Narrative in First-Person Shooters', by Jo Bryce & Jason Rutter), although the emphasis here is on the specific generic context of the first-person shooter. The same genre is the main point of focus of the fourth chapter ('First-Person Shooters — A Game Apparatus', by Sue Morris), which offers a broad typology of differences between cinema, games and television, and argues for the strongly immersive character of the experience, especially in the multiplayer variant. A return to issues of narrative, in the specific context of the visual qualities of games, is found in the following chapter ('Vision and Virtuality: The Construction of Narrative Space in Film and Computer Games', by Wee Liang Tong and Marcus Cheng Chye Tan), which argues that a distinctive form of narrative is constructed through the processes of visualisation adopted by games. The role of cut-scenes is also considered by Wee and Tan, a subject taken up more centrally in the next chapter ('Watching a Game, Playing a Movie: When Media Collide', by Sacha A. Howells).

Issues arising from the animated nature of videogames, including various claims to the status of 'realism', are explored in the following chapter ('Videogames as Remediated Animation', by Paul Ward), a contribution followed by analysis of the often neglected role of music in games ('What's That Funny Noise? An Examination of the Role of Music in *Cool Boarders 2*, *Alien Trilogy* and *Medievil*', by David Bessell). The two chapters that follow each focus on one individual film in the light of videogames ('From Hardware to Fleshware: Plugging into David Cronenberg's *eXistenZ*', by Steve Keane, and 'Run Lara Run', by Margit Grieb), the former focusing centrally on games hardware, both real and fictional-imaginary, the latter examining game influences on *Run Lola Run*. The last four chapters move across the terrain of gender and genre, sometimes considering the two in combination. A reading of the *Tomb Raider* games in the light of cine-psychoanalytical theory ('Playing With Lara', by Diane Carr) is followed by an analysis of the James Bond franchise ('"Oh, Grow up 007": The Performance of Bond and Boyhood in Film and Videogames', by Derek A. Burrill) in relation to theories of the development of the performance of masculinity. Questions specific to the genres of Hong Kong martial arts and horror are explored, in relation to wider issues, in the final chapters ('"I Know Kung Fu!": The Martial Arts in the Age of Digital Reproduction', by Leon Hunt, and 'Hands-On Horror', by Tanya Krzywinska).

We have encouraged contributors to this volume to use the exploration of the interface between cinema and games as an opportunity to question certain assumptions or orthodoxies relating to both media forms — the more established terrain of cinema as well as the emergent field of games analysis. One option when considering cinema in the light of games is to offer a reductive and over-simplistic comparison that reifies certain theoretical approaches to the former. The most obvious example of this, as already mentioned, is the temptation to invoke a concept of film-viewing as 'passive' in contrast to the more obvious 'interactivity' required by games. Forms such as games and cinema exist in complex and multidimensional relationships. In some respects, clear points of similarity can be identified. In others, divergences are sharp. In between, however, lie many shades of overlap, areas of relevance not just to the analysis of this particular conjuncture but to the interrelations between contemporary media forms more generally.

notes

1   We use the term 'videogame' as a general term to embrace what are sometimes known as either 'videogames' or 'computer games' (the former usually in reference to console or arcade-based games, the latter usually in reference to games played on a personal computer). Throughout this collection the two terms are used interchangeably, unless otherwise indicated (for instance, in the essay by Sue Morris that focuses specifically on games played on PC).

2 The first videogame, which was later to become *Spacewar* (1962), was created in 1958, according to Steven Poole (2000: 29). The first major commercial success was *Pong* (1972) (Poole 2000: 33—4).

3 Throughout this collection game references are given in parentheses in the following order: main developer, publisher and date. Where a game's developer and publisher are the same, only one name appears. Our main source for these is gamespot.com.

4 See, for example, Greg Howson 'Max Payne: the best PC game ever', *The Guardian*, Online, 9 August 2001, 6.

5 Our thanks to Sue Morris for this observation.

6 A product in this case, it seems, of the role Jenkins has played as an academic 'expert' called into not very enlightened political debate in America on the old question of the 'effects' of videogames.

7 See http://www.idsoftware.com/corporate/idtech for information on id Software's license agreements with third parties, including costs.

citations

Aarseth, Espen (1997) *Cybertext: Perspectives on Ergodic Literature*. Baltimore: Johns Hopkins University Press.

___ (2001a) 'What kind of text is a game?' 'Game Cultures' conference. Bristol, June.

___ (2001b) 'Computer Game Studies, Year One.' *Game Studies*, 1, July. Available on-line at: http://www.gamestudies.org/0101/editorial.html.

Altman, Rick (1999) *Film/Genre*. London: BFI.

Bolter, Jay David, & Richard Grusin (1999) *Remediation: Understanding New Media*. Cambridge, Mass.: MIT Press.

Bordwell, David (1985) 'The classical Hollywood style, 1917—60', in David Bordwell, Janet Staiger & Kristin Thompson, *The Classical Hollywood Cinema: Film Style and Mode of Production to 1960*. London: Routledge.

British Board of Film Classification 'News Releases', Carmeggedon. Available on-line at: http://www.bbfc.co.uk.

Buckland, Warren (2000) 'Video Pleasure and Narrative Cinema: Luc Besson's The Fifth Element and Video Game Logic', in John Fullerton & Astrid Soderbergh Widding (eds) *Moving Images: From Edison to the Webcam*. London: John Libbey, 2000: 159—64.

Donahue, Ann & Tim Swanson (2000) 'H'wood hits paydirt in playtime', *Variety*, 18—31 December: 9, 74.

Edge (2002) 'Mayan attraction', June, 10—11.

European Leisure Software Publishers Association. 'Video Standards Council: Codes of Practice', www.elspa.com.

Eskelinen, Markku (2001) 'The Gaming Situation', in *Game Studies*, 1, July 2001. Available on-line at: http://www.gamestudies.org/0101.

Entertainment Software Rating Board 'About ESRB', 'ESRB video and game ratings'. Available on-line at: http://www.esrb.com.

Evans, Brian (2001) 'Review of GeForce 3', 3DGPU website. Available on-line at: http://www.3dgpu.com/previews/gf3_tech5.cfm.

Financial Times (2001) 'Survey — Creative Business: The computer games industry', 14 August. Available on-line at: http://globalarchive.ft.com/globalarchive/article.html?id

=010814001476&query=computer+games.

Fuller, Mary & Henry Jenkins (1995) 'Nintendo and New World Travel Writing: A Dialogue', in Steven Jones (ed.) *Cybersociety: Computer-Mediated Communication and Community.* Thousand Oaks: Sage, 57–72.

Gamespot, www.GameSpot.com.

Gaudiosi, John (2002) 'CAA helping Xbox go H'wood', *The Hollywood Reporter East*, 5 March, 3

Hague, James (2000) 'Gaming and Graphics', in SIGGRAPH Computer Graphics Newsletter, May. Available on-line at: http://www.siggraph.org/publications/newsletter/v34n2/columns/gaming.html.

Hazelton, John (2000) 'Hollywood game players battle again', *Screen International*, 11–17 August, 1, 4.

id Software. Available on-line at: http://www.idsoftware.com/corporate/idtech.

Internet Movie DataBase, www.imdb.com

Howson, Greg (2001) 'Max Payne: the best PC game ever', *The Guardian*: Online, 9 August, 6.

Jenkins, Henry (2001) 'The Game as Object of Study', 'Game Cultures' conference, Bristol, June.

Juul, Jesper (2001) 'Games Telling stories? A brief note on games and narratives', *Games Studies*, 1, July. Available on-line at http://www.gamestudies.org/0101/juul-gts.

Kinder, Marsha (1991) *Playing with Power.* Berkeley/LA/Oxford: University of California Press.

King, Geoff (2000) *Spectacular Narratives: Hollywood in the Age of the Blockbuster.* London: I.B. Tauris.

____ (2002) *New Hollywood Cinema: An Introduction.* London: I.B. Tauris.

Klevjer, Rune (2002) 'In Defense of Cutscenes', in Frans Mäyrä (ed.) *Computer Games and Digital Cultures.* Tampere: University of Tampere Press.

Krzywinska, Tanya (2000) *A Skin for Dancing In: Possession, Voodoo and Witchcraft in Film.* Trowbridge: Flicks Books.

Lindley, Craig (2002) 'The Gameplay Gestalt, Narrative, and Interactive Storytelling', in Frans Mäyrä (ed.) *Computer Games and Digital Cultures.* Tampere: University of Tampere Press.

Murray, Janet (1997) *Hamlet on the Holodeck: The Future of Narrative in Cyberspace.* Cambridge, Mass.: MIT Press.

Neale, Steve (2000) *Genre and Hollywood.* London: Routledge.

nVidia Corporation (2001) Press release. Available on-line at: http://biz.yahoo.com/bw/010814/140198.html.

Office of Film and Literature Classification, 'Classification Information: computer games'. Available on-line at: www.oflc.gov.au.

P2 (2000a) 'Konami Makes the silver Screen Scream', December, 10.

P2 (2000b) 'Red Faction', December, 59.

Poole, Steven (2000) *Trigger Happy: The Inner Life of Videogames.* London: Fourth Estate.

Rouse, Richard (2001) *Game Design: Theory and Practice.* Plano, Texas: Wordware Publishing.

Sony Corporation (2000) Annual Report.

Stables, Kate (2001) 'Run Lara Run', *Sight and Sound*, August, 18–20.

chapter one

Technological Pleasure: The Performance and Narrative of Technology in *Half-Life* and other High-Tech Computer Games

andrew mactavish

A common strategy for academics studying computer games is to ask questions within the context of narrative: are computer games narratives? If so, in what ways are they like and unlike written narrative, oral narrative and cinematic narrative? How does computerised interactivity reorganise literary models of narrative in which the reader's role in shaping the story is normally circumscribed by the relatively linear flow from author-narrator-narratee to reader? These important questions extend those posed by hypertext theorists who claim a convergence between post-structuralist literary theory and interactive fiction.[1] But these questions also tend to reduce computer games to narrative meaning and to ignore the dimensions of visual and auditory experience such as spectacle and kinaesthetics.

The study of narrative in computer game scholarship exposes a tendency to ignore what many game designers, industry pundits and gamers say about computer games. As guides to game design and game reviews illustrate, narrative is certainly an important element in many computer games, but it is only one in a mixture contributing to the gaming experience. Indeed, in many computer games, if narrative exists at all, it plays a secondary role to graphics, audio and gameplay (a broad notion which can include graphics and audio, but that also covers a game's artificial intelligence (AI), physics, interface, user control and other elements that make a game fun to play). First-person shooters such as *Unreal Tournament* (Epic MegaGames & Digital Extremes/GT Interactive, 1999) and *Quake III* (id Software/Activision, 1999) have almost no story at all, yet they rate as some of the most popular and entertaining computer games currently on the market. A narrative framework would do little to explain their appeal or even their representations of violence and social order. Conversely, recent games such as *The Longest Journey* (Funcom, 2000) and *Deus Ex* (Ion Storm/Eidos, 2000) include compelling storylines, but narrative remains only one ingredient in the blend. While these games may require the user to act within a narrative space, they also provide a plentitude of visual and auditory effects that contribute less to a narrative experience than to an astonishment at technological display. This is especially the case today as advances in visual and audio technologies work hand-in-hand with the gaming industry to build increasingly sensory-rich gaming environments.

Theorising computer gameplay without considering narrative, however, would lead to an account as unbalanced and imprecise as those that privilege narrative. In the following pages, I contribute to a more inclusive theory of computer gameplay by focusing on the intersection of narrative, technology and interactivity to demonstrate that the widespread appeal of computer games is based less upon internal narrative meaning than some critics argue. Rather, I contend that a significant and relatively unexplored component of the pleasure of computer gameplay is our astonishment at visual and auditory technology, at our participation in technological spectacle, and in the story of its development. In doing so, I describe the ways in which game designers use visual and auditory display to immerse players into a frenetic virtual world but also to draw attention to the game's virtual world *as virtual*. The thrill of playing computer games involves more than problem-solving, combat, hand-eye coordination, or participation in a narrative world. For many gamers, the pleasure of computer gameplay is substantially composed of admiration for, and participation within, the game's exhibition of advanced visual and auditory technology. The feeling of agency, therefore, is less one of power over internal narrative sequence, as many critics of interactive fiction might argue. Rather, agency in computer games involves the gamer's participation within a virtuoso performance of technological expertise.

My argument cannot be applied to all computer games. The thrill of playing a fast-paced, high-tech game like *Quake III* is too dissimilar from the pleasures of *Tetris* (Pajitnov, 1989) to be included under a single category in which performative agency and technological effect are central to the gaming experience. In this essay, I am mainly interested in those high-tech computer games that, for the most part, present plausible, three-dimensional virtual worlds in which players operate characters, animals or machines from a first-person, third-person, or omniscient perspective. My arguments do not apply to many text-only games, although high-tech games can include substantial textual elements. Nor do they necessarily apply to computer gaming since its beginnings in the 1960s. Computer games have often been an expression of technological progress where one game or console ups the ante for the next. In this respect, part of the pleasure of playing computer games has always been the pleasure of their technological mediation. But recent developments in the gaming industry have focused on improvements in visual and auditory technologies for the realistic display of virtual worlds, meaning that sensational effect is now, more than ever, one of the central components of gameplay.

While my argument is applicable to many of today's high-tech computer games, I focus mainly on one: Valve Software's *Half-Life* (Valve/Sierra), the extraordinarily successful first-person shooter launched in 1998 and still a top-seller at the time of writing. I have chosen *Half-Life* for a variety of reasons, not the least of which is that I have spent many hours playing the game. But there are other, perhaps more academically suitable reasons for my selection. *Half-Life* has had a substantial impact on the gaming industry. It continues to raise the level of technological and gameplay development (although, according to my own argument, it inevitably will be superceded) and has resulted in one of the largest gaming communities in the short history of computer games. This large community provides a substantial amount of data in the form of game reviews from magazines and online gamer communities for investigating the pleasures of playing *Half-Life*. Indeed, it is my hope that, by considering the discourse of *Half-Life*, I can gain a clearer picture of what gamers find pleasurable not only in *Half-Life* but in playing other high-tech computer games as well.

Computer games and post-structuralist hypertext theory

Academics may be late to the scene, but scholars have recently begun to define identifiable and legitimate topics of computer game scholarship. Conferences, listservs, book-length studies, and collections of articles like the one you are reading assemble communities of scholars, designers and gaming experts, frame topics of inquiry and, ultimately, confer academic legitimacy on a field in the early stages of development. Yet, as exciting and empowering as this may be for some academics — especially in an industry so dependent upon peer recognition — we should heed Espen Aarseth's caution against the oft-repeated mistake he finds in recent approaches to digital media:

> The race is on to conquer and colonize these new territories for our existing paradigms and theories, often in the form of 'the theoretical perspectives of [fill in your favorite theory/theoretician here] is clearly really a prediction/description of [fill in your favorite digital medium here]'. [...] Instead of playing the combinatorial game and applying this or that paradigm to the new phenomena ... we must step back from our theories if we are to see something not already inscribed in them. (1999: 31–2)

Putting Aarseth's caution aside for the moment, however, we need to recognize that the 'combinatorial game' is helping to legitimate the practice and theory of digital expression within the arts and humanities, which look less skeptically at digitalization through the lens of established paradigms and theories. To date, the most common perspectives applied to interactive multimedia find their basis in post-structuralist theories of linguistics and narrative, theories developed mainly within the context of written and verbal text. For all the problems that may arise from applying theories of written or verbal text to interactive multimedia — with its combination of various media types and regular emphasis upon non-verbal elements — early linguistics-based attempts to theorize the digital arts have helped create a recognized field of academic inquiry. For instance, hypertext theorists such as George P. Landow, Jay David Bolter and Stuart Moulthrop may make contestable claims for hypertext's embodiment of the post-structuralist notions of intertextuality, multivocality, and the decentered subject, but these arguments have found a well-primed audience in the arts and humanities, where literary post-structuralism has been the dominant theoretical framework.[2] The positive result, albeit less than ideal, is a fertile field of study where new theories can take root.

The less fortunate consequence of post-structuralist hypertext theory, however, has been the framing of digitally interactive expression within semiotic models of linguistics, which ultimately prove inadequate to theorising sensory-rich interactive works like many of today's computer games. Many strains of linguistics-based post-structuralist theory maintain that language is fundamental to subjectivity, or as Martin McQuillan argues, 'it is through language that the subject constructs meaningful realities and cognitive processes' (2000: 7). Linguistics-based theories of meaning, therefore, risk reducing the multi-sensory experiences of digitally interactive expression to language, a risk that has not gone unnoticed in recent critiques of the linguistic turn. According to Barbara Maria Stafford, 'the conjunction of *psyche* with *logos*' has had the consequence of 'collapsing diverse phenomenological performances, whether drawings, gestures, sounds, or scents, into interpretable texts without sensory diversity' (1996: 6). When all meaning is reduced to language, there is very little room left to imagine a phenomenology of sensual experience that can account for the intensely visual and auditory performances that characterise even the most strongly narrative of today's media-rich computer games.[3]

Narrative and special-effects cinema

An offshoot of the privileged status of linguistics-based theory has been the privileging of narrative in the theoretical models applied to multiple-media works like film, drama and computer games. But, as recent science-fiction film theorists have argued, narrative theory cannot encompass the multi-sensory and technological dimensions of all film experience.[4] One of the most notable elements of much sci-fi film is the prevalence of special effects, whether they come to us as ape suits, blue-screen film techniques, digital film manipulation, 3D computer animation or the latest in surround-sound audio standards. Yet, as Angela Ndalianis documents, sci-fi film has often felt the brunt of narrative-based criticism, which tends to cast 'spectacle as serving a hollow purpose because it serves no "higher" narrative function' (2000: 258). Rather than build a critical apparatus to support sci-fi film's unique visual and auditory qualities, many film theorists and reviewers tend to adopt criteria used to evaluate classic realist film, as if narrative is the single most important criteria for evaluating all film in general.[5]

Since the publication in 1986 of Tom Gunning's 'The Cinema of Attractions: Early Film, Its Spectator, and the Avant-Garde', some film critics have begun to rescue sci-fi film from the hegemonic grasp of narrative film theory. Gunning questions what his collaborator, André Gaudreault, calls 'the privileged relationship between cinema and narrativity' by arguing that pre-1906 cinema is not primarily narrative (1990: 68). Rather, it is primarily visual, a cinema of attractions that 'directly solicits spectator attention, inciting visual curiosity, and supplying pleasure through a visual and exciting spectacle' (1990: 58). Gunning uses Méliès' trick film, *Voyage dans la lune* (1902), to argue that: 'The story simply provides a frame upon which to string a demonstration of the magical possibilities of the cinema' (1990: 58). In the cinema of attractions, then, narrative is structural support for the spectacle.

Importantly, part of the allure of the cinema of attractions is the very technology of display itself. As Gunning notes: 'Early audiences went to exhibitions to see machines demonstrated (the newest technological wonder…), rather than to view films' (1990: 58). A similar situation exists today in special effects films like *Toy Story* (1995), *The Matrix* (1999), and *Titanic* (1997), not to mention most IMAX films, where the film's technology is at least as attractive as its storyline. Indeed, much of the driving force behind these films' highly successful box-office returns and video rentals is a general fascination with their technical expertise. The web site for *Star Wars: Episode I – The Phantom Menace* (1999) is filled with statistics detailing the production's number of computer artists (250), its record-breaking number of shots (2000), and the percentage of frames employing digital work (95 per cent).[6] Many of today's movie-goers are captivated by uses of the computer for realistic display and, in some cases, by being tricked into asking if it's real or if it's digital. As Ndalianis states: 'Contemporary effects cinema is a cinema that establishes itself as a technological performance, and audiences recognize and revel in the effects technology and its cinematic potential' (2000: 258). And further: 'We remain astounded at the effortless magic of the transformations we see before us, yet these very transformations also remind us that they are special effects and ask us to be astounded at the technology that produces such magic' (2000: 260). Part of the experience of recent sci-fi film, then, is what Gunning calls an 'aesthetic of astonishment' (quoted in Ndalianis 2000: 258), which amounts to the viewer's oscillation between illusionary immersion and technological awe.

What's the story with computer games?

Special effects film theory can be very useful for theorising computer games, not only because computer games can be understood within the context of an oscillatory aesthetic of astonishment – a point I will return to shortly – but also because computer games have suffered from a similar narrative bias that shapes traditional film criticism. Ironically, one of the most important recognitions of the power of special effects in computer games is also one of the best examples of the power of narrative theory to shape computer game criticism. In *Hamlet on the Holodeck: The Future of Narrative in Cyberspace*, Janet Murray clearly recognises the importance of visual and auditory effect in computer games and other forms of high-tech entertainment, stating that the 'experience of being transported to an elaborately simulated place is pleasurable in itself, regardless of the fantasy content' (1997: 98).[7] Ultimately, however, Murray grieves the narrative weakness of most high-tech computer games: 'Although economic and social forces may never move the established game industry far past the lucrative shoot-'em-ups and puzzle mazes, there is no reason why more sophisticated developers could not make stories that have more dramatic resonance and human import to them' (1997: 54).

Murray's right. Technically there is no reason why games with deeper and more seamlessly integrated narratives could not be developed. Yet, if high-tech computer games in general are so weak in narrative, and if, as Murray implies, they would be better with stronger narrative, then why is the computer game industry so successful? Surely game developers are creating something that players like, and, if it is not narrative, then there is something else that moved North Americans to spend $6 billion on electronic games in 2000 (Interactive Digital Software Association).[8] It would be a perilous generalisation to lump all computer games into one grouping where narrative is equally important, but there is a growing tendency for many game publishers to develop works with deeper narrative, more expansive and convincing settings, and more complex character development. Yet, even in the most strongly narrative of today's high-tech computer games, narrative frequently remains only one element in a mixture contributing to gaming pleasure. This is borne out by most game review magazines, whose criteria for evaluating games normally emphasise visual and auditory elements over narrative, which is frequently lumped into the all-inclusive category of gameplay.[9] In the host of annual game awards where games are selected according to one element of game design, story normally figures in only one category among many that emphasise graphics, audio and other technical elements. For instance, of the eight special achievement honours in GameSpot's annual Best & Worst awards, only one goes to the best story while no fewer than four cover visual and auditory technologies (audio, music, artistic graphics and technical graphics) (CNET). Even GameSpot's review of *Planescape: Torment* (Black Isle Studios/Interplay), its 1999 Best Story award winner, focuses mainly upon the visual and aural qualities of the game, progressing from its graphics engine, art work, scenery and special effects to its interface and close-up isometric perspective before even mentioning its 'original plot, well-written, descriptive dialogue, and likeable characters' (Kasavin 2001). Although the storyline is apparently so strong in *Torment*, Greg Kasavin gives it rather faint praise: 'It's fortunate that Torment's dialogue reads well, because there's a lot of it to read. [...] You might wish the game had a more frequent tendency to show-not-tell; however, its combination of great graphics and writing is generally very effective' (2001). Written narrative seems somehow out of place for Kasavin. It is the thrilling nature of dynamic graphics that he finds most important to the game.

One of the most successful computer games of all time, Valve Software's *Half-Life*, has also been widely praised for the strength of its narrative. As one game reviewer writes: 'Unlike other first-person shooters ... the story is not abandoned in the middle of the game for bigger weapons and constant mayhem' (Hubble 2001). Instead, the storyline develops as the player reaches new levels in the game and learns important narrative details from dialogue with friendly non-playing characters and overheard conversations. However, even though the storyline is sustained more seamlessly across the duration of the game, the narrative in *Half-Life* remains rather simplistic (government-funded secret experiments in teleportation go horribly wrong, alien monsters appear and the government tries to cover it up) and secondary to the actual gameplay itself (destroy progressively more dangerous enemies, solve progressively harder problems, interact with a spectacularly rendered virtual space).[10] And, contrary to the reviewer's praise for *Half-Life*, players do indeed gain bigger weapons over time, but, more significantly, the visual splendour of the game's monsters intensifies with each level, an escalation echoed in part by increasingly elaborate visual environments and auditory effect. As the game progresses, opponents increase in complexity and danger from small and easy-to-kill headcrabs and lethargic zombies, to more deadly and visually interesting houndseyes, barnacles and bullsquids, to the tactically accurate and technologically advanced military killing squads, to nearly indestructible gargantuans, ichthyosaurs and alien grunts, and finally to the omnipotent Nihilanth, the enormous infantile monster that rules the alien world of Xen. Ironically, but acting as the exception that proves the rule, the truly indestructible opponent ends up being the least visually interesting character: a government man in a blue suit.

Immersion breaks

While narrative certainly helps to structure one's progress through *Half-Life*, the game's stronger structural agent — and this holds for most high-tech games — is rooted in the close relationship between the progression of visual and auditory effect and increasingly difficult obstacles. In other words, the formalised reward for progressing through these games — solving puzzles, discovering correct routes and defeating opponents — is access to even more challenging obstacles and further, often more dazzling spectacle. Aarseth's dialectic of aporia and epiphany provides a useful model for thinking about the structural role of obstacles in *Half-Life* in particular and in computer games in general. For Aarseth, aporias are not 'informal structures, semantic gaps that hinder the interpretation of the work', but are 'formal figures, localizable "roadblocks" that must be overcome by some unknown combination of actions' (1999: 38). When players overcome an aporia, they experience an epiphany, not quite as soul-rendering as a character's epiphany in a James Joyce novel, but still 'a sudden, often unexpected solution to the impasse' (Aarseth 1999: 38). So, when a gamer confronts a situation in which there seems to be no way forward, such as facing the Nihilanth in *Half-Life*, he experiences an aporia. When he learns the right way to defeat his opponent, likely after several failed attempts, he experiences an epiphany — frequently intensified by special effect — that allows him to progress closer to completing the game.

What Aarseth does not account for sufficiently, however, is the integral role of visual and auditory effect during periods of aporia and epiphany, or even during moments when players are not solving puzzles or defeating opponents. For instance, a player may opt to consult game guides or walkthroughs that give step-by-step instructions for completing the game or she may invoke cheat codes — available in most games — that make her game character invincible. These gameplay strategies may lessen or even eliminate feelings of aporia and epiphany, but they obviously do not make the game completely pleasure-free; otherwise, players would not use them. These strategies suggest that a player's interaction within a game's virtual environment, regardless of formalised aporia, can provide significant pleasure in itself. In other words, a key component of delight in computer games is user-driven exploration and discovery within a virtual space. So, while *Half-Life* may require a gamer to overcome obstacles if she hopes to proceed from level to level, it also provides a virtual space that elicits amazement at its splendorous display and the kinaesthetic effects of its three-dimensional event space. As Amer Ajami puts it:

> *Half-Life*'s environments are beautifully modeled, with both the indoor and outdoor scenes conveying a great sense of believability. Character models feature realistic movements; Aliens scamper, grunts aim and assassins do back flips in a display that almost flaunts Valve's own skeletal animation system. (2001)

As Ajami's remarks suggest, the visual and auditory environment itself provides a significant level of sensational stimulation, or to repeat Murray, the 'experience of being transported to an elaborately simulated place is pleasurable in itself, regardless of the fantasy content' (1997: 98).

The pleasure of psychological transportation — or immersion, as it is commonly called — in high-tech computer games clearly depends upon the visual and auditory elements that make the virtual environment convincing to the senses, but it is not only the look and sound of the space that create and sustain the illusion. Other technical elements also make a game more or less immersive, such as level design, the logic and consistency of the space and the artificial intelligence defining the non-playing characters. The virtual space and the characters that inhabit it must seem plausible not only to the senses, but also to logic. It is the strength of these features in *Half-Life* that inspired Ron Dunlin to open his review of *Half-Life* with a general statement about computer games and illusion:

> A major goal in any game is to create the illusion of reality, a fact that is especially true for first-person shooters. The whole point of the genre is to put you, literally, in the role of the protagonist. [...] Through a series of subtle and artistic design decisions, *Half-Life* creates a reality that is self-contained, believable, and thoroughly engaging. (2001)

The remainder of Dunlin's review is essentially a list of visual, auditory, architectural and puzzle elements that make *Half-Life* so impressively believable: the many puzzles 'always seem plausible in the world Valve has created'; the alien monsters 'truly look like organic beings'; 'antagonists act in a manner that is frighteningly realistic'; and the 'weapons look and sound great' (Dunlin 2001).

Dunlin's list of elements that contribute to the digital illusion of reality assumes that the ideal experience of computer gameplay, especially for games using a first-person perspective, involves deep immersion within an interactive and convincing virtual space. Andrew Darley makes a similar claim in *Visual Digital Culture* where he argues that 'the increased sense of presence in a three-dimensional world that *the best games* offer' comes when interactivity and visual realism combine to 'augment the impression of kinaesthetic presence or involvement in the image' (Darley 2000: 159, emphasis added). While Dunlin and Darley both see immersion as a central quality in computer games, Darley recognises the importance of visual stimulation to feelings of kinaesthetic presence, even if he does overlook the increasingly important role of audio in creating the impression of a virtual but seemingly present space.[11] Regardless of how they understand immersion, it remains that both Dunlin and Darley see it as a qualitatively defining element of computer gameplay.

In many respects, then, graphical computer games like *Half-Life* can be evaluated for the quality of immersive experience they offer. But if we are to understand the relationship between the feeling of immersion in a game and its engineering (level design, AI, and so on) and visual and auditory elements, then we also need to ask how these features might simultaneously disrupt immersion or even create a different order of immersion. Neither Dunlin nor Darley address the issue of interruptions in the player's immersion in a game, which suggests that, for them, when the illusion of reality is broken, the immersive experience is weakened and the game is less impressive. Yet, as much as immersion in a virtual space is integral to high-tech computer games like *Half-Life*, breaks in this immersive state are inescapable and often a necessary and important component of gameplay. While the immersive state can be broken in a variety of undesirable ways — poor game design, insufficient hardware, or real-world elements like a ringing telephone — not all breaks in the immersive illusion signify weakness or are undesirable. Indeed, aporias seem by nature opposed to immersion within a game's virtual world. Even the most environmentally consistent aporias — some thrilling, some aggravating — often require players to interrupt the temporal flow of the game and, in so doing, draw attention to the game's artifice. A common strategy for experienced gamers is to save games frequently in anticipation of aporias with irrevocable consequences and in avoidance of being forced to replay significant sections of the game before returning to the problematic obstacle. Like invoking cheat codes, game saving can lessen the power of an aporia and epiphany, but it can also interrupt the player's feelings of immersion since saving can frequently involve extended pauses in gameplay.[12] Some aporias, therefore, are formalised breaks in a player's immersion that increase rather than lessen the satisfaction of gameplay.

Ironically, the very spectacular elements that make a game such a convincing illusion can also interrupt our immersion within a virtual space. Like the aporia that draws attention to a game's artifice, spectacular display can lead players to levels of astonishment that exceed the boundaries of a virtual reality. Even when spectacular displays of a game's technology are consistent with the virtual environment, they can trigger moments that disrupt immersion in a believable world but create exultation in the breathtaking demonstration of special effect. These moments of exultation may ultimately contribute to one's immersion in a game, but they can simultaneously remove players from a game's virtual world into the meta-space of technological admiration. Indeed, the 'realism' of an explosion can remove a player from a virtual space at the same time that it increases her feeling of presence within it. Murray agrees that 'Spectacle is used to create exultation, to move us to another order of perception, and to fix us in the moment' (1997: 112), and her account of immersion as a 'threshold experience' can help to explain the relationship between our astonishment at technological display and our immersion in a virtual environment. She sees spectacle as creating a 'boundary of the immersive reality' (113) that keeps the real and the virtual apart so that we may project our internal feelings upon safely external realities. 'The more present the enchanted world, the more we need to be reassured that it is only virtual' (103). While I remain cautious about positing a direct correlation between the seeming realness of the virtual and a psychological need to be reminded of its artifice, I agree with Murray's characterisation of the relationship between immersion and astonishment as a threshold experience. But rather than explain the phenomenon of technological astonishment as a necessary 'fourth wall' sustaining the apparently higher purpose of an immersive trance, we should not underestimate the joy we take in the virtuoso display of technological wizardry in and of itself.

The differences between the two psychological spaces I am describing should not be understood as a conflict between immersion and non-immersion, for the astonishment we feel at a game's technological spectacle is also a form of immersion, not in a continuously present virtual environment, although special effects can certainly contribute to building a convincing space. Instead, it is a temporary, rapturous immersion in the game's expert performance of technology. When we watch the particle beam generator in the opening level of *Half-Life* explode in a stunning display of graphic artistry, we might find ourselves both mesmerised and horrified by the imminent chaos at the Black Mesa Research Facility, but also by the fact that the animation continues smoothly while we move around the room admiring the spectacle. When we enter the teleporter room in Lamba Core, we experience a mixture of terror at the several flying alien beasts screeching as they try to kill us and delight at the beautifully rendered room with its impressive and smoothly animated effects. Similarly, when we first teleport to the alien world Xen, we momentarily look in awe, perhaps even letting a 'wow' or 'cool' slip from our lips as we admire the bizarre world of rocks revolving in purple gaseous suspension. In each case, we oscillate back and forth between immersion in the game's world and astonishment at the technological performance.[13]

Story material: the narrative *of* computer games

Recent scholarship on special effects cinema also reflects on the relationship between immersion in a virtual space and astonishment at technological display, a relationship Brooks Landon names the 'aesthetic of ambivalence', where the spectator oscillates between being immersed in the film's fantasy world and being in awe of its special effects. Responding to narrative-based criticism of special effects film, Landon demonstrates that some special effects are 'so striking that they interrupt the narrative or actually work to undermine it' (1992: 68). We might be lead to think of the long spaceship scenes in *2001: A Space Odyssey* (1968), the extended urban shots in *Blade Runner* (1982), or, as Annette Kuhn has noted, the long spaceship landing sequence in *Alien* (1979), 'whose only function must be to invite the spectator's awed gaze' (1990: 148). Rather than being internal narrative elements, these 'show-stoppers' act as 'a kind of counter-narrative that often conflicts with the ostensible discursive narrative' (Landon 1999: 39). Importantly, they also act as episodes in a meta-story of special effects, or what Landon calls 'the special effects story that the film is 'really' about' (1999: 69). As Ndalianis documents, George Lucas's *Star Wars* series provides an excellent example of how the story of Hollywood special effects gets told from one film to the next. After the relatively computer-free effects in the original *Star Wars* (1977), Lucas's film effects company, Industrial Light and Magic (ILM), began employing more digital effects, ultimately taking the original *Star Wars* trilogy and digitally re-mastering their effects for re-release twenty years later in 1997. Ndalianis calls this re-release 'an homage to the changes that have occurred in computer graphics ... and a virtuoso performance that takes a bow for the "improvements" in special effects the film has introduced' (2000: 259). *The Phantom Menace*, with 95 per cent of its frames employing digital effects of some kind, is the latest magic performance from a company that has been writing the story of Hollywood special effects.

A similar meta-story of effects technology shapes the computer gameplay experience, at least for gamers who play on more than a casual basis. Indeed, the most powerful narrative element of computer games is neither a game's story line nor the retelling of a player's gaming episode, the story he created within the narrative boundaries of the explorative game world. Rather, the striking narrative of computer games is the continuously climaxing state of the art of computer game technology performed in spectacular fashion and for the sake of astonishment whenever the game is played. This narrative is always performed live by the game and the player, and relived repeatedly in gamer community venues such as game review web sites and online newsgroups.[14] This is not the sort of narrative that interests Murray, for it exceeds an individual game's story line. Rather, it is a narrative about special effects and our astonishment over new developments in special effects technology. In other words, it is not the narrative *in* computer games; it is the narrative *of* computer games.

Just as the *Star Wars* series tells the story of cinematic effects development, so too do computer games tell the story of gaming technologies. This narrative is exemplified by the development of 3D first-person shooters in the 1990s. The progression from *Wolfenstein 3D* (Apogee/id software, 1992), to *Doom* and *Doom II* (id software, 1993, 1994), to *Duke Nukem 3D* (3D Realms/GT Interactive, 1996), to *Quake, Quake II,* and *Quake III* (id software, 1996, 1997, 1999), to *Unreal* and *Unreal Tournament* (GT Interactive, 1998, 1999), and to *Half-Life* is the story of 3D game engines, video card technology and game genre design. Each new major game release marks a new episode in game development and an attempt to out-do its predecessors by offering enhanced game play, more immersive graphics and audio, and better overall special effects. In addition, each new graphic or sound effect is often a reflection upon previous games and an attempt to surpass them technologically. Game developers know that many gamers will inevitably compare their new game to previous releases in the genre. Indeed, reviews of *Half-Life* inevitably point back to its predecessors, whether to say that, until *Half-Life,* 'Quake has long been the standard' (Skinner 2000) or, until *Half-Life,* 'Games like *Quake* and *Quake 2, Doom* and others, haven't really captivated me' (Jaco 2001). Others reflect more directly upon the evolution of the technology, claiming that *Half-Life* is 'an excellent utilization of the *Quake II* engine ... with interesting nonplayer character, AI' (O'Neal 2000). *Half-Life,* or almost any other computer game for that matter, exists within a narrative of computing technology, a narrative that is in many ways the seemingly never-ending story of digital technology's constantly changing scenery.

Performative agency

When we consider the role of technological astonishment in computer gaming (it simultaneously interrupts and deepens immersion and it functions as a significant element of narrative), then we begin to see the importance of the materiality of technology to the experience of gaming. Computer games are certainly not unique in this respect. Indeed, no cultural artefact exists separately from the material conditions of its production and consumption. But where some cultural forms, such as the realist novel, may try to conceal or simply reduce the interruptive potential of these material conditions, computer games tend to flaunt them. Indeed, rather than seeing their presentation technology as a possible hindrance to ideal consumption — for some, a novel's physical characteristics should not detract from one's immersion in the story — computer game publishers and designers tend to emphasise the materiality of their games. For example, game publishers frequently use magazine advertisements, web sites and other promotional material to tout a game's technological advances, including its support for the latest hardware. And game designers normally provide advanced user settings for adjusting visual and auditory quality, including colour depth, texture quality, video resolution and three-dimensional sound. While these settings ostensibly allow users with less powerful hardware to play a game, they also imply that the best gaming experience is available only to those with the most powerful computers. Where last year's graphics adapter and sound card may be enough to run a game, the latest graphics adapter and sound card, according to Sierra Studios' *Half-Life* promotion, will make things look and sound 'mind-bogglingly cool' (Sierra Studios 2001). If the experience of gaming, therefore, is closely tied to visual and auditory effect, and if the best experience depends upon the best technology, then it seems fair to say that the experience of gaming is also closely tied to the material technology of its consumption.

It is here where the experience of special effects film and computer games begin to diverge, not so much because one flaunts its technology more than the other. Indeed, recent developments in home theatre technology highlight the materiality of the film experience just as computer games do, especially when movies are made to take advantage of technologies such as Dolby digital audio and interactive DVD. Where computer games differ significantly is in their fundamental reliance upon user participation. Certainly, some DVD videos include interactivity to expand the viewing experience beyond the basic start-pause-rewind interactivity of a VHS video. In the DVD release of *The Matrix*, for instance, a white rabbit periodically pops onto the screen to signify that, if the viewer presses the right button on her remote control, she will jump to a behind-the-scenes explanation of the scene's technical construction. But this form of interactivity is necessary neither to the movie's internal narrative development nor to its display of technological effect, although it certainly highlights the movie's technology. In computer games, however, interactivity is necessary not only for the game to proceed — in most games, players must use interface devices to guide a character, animal or machine through a game's virtual spaces. Interactivity in computer games is also necessary to the performance of technological splendour, a performance that is shared between the player and the game's designers. In this respect, a game's spectacular display of technological effect is both scripted and partially performed by the game developer, who programmes and arranges the game's potentialities, and the player, whose interactions with the game help determine the timing, quantity and even the quality of these potentialities. So, where the movie viewer and gamer may share a *psychologically* active oscillation between immersion and technological awe, the gamer is more deeply involved in a *physically* active performance.

In some gamer communities, the lines that distinguish the performative work of a gamer from that of a game designer are very difficult, even if useful, to determine. This is especially so in games that provide players with varying degrees of access to the game's low-level design technology. In these cases, the performance of a game's technology includes deep levels of user-customisation, such as the design of new character appearances (skins) and the creation of new levels, spaces, and scenarios (mods). In the enormous *Half-Life* community, there are literally hundreds of skins and mods that users share over the internet, most built using the Worldcraft level editor supplied with the *Half-Life* game.[15] Like game designers, players who build their own game modifications are both performing and choreographing the game's underlying technology in that their choreography of the game engine's potentialities is also a virtuoso performance of skill with gaming technology. The temptation may be to explain the blurring of lines between the player (performer) and game developer (choreographer) in terms of a politics of power, an approach taken by many hypertext theorists to explain the relationship between readers and authors of interactive texts.[16] Such an account, however, would assume a prior state in which the game player did not have the power to influence a game's demonstration of visual and auditory effect. Rather than thinking of computer gameplay in terms of before and after agency, it is more useful to think in terms of degrees of agency. Indeed, game developers who supply level and character editors with their games clearly recognise that the feeling of performative agency is fundamental to the computer gaming experience.

Deep levels of user-customisation emphasise, as do the other elements of gameplay I have been discussing, that the pleasure of today's high-tech computer games is significantly steeped in the pleasure of experiencing and participating in the performance of visual and auditory technologies. Immersion within a fictional space is clearly part of the pleasure, but many action-adventure games — and most current computer games in other genres — present themselves as performances and choreographies of technological wizardry. They elicit astonishment, seek admiration and invite participation in the performance. While these fictional spaces may rely upon narrative to provide logical context, narrative in most action-adventure computer games, as Gunning (1990) has demonstrated of early trick films, is frequently relegated to a back-story upon which to arrange a technological performance. This does not mean that internal narrative is not important to computer games, but it does suggest that it is not the only or even the central element of computer gaming pleasure. The more fascinating story for many dedicated gamers is the story of gaming technology itself, a story in which players participate through their own performance of the game's technology. This feeling of participation may be illusory, since the game's potentialities are defined by its designer and the player's participation is shaped significantly by access to the latest personal computing technology. In this sense, player participation in computer gaming may seem to offer up a virtual freedom of movement when it really acts as a means to promoting sales in the computer industry. The story of computer gaming, therefore, can be understood as a story of technological progression where participating in the story involves more than the pleasure of playing technology, but also the pleasure of accessing it.

The pleasure of computer games, therefore, is a technological pleasure. It is a pleasure of accessing, witnessing and performing technologically mediated environments. Inasmuch as players take pleasure in performing game technology, they also take pleasure in game technology performing them: their physical movements, emotional responses and financial investments. It is a pleasure of control, but also of being controlled. But most of all, it is a technological pleasure propelled by the computer gaming industry's apparent mission to provide more realistically rendered environments, deeper feelings of performative agency and even greater levels of astonishment.

notes

1   See Landow 1997; Bolter 1991; Joyce 1995; Douglas 2000; and Moulthrop 1989; 1994.
2   See Grusin 1994.
3   Andrew Darley argues that a distinctive characteristic of three-dimensional computer games is their lack of semantic meaning (2000: 147—66).
4   See Landon 1992 and 1999; Ndalianis 2000.

5 Geoff King (2000) makes a compelling argument for the narrative capacity of special effect in *Spectacular Narratives: Hollywood in the Age of the Blockbuster*.

6 For detailed technical discussion of *The Phantom Menace* see Lucasfilm Ltd. 2001.

7 For other treatments of narrative in computer games, see Aarseth 1997 and Douglas 2000.

8 Figures are in US dollars.

9 At Gamespot.com (Ziff-Davis's online repository for game review from their collection of print game magazines *Computer Gaming World, Official US PlayStation Magazine, Expert Gamer*, and *Electronic Gaming Monthly*), games are evaluated for gameplay, graphics, sound, value, and reviewer's tilt; the Adrenaline Vault relies upon graphics, interface, gameplay, multiplayer implementation, sound f/x, musical score, intelligence and difficulty, and overall impression; and PCGameReview, a site for user reviews, requires that users evaluate games upon the basis of graphics, sound, gameplay, and an overall rating.

10 Not all reviews of *Half-Life* are so enthusiastic about its narrative, but even those that criticize it inadvertently praise it, as in Ron Dunlin's review from *GameSpot*: 'Suffice it so say that *Half-Life* isn't a great game because of its story; it's a great game because of how it presents that story' (2001).

11 One of the more important gaming technology developments in recent years has been the development of three-dimensional environmental audio standards such as Creative Labs' Environmental Audio Extensions (EAX) and Microsoft's DirectSound.

12 Many games include a quick-save feature which allows players to hit a single key to save their spot in the game. While this significantly overcomes the interruptive process of invoking menu systems and naming files, most computer games limit the number of quick-saves to one or a few, and some do not store quick-saves between game-playing sessions. Some games do not allow users to perform any saving at all until the player finishes a level, which can be remarkably frustrating during particularly difficult moments in a game.

13 We might think of this oscillation in terms of the sublime, that pleasurable feeling we experience when we see in representation what we believe would be too dangerous, painful, or terrifying in reality. For eighteenth-century philosopher Edmund Burke, the sublime finds its source in 'Whatever is fitted in any sort to excite the ideas of pain, and danger, that is to say, whatever is in any sort terrible, or is conversant about terrible objects, or operates in a manner analogous to terror' (Burke 1759: 58). And it results in 'the strongest emotion which the mind is capable of feeling' (*Ibid.*). The sublime is the deep feeling of delightful terror we experience in works that bring us to intensely emotional and terrifying, but still satisfying, moments of climax that, in William Wordsworth's words, lead us to 'elevated thoughts; a sense sublime/ Of something far more deeply interfused' (Wordsworth, ll. 95—6). Importantly, Burke uses the term 'astonishment' to describe our experience of the sublime. For Burke, astonishment is 'that state of the soul, in which all its motions are suspended, with some degree of horror' and the 'mind is so entirely filled with its object, that it cannot entertain any other, nor by consequence reason on that object which employs it' (1759: 95). In other words, astonishment is a feeling of immersion in the object of contemplation, for we are so filled with astonishment and amazement that we can think of nothing else.

14 One way in which game players gain some of the visibility of professional game reviewers is on web sites that support player reviews of games. GameSpot.com and

PCGameReview.com encourage readers to contribute their own reviews and ratings of games, which amounts to the telling of the story of game technology. These reviews are not normally reflections upon one player's experience of blowing away a particular alien or of figuring out a specific puzzle, although they do comment on these moments. Instead, as with professional reviews, they focus on a game's technical merit, hardware requirements, and, of course, its level of challenge and fun.

15 At the time of writing, there were over 240 mods listed at *EspaceMOD* (http://www.planethalflife.com/espacemod/).

16 See Landow 1997.

citations

Aarseth, Espen J. (1997) *Cybertext: Perspectives on Ergodic Literature*. Baltimore: Johns Hopkins UP.

___ (1999) 'Aporia and Epiphany in *Doom* and *The Speaking Clock*: The Temporality of Ergodic Art', in Marie-Laure Ryan (ed.) *Cyberspace Textuality, Computer Technology and Literary Theory*. Bloomington, Indiana: Indiana UP, 31—41.

Ajami, Amer (2001) 'Half-Life Review', *SharkyExtreme.com*. 5 August. Available on-line at: http://www.sharkyextreme.com/games/valve_halflife_r/.

Bolter, Jay David (1991) *Writing Space: The Computer, Hypertext, and the History of Writing*. Hillsdale, New Jersey: Lawrence Erlbaum Associates.

Burke, Edmund (1759) *A Philosophical Inquiry into the Origin of our Ideas of the Sublime and Beautiful*, 2nd edn., London: R. & J. Dodsley.

CNET Networks Media Property (2001a) *GameSpot.com*. 5 August. Available on-line at: http://www.gamespot.com.

CNET Networks Media Property (2001b) *GameSpot.com: The Best & Worst of 1999*. 5 August. Available on-line at: http://www.gamespot.com/features/1999/index.html.

CNET Networks Media Property (2001c) *GameSpot.com: The Best & Worst of 2000*. 5 August. Available on-line at: http://gamespot.com/gamespot/features/pc/bestof_2000/.

ConsumerREVIEW Inc. (2001) *PCGameReview*. 5 August. Available on-line at: http://www.pcgamereview.com/.

Darley, Andrew (2000) *Visual Digital Culture: Surface Play and Spectacle in New Media Genres*. New York: Routledge.

Douglas, J. Yellowlees (2000) *The End of Books — Or Books Without End: Reading Interactive Narratives*. Ann Arbor, Mich.: U Michigan P.

Dunlin, Ron (2001) 'Half-Life.' *GameSpot.com*. 5 August. Available on-line at: http://gamespot.com/gamespot/stories/reviews/0,10867,2537398,00.html.

EspaceMOD (2001) 5 August 2001. Available on-line at: http://www.planethalflife.com.

Gaudreault, André (1990) 'Film, Narrative, Narration: The Cinema of the Lumière Brothers', in Thomas Elsaesser with Adam Barker (eds) *Early Cinema: Space, Frame, Narrative*. London: BFI, 68—75.

Grusin, Richard (1994) 'What is an Electronic Author? Theory and the Technological Fallacy', *Configurations*, 2, 3, 469—83.

Gunning, Tom (1990) 'The Cinema of Attractions: Early Film, Its Spectator and the Avant-Garde', in Thomas Elsaesser with Adam Barker (eds) *Early Cinema: Space, Frame, Narrative*. London: BFI, 56—62.

Hubble, Calvin (2001) 'Half-Life, Not Half Bad', *Game Revolution*. 5 August. Available on-line at: http://www.game-revolution.com/games/pc/action/half-life.htm.

Interactive Digital Software Association (2001) *State of the Industry Report, 2000–2001*. 5 August. Available on-line at: http://www.idsa.com/releases/SOTI2001.pdf.

Jaco (2001) 'Half-Life.' *Gamer's Edge*. 5 August. Available on-line at: http://gamersxtreme. virtualave.net/reviews/action/half%20life/halflife.htm.

Joyce, Michael (1995) *Of Two Minds: Hypertext Pedagogy and Poetics*. Ann Arbor, Mich.: U Michigan P.

Kasavin, Greg (2001) 'Planescape: Torment', *GameSpot.com*, 5 August. Available on-line at: http://www.gamespot.com/rpg/torment/review.html.

King, Geoff (2000) *Spectacular Narratives: Hollywood in the Age of the Blockbuster.* New York: I.B. Tauris.

Kuhn, Annette (ed.) (1999) *Alien Zone II: The Spaces of Science Fiction Cinema.* New York: Verso.

___ (ed.) (1990) *Alien Zone: Cultural Theory and Contemporary Science Fiction Cinema.* London: Verso.

Landon, Brooks (1992) *The Aesthetics of Ambivalence: Rethinking Science Fiction Film in the Age of Electronic (Re)production.* Westport, Conn.: Greenwood Press.

___ (1999) 'Diegetic or Digital? The Convergence of Science Fiction Literature and Science Fiction Film in Hypermedia', in Annette Kuhn (ed.) *Alien Zone II: The Spaces of Science Fiction Cinema.* New York: Verso, 31–49.

Landow, George P. (1997) *Hypertext 2.0: The Convergence of Contemporary Critical Theory and Technology.* Baltimore: Johns Hopkins UP.

Lucasfilm Ltd. (2001) *Star Wars: Episode I: Episode I Feature Archive.* 5 August. Available on-line at: http://www.starwars.com/episode-i/feature/.

McQuillan, Martin (2000) 'Introduction: Aporias of Writing: Narrative and Subjectivity', in *The Narrative Reader.* New York: Routledge, 1–33.

Moulthrop, Stuart (1989) 'In the Zones: Hypertext and the Politics of Interpretation'. Available on-line at: http://www.ubalt.edu/ygcla/sam/essays/prezones.html.

___ (1994) 'Rhizome and Resistance: Hypertext and the Dreams of a New Culture', in George Landow (ed.) *Hyper/ Text/ Theory.* Baltimore: Johns Hopkins UP, 299–322.

Murray, Janet (1997) *Hamlet on the Holodeck: The Future of Narrative in Cyberspace.* Cambridge, Mass.: MIT Press.

Ndalianis, Angela. 'Special Effects, Morphing Magic, and the 1990s Cinema of Attractions.' *Meta-Morphing: Visual Transformation and the Culture of Quick Change.'* Ed. Vivian Sobchack. Minneapolis, MN: U Minnesota P, 2000, pp. 251–71.

Newworld.com Inc. *The Adrenaline Vault.* 5 August 2001. Available on-line at: http://www.adrenalinevault.com/.

O'Neal, William. 'Half-Life.' *Gamecenter.com.* 9 April 2000. Available on-line at: http://www.gamecenter.com/Reviews/Item/0,6,0-2289,00.html.

Sierra Studios. *Half-Life Overview.* 5 August 2001. Available on-line at: http://www.sierrastudios.com/games/half-life/bot.html.

Skinner, Reed (2000) 'Half-Life', *The Gamers View.* 15 May. Available on-line at: http://www.gamersview.net/reviews/halflife.htm.

Stafford, Barbara Maria (1996) *Good Looking: Essays on the Virtue of Images.* Cambridge, Mass: MIT Press.

Wordsworth, William (1967) 'Tintern Abbey', in David Perkins (ed.) *British Romantic Writers.* New York: Harcour Brace Jovanovich, 209–11.

chapter two

Die Hard/Try Harder: Narrative, Spectacle and Beyond, from Hollywood to Videogame

geoff king

Debates about the relationship between narrative and spectacle in contemporary media products, particularly those associated with new digital technologies, have provided one prominent point of intersection between the study of cinema and videogames. The aesthetic of games, generally, is associated with an attenuation of narrative dynamics in favour of the production of qualities such as sensation and spectacle, among others. The same is often said to have become a dominant characteristic of many special-effects or action-oriented Hollywood films. A causal connection might be suggested, as a result of mutual influences and borrowings between Hollywood and the games industry, both aesthetic and in terms of the corporate links between the two media. Alternatively, the dominance of spectacle and sensation over narrative, in these cases, is seen as part of a broader historical tendency in particular sectors of contemporary visual media culture (see Darley 2000). Claims about the diminishment of narrative in the contemporary Hollywood blockbuster have been greatly overstated, as I have argued elsewhere (see King 2000, 2002). Narrative, *combined with* spectacle, remains centrally important to even the noisiest and most special-effects and action reliant of big-screen blockbusters. How exactly, though, do qualities such as narrative and spectacle operate in videogames?

Narrative and spectacle are both present in videogames, but their situation in the interactive environment of the game creates a number of differences and distinctions, in each case, from their role in Hollywood cinema. One way to approach this question, to highlight such differences, is to examine games based directly on major film franchises. The structure of some film-based games is modeled quite closely on sequences from the films themselves, which provides a good opportunity to compare and contrast the specific qualities offered by the two forms. This chapter will focus principally on the experiences offered to the viewer or participant by the PlayStation games *Die Hard Trilogy* (Probe/Fox Interactive, 1996) and *Die Hard Trilogy 2* (n-Space/Fox Interactive, 2000) and the three *Die Hard* films (1988, 1990, 1995). Some other examples will also be used, including *Max Payne* (Remedy/GodGames, 2001), a strongly narrative-driven game that occupies much the same generic territory as the *Die Hard* franchise.

From linear narrative to repetition

Narrative plays a part in the construction of the pleasures offered by the two *Die Hard Trilogy* games, but it is both differently located and less central to the experience of the game than it is to the films. The *Die Hard* games, like many others, provide narrative frames for the gaming experience. A fairly minimal 'backstory' is supplied, giving some context for the action. Narrative components are provided, to varying extents, as the events progress (to a greater extent in *Die Hard Trilogy 2* than in the original, a distinction to which I return later). The role of narrative, however, is primarily one of setting up situations of gameplay from which narrative itself tends largely to be absent.[1] A narrative dimension is found in many games of this kind, but it tends to take a backseat in the design process to the demands set by the provision of particular forms of gameplay or the parameters set by existing technological resources (see Rouse 2001: 44–7). The main 'business' of the *Die Hard* games is engagement in the specific challenges set by each of the three components: a third-person action-adventure game, a first-person rail-shooter and a high-speed 'extreme driving' game. The overall narrative framework is built into the infrastructure of the game and is inviolable, as is the case in many games. Part of the task of the player is to realise the pre-set narrative fabric, through successful completion of each level, but little if anything is offered in the way of interactivity at the narrative level itself. Only one route is permitted through the game. The dimension of interactivity is located, instead, in the ongoing action that occurs within this narrative frame and that constitutes the bulk of the game-playing experience.

The balance of emphasis here is very different from that found in the films, in which an important dimension of pleasure is founded on the fact that the viewer cannot control or shape *any* aspects of the on-screen events. This is a major component of the narrative infrastructure of Hollywood-type films. A central premise of the *Die Hard* films, for example, is that the hero *will* ultimately prevail. We know that pretty much for certain, as a basic narrative convention in the mainstream action movie. Because we have this certainty, we can enjoy all sorts of difficulties on the way. We can enjoy the various sufferings and setbacks faced by a hero such as McClane in the safe knowledge that it will all turn out well, even if we do not know exactly *how* he will overcome any particular difficulty. A balance is established between narrative elements of suspense and uncertainty and of confident security. A real sense of suspense and *localised* uncertainty is mobilised by the film. In one sequence in *Die Hard*, for example,

51

McClane dangles in a lift shaft, suspended on a belt tied to a gun wedged in the doorway. The gun is not very securely placed. It starts to slip, detail picked up in cutaway shots from McClane that create a situation of suspense for the viewer. At the same time, one of the bad guys is seen getting closer... Eventually the gun does slip but McClane manages to gain a hand-hold and finds his way into a ventilation duct — from which the film moves to its next sequence of will-they-or-won't-they-find-him suspense.

The narrative dynamic of sequences such as these is dependent on the fact that the viewer has no direct influence over the course of events. The film viewer performs none of the active, *shaping* role that is permitted in the game, even if the game only allows this within pre-structured limits (the degree of freedom offered to the player within such constraints can vary considerably from one game to another). Film viewing is not an entirely passive experience, as is sometimes implied in comparisons between cinema and games. It involves a variety of cognitive activities, conscious and subconscious, through which we bring to the text a range of expectations and various engagements with the ongoing events and their likely consequences (for more on this, see Branigan 1992); events might be understood in more ways than one, but this is not the same as the viewer having any ability to alter what actually happens on screen.

The experience of the game is rather different. If we can be sure that McClane lives up to the *Die Hard* title in the movie, the opposite tends to be the case in the game. The figure of McClane, loosely occupied by the player, dies repeatedly. This is a basic structural assumption that marks a major distinction between films and games of this kind. The game does not offer the same kind of narrative-based security as that found in the movie, although it might offer other forms of its own. The experience of the game involves a great deal of nervous anxiety amid the finger-twitching, because the fate of the avatar is (literally) in the hands of the player and is genuinely in doubt, depending on the skill and experience (or otherwise!) of the player. The films offer a combination of tension, uncertainty and underlying security, in a very particular balance that I would suggest is one factor central to the appeal of the form.

Some aides are given to the game-player, such as the map-insert in the third-person *Die Hard* component that indicates the presence of enemy figures and where to find goodies such as weapons and health restoration. This adds to the difference between movie and game experiences, however, because it gives the player another thing to worry about. The player has to decide whether to focus attention on the immediate situation on the main screen or the wider picture offered by the insert, or some kind of combination of the two: the kind of choice that is usually taken out of our hands in the movies. This, in my experience, creates a rather uncomfortable state of trying to watch both at once, an experience rarely created more than fleetingly in the cinema.[2]

A sense of predictability or security is achieved through a process in which the player, given sufficient time and competence, eventually masters the game and moves on to another. Much repetition is usually involved: going back and starting again, whole levels or parts of levels, depending on the 'saving' regime permitted by any particular game or platform. Repetition occupies a central place in the regime of game-playing and might be said to perform something like the function of the establishment of narrative-convention-based security in the film. In both cases, an element of predictability is also established through repetition from one *text* to another. Familiarity with the game genre helps to build competence, with many action-adventure games such as *Die Hard Trilogy* deploying broadly similar conventions and requiring the performance of similar tasks. The same is true in popular cinema, familiarity with genre-specific or broader Hollywood conventions being one of the main sources of the ultimate predictability of narrative outcomes in a film such as *Die Hard*. The difference is that experience of the film is less likely to involve repetition of the single text; or, at least, to be in any significant way *dependent upon* repetition.[3] Mastery of the game does in most cases require multiple repetitions: an injunction to learn, to keep going, to try harder. Without that great investment of time, or even during it, the gaming experience can be a source of frustration. Games have learning curves that are variable, more or less steep or shallow, a dimension that features quite importantly in the reviews, indicating the degree of time/commitment that is likely to be required. A strategy that is learned quite quickly in the third-person action-adventure component of *Die Hard Trilogy*, for example, is that it should be played in a manner that does reflect a central element of the films: that is, to adopt a careful hide-and-seek approach, sneaking around and picking off enemies from positions, rather than attempting frontal assault that is likely to end in the death of the avatar.

The fact that the experience of games can entail large measures of anxiety and uncertainty — to an extent not usually found in the cinema, because of its particular narrative regime — has been linked by some commentators to the role they might perform in the socialization process for adolescent males. Playing a game such as *Die Hard Trilogy*, persistently, to achieve mastery in the face of the stresses and anxieties it creates, is seen as one way of practicing the 'performance' of dominant versions of masculinity (see Jenkins 1999; Burrill 2002). This is a useful perspective on some of these specific qualities of gameplay in formats such as action-adventure-shooting that tend to appeal primarily, if far from exclusively, to young males. One element often left out of consideration, however, here and in analysis of games more generally, is the range of ways in which games can be played. There are other ways of engaging with a title such as *Die Hard Trilogy*, some of which might counter the characteristics I have emphasised so far and that play a central role in these gender-based readings.

'Cheating' is a process that has become institutionalised in the game-playing world. Official strategy guides are available for many games, requiring a considerable outlay on top of the price of the game itself. Or, increasingly, cheats and walk-throughs are available free of charge from a number of internet sources.[4] This is an important and distinctive element of the game-playing experience. With the aid of cheats, the nature of the experience can be very different. There is no great need for subtlety if you play *Die Hard Trilogy* in 'god' mode, for example: you can just stand and blast enemies in the knowledge that you are beyond harm. Cheating permits a faster passage through the game that can be more satisfying on one level. It removes most if not all of the anxiety. It saves much of the need to keep repeating sequences because your avatar has died. But, of course, cheating removes the real sense of achievement that can result from success earned the longer and harder way, and much of the dynamic of stress/anxiety/mastery on which some gender-socialisation accounts focus.

A variety of modes of engagement are possible. Games can be played 'straight', without any cheating, or with cheats of different kinds or extents. It is also possible to combine different types of play. Cheats or walk-throughs might be used to gain an initial sense of orientation, for example, before reverting to a 'straight' mode of play; or in cases of particular difficulty for the individual gamer. An interesting area for empirical research would be to try to establish what the main tendencies of play are in this sense, or exactly how varied they might be. The type of play used in any particular case depends partly on the level of investment put in by the player — investment of both time and money. A difference might be found in attitudes towards games that have been bought, at quite a high cost, and to which the player has unlimited access, and those that have just been hired for a weekend or borrowed. Being open to more than one approach seems to be important to the games industry, not limiting enjoyable access to just the most 'serious', sustained or time-consuming modes of engagement.

Audience-oriented approaches have demonstrated that the uses of media such as film and television are far from entirely fixed by the characteristics of the text itself. Different viewers might 'do' different things with the same textual material. To some extent, this potential variety of use can be structured-in at the textual level. Hollywood films, for example, often offer a range of potential appeals in the hope of reaching the largest possible audience. Games appear to be structured with this in-built variety of uses more overtly in mind, a factor largely of the greater commitment of time and effort they demand on the part of the player. There are big differences between film and game, but these are not simple or singular. The fact that the game can be played in different modes complicates the picture and raises many questions.

The interactive dimension of games, in the form of the responsibility taken by the player, does open up a large gulf between the two media, however, especially at the level of narrative or its relative absence, whichever way the game is played. The distinctions highlighted above pose a number of questions about the likely appeal or structure of possible future hybrids between film and more interactive media such as videogames. To introduce *substantial* interactivity — in terms of the viewer/player shaping what happens — offers all sorts of new potentials. But it also means the loss of one key source of the appeal of popular narrative cinema: the enjoyable process of having the balance of events taken entirely out of our hands. It might well be fun, as a novelty, for the film viewer to be able to make certain decisions about the outcome of the movie, for example, through the design of branching narrative forms. This is something that has been explored in various ways, including some Net-based serials and the occasional interactive DVD movie. But to do so might be to risk undermining pleasures such as those of carefully balanced and organised tension and suspense; of wondering what exactly is going to happen or when *without* being able to influence it at all.

Tension and suspense can be created in games in a number of ways, including musical cues and other warnings of imminent but not necessarily certain danger (for example, devices similar to those used by characters in *Alien* (1979) to alert the player to the presence of aliens in *Alien Trilogy* (Probe/Acclaim, 1996) and *Aliens vs. Predator* (Rebellion/Fox Interactive, 1999)), or simply the knowledge that something nasty is likely to happen before long in horror or action-adventure based titles. The experience of such qualities is very different from that found in film, however, because of the influence active intervention by the player usually has on crucial factors such as the precise timing of movement (and, hence, in many cases, events) and the simple fact that the player can often choose one response or another. The aim for potential hybrid media might be to achieve an appropriate balance between different kinds of pleasure: the pleasure of close interactivity and control and the Hollywood-movie-type pleasure of safely underpinned loss of control over the unfolding of the action.

Some games do already seek to establish something closer to this kind of combination of narrative-led and interactive appeals. An element of this is found in the sequel to the *Die Hard Trilogy* game, *Die Hard Trilogy 2*. The sequel is not based on events in the films but follows the same basic structure as the first game: a third-person adventure game, a shooting gallery and a driving game. The principal addition is the ability to play in what the game calls 'movie mode', a significant choice of phrase in this context. This involves a combination of all three games, starting in the action-adventure mode and interspersing progress through this dimension with bursts of shooting gallery, driving and the obligatory (rather low quality) movie-style pre-rendered cut-scenes. This offers something a little closer to a movie-type experience. It strengthens the sense of building some kind of narrative development, or assembly of components, that might be expected in an action movie.

A sense is established in 'movie mode' that what happens in one segment *leads to* that which occurs in the next. Completion of a third-person adventure level appears to *set up* a driving chase, for example, that *ends in* or *leads to* a confrontation that takes the form of a shooting gallery sequence. Play in this mode offers a balance between different kinds of activities that has something in common with the balance you might find in a *Die Hard* type movie: cat-and-mouse sequences, chases, all-out gun battles — some, if far from all, of the ingredients of the films.[5] There is also a sense here of the *unfolding* of the game and the movement between different components, at least, being taken out of the hands of the player. The experience is very different from choosing to play just one of the games, repeating its basic characteristics through different levels, and then choosing to move to another. There is a sense of *rhythm* and variety that's set up *for* the player. Establishing an appropriate rhythm across the length of the game is an important aspect of game design if interest is to be maintained, including the right balance of challenge and reward (see Poole 2000: 198–201).

How exactly this works in the case of *Die Hard Trilogy 2* is, again, subject to a number of qualifications. It depends, as always, on how the game is played. The sense of anything approaching a movie rhythm is lost if the game is played by a not very competent or committed player in anything other than 'invincibility' mode: too much dying, stopping, reloading, impatience and starting again breaks up any strong sense of forward-moving dynamic. Even in 'invincibility' mode, it is still easy to get excessively and frustratingly delayed by inability to solve a particular puzzle in the third-person adventure segments, and the strategy guide is not always so easy to obtain (or to understand, in some cases) at the moment when it is required. But there is, here, the possibility of something that, while not being in any way the same as a movie, offers *some* similar qualities of experience. It is significant that the term 'movie mode' is employed, suggesting some investment on the part of the games industry in playing on associations with Hollywood movies at a level that is not entirely superficial (the use of the term can be explained to some extent in this case, of course, by the fact that the game is part of a movie franchise, and hence might be expected to be more likely than some to attract buyers anticipating some specific connection with the movie experience).

The PC game *Max Payne* takes these movie-like qualities a significant stage further, moving much more rapidly between instances of interactive gameplay (primarily searching, exploring and shooting) and of narrative development that is taken out of the hands of the player. In the opening scenes, for example, flashbacks cut in on the active gameplay. Narrative generally is pushed forward quite rapidly, through cut-scenes and hard-boiled 'graphic novel' sequences. It is noteworthy that the game is sold partly on this basis, along with its high-quality graphics; it is a relentless 'story-driven game', according to the cover blurb, a dimension highlighted also in the introductory text of the manual. The relatively more cinematic rhythm of the game is heightened by its rapid save and re-start regime. The game can quickly be saved at any point in the active gameplay, obviating the need to replay large sections in the event of the death of the avatar (a regular occurrence), and can be re-started instantaneously. The result is, generally, a much more fast and frenetic pace, without recourse to the use of 'cheats', although this does not remove the possibility of slower and more frustrating periods in which the player gets stuck in one location or another (the sense of being stuck is, if anything, accentuated by the otherwise rapid pace of the game).

Spectacle, sensation and beyond

If narrative plays a less prominent role in games than in films, what about the dimensions of spectacle and sensation? Games appear, generally, to have a larger investment in these qualities than in those based on narrative dynamics, even more story-driven games such as *Max Payne*. In some cases, similarities can be suggested with the mobilization of spectacular or sensational qualities in Hollywood blockbuster films. But, again, important differences also need to be identified, as a result of the interactive dimension of games and the variable forms of play. A useful starting point here is to distinguish between two different modes in which spectacle is often generated in contemporary Hollywood action or special-effects oriented cinema (for more detailed elaboration of these in relation to individual films and the contexts in which they appear, see King

2000). Some forms of cinematic spectacle invite the viewer to sit back in a state of admiration/astonishment, contemplating the scale, detail, convincing texture or other impressive attributes of the image. Others seek to create a more aggressive, explosive and 'in your face' variety of spectacular impact. The distinction is far from an absolute one, the two styles sometimes being used in conjunction and the boundary between one and the other not always clear cut. In general, however, the more contemplative form tends to offer longer and more lingering spectacular vistas while the latter is more reliant on rapid montage-style editing and/or camera movement to create its visual impact.

A broad distinction can be made between the kind of experience offered to the viewer by these two forms of spectacular audio-visual effects, a distinction of relevance to the production of spectacle and sensation in videogames. The more 'contemplative' brand of spectacle emphasises and invites the *look* of the viewer; it is designed to create a 'wow' reaction that entails a subtle dialectic between awareness of spectacle *as* impressive artifice and being (or allowing ourselves to be) 'taken in' by, and thus 'taken into', the fictional world of which the images is a part (for more on this, see King 2000: 54—6; Darley 2000: 104—5). The 'impact aesthetic' created by the more explosive 'in your face' variety offers something closer to an assault on the sensations of the viewer, a vicarious impression of participation in the spectacular action/destruction on screen. The spectacular/sensational qualities of videogames share some of these qualities, but with a number of significant distinctions.

Spectacle of the contemplative variety is offered by some videogames, although rather less in the *Die Hard* games on which this chapter has focused than in some others. One of the pleasures of games is the ability they offer the player, vicariously but with some control over the experience, to explore strange and often visually striking and spectacular worlds of digital animation. The *Die Hard* games are not noted for the quality of their graphics; most of the environments on offer are rather dingy or industrial-functional in nature: office spaces, warehouses, maintenance levels, scientific laboratories, and so on. The driving game in *Die Hard Trilogy 2* is set around the potentially spectacular urban landscape of Las Vegas, but little of the glitter and glitz of the city is rendered in any striking form. The same goes on one level for *Max Payne*, set in 'the gritty bowels of New York', as the cover copy puts it. The settings themselves are unspectacular, but a 'wow' reaction is invited at the degree of resolution with which they are reproduced, especially on higher-end graphics cards at the time of release such as the nVidia GeForce3. This effect, like that of many other forms of visual or audio-visual spectacle, is relative rather than absolute, the 'spectacular' in games often being a function of comparison between one work and predecessors created with less powerful graphics engines or played on machines with inferior capacity. Other game genres offer environments that are, intrinsically, more impressive and spectacular — the exotic locations of the *Tomb Raider* series (Core/Eidos, 1996—2000) or the swirling voids and strange underworld landscapes of *American McGee's Alice* (Rogue/Electronic Arts, 2001), for example — but the same dynamic of relative comparison and contrast is also in operation, between 'previous versions' and the 'state-of-the-art' spectacle promised by each new entry in the series. The pleasure of contemplative spectacle can be a selling point, a way of emphasizing quality of graphics more generally, as in a television advert for the PlayStation 2 racing simulator *Gran Turismo 3* (Polyphony/SCEA, 2001) in which one of the competitors pulls over to the side of the road to watch the sunset.

New or unfolding spectacular vistas — including cut-scenes — are frequently offered as reward and incentive for the completion of particular tasks, subsections, levels or entire games. The aesthetic qualities of digitally rendered environments are, generally, an important factor in videogames, in terms of both player enjoyment and industrial strategy. Improved graphics (along with improved gameplay options) is one of the lures with which the industry sells new titles and, especially, new generations of hardware, such as expensive graphics cards or platforms such as the PlayStation 2 and the X-Box. In this sense the experience and underlying economics have a good deal in common with the production of cinematic spectacle, particularly that which involves the use of new generations of special effects technologies. Spectacular films and games sell the promise of both greater 'realism' — effects that are more 'convincing', relatively speaking — and more impressive varieties of artifice.

The potential pleasures of contemplative spectacle are often interrupted, however, sometimes literally, by the interactive dimension of gameplay. Too much idle enjoyment of spectacular environments can be bad for the health of the avatar, who is liable to be shot, eaten or to face some other unpleasant fate in many games if attention is directed solely to the quality of the surroundings. Intense interactive engagement does not always leave much time for contemplation, although even frenetic first-person shooters figure among the games most highly rated for the spectacular qualities of their visuals; Gamespot's ten 'best-looking' games poll of 2001 included *Unreal* (Epic/GT Interactive, 1998), *Half-Life* (Valve/Sierra, 1998), *Unreal Tournament* (Epic/GT Interactive, 1999) and *Quake III Arena* (id/Activision, 1999), as well as *Myst* (Cyan/Broderbund, 1993) and *American McGee's Alice*. On the other hand, the tedium and frustration that can result from unsuccessful stretches of gameplay can be such that enjoyment of even the most splendid environments begins to wane as a level or section is failed and restarted for the umpteenth time. One of the values of background, environmental spectacle is its ability to maintain visual interest during repeated attempts at a particular task, but there is a limit (in my experience) beyond which its continued appeal is lost.

The location of spectacle/sensation in relation to the player/viewer can also shift in the transition from film to game, although this is a potentially ambiguous ingredient in both forms. In the *Die Hard* films, fireball explosions and kinetic gun battles — the basic currency of the contemporary action movie — offer one of the principal forms of pleasurable spectacular impact. In terms of narrative situation, the attitude the viewer is encouraged to take to explosions, in particular, is variable and far from clear-cut, depending only partly on the identity of the perpetrator. One major fireball in *Die Hard* is unleashed against the 'terrorist' criminal gang by McClane (explosives launched down a lift-shaft), an act designed to be cheered-on by the audience. Another is the work of the bad guys, in an attempt to kill a large number of hostages gathered on the roof of the building, although it is still offered as a source of spectacular attraction for the viewer. More ambiguous might be the status of the fiery destruction of a crowded passenger jet, with much 'innocent' loss of life, in *Die Hard 2*. The sequence is one of the most spectacular in the film, yet narratively coded as tragic and the work of 'evil' terrorist-criminals. McClane's actions for the remainder of the film are intended to avoid a repeat of the incident, just as his objective in *Die Hard with a Vengeance* is to prevent the threatened bombing of a school.

The dynamics of narrative and spectacle appear to be at odds in some of these instances. Narrative quest to prevent destruction vies with viewer pleasure in its spectacular representation. Reconciliation is often found, however, in the form of climactic spectacular explosions in which McClane eventually destroys the opposition. In *Die Hard 2*, for example, poetic justice ensures that the only other aircraft engulfed in spectacular conflagration is that being used in the attempted escape of the bad guys (not only that, but the flames unleashed act as a beacon to help dozens of stranded aircraft to land safely, including the one on which McClane's wife is a passenger). What about the games? Here, gunfire and explosions often represent more immediate hazards to the avatar, and thus to the player. The task on each level of the third-person action-shooter level of *Die Hard Trilogy* is precisely to avoid spectacular explosion: a bomb has to be defused, against the clock, after all 'terrorists' have been dispatched. A similar mission organises the 'extreme driving' component of the trilogy. Other explosions and spectacular events might be offered along the way, but the unleashing of spectacle that has most in common with that of the films occurs at the moment of failure. In both cases, the climactic explosion is mounted in a manner similar to the Hollywood action-movie style.

Figure 6 Fireball engulfs the Nakatomi Plaza tower, coming out to fill the screen, in the cut-scene after failure of the mission in *Die Hard Trilogy* (Probe/Fox Interactive, 1996)

Figure 7 Fireball and debris explodes out towards the player, action-movie style, in *Die Hard Trilogy* (Probe/Fox Interactive, 1996)

The end-of-level conflagration that occurs when time runs out in third-person action-adventure-shooting mode starts as a fiery rush outwards, across the setting of the level and towards the screen. The player is then presented with a pre-rendered sequence in which a digital version of the Nakatomi Plaza tower blows up, sending another fiery mass out towards the player. Timed-out failure in the driving game also ends in an explosion that generates a wall of flame that comes out at the screen, carrying with it cars and other debris in a manner that replicates almost exactly a style widely adopted by the contemporary Hollywood action-spectacular (for more on this in relation to Hollywood, see King 2000: 91–104).

These incidences of spectacular impact, the most cinematic in the game, offer a potential mixture of pleasure and irritation; a enjoyable *frisson*, but located at a moment likely to be that of maximum frustration, following the anxiety-inducing final moments of the countdown. This might be experienced as compensation for the frustrating experience of having failed, and having to start the level again, although the reaction might be a more complex mixture of pleasure and annoyance (the same can be said of the spectacle of the death of the avatar in numerous other games, including *Max Payne*, in which the central character often performs a satisfying pirouette movement on being shot or burned to death, and the *Tomb Raider* games, in which aural qualities such as the

Figure 8 The spectacle of death: Max comes to grief ... again, in *Max Payne* (Remedy/GodGames, 2001)

sound of being impaled on a spike contribute to the aesthetics of virtual death). It is a more satisfying way to conclude a failed level than the equivalent in *Die Hard Trilogy 2*, for example, in which any such effect is conspicuous by its absence. Failure in a third-person sequence set in a 'bio-lab' ends in the activation of an auto-destruct mechanism that is marked by no satisfying manifestation of destruction, merely the words 'out of time' and a fade to black. The same anti-climax concludes unsuccessful efforts at the driving game.

An interesting and unusual example of a game that seeks deliberately to avoid the potential moral quandary of offering pleasurable spectacular display at the point of avowed failure – and, in this case, mass destruction and death in the game-world – is *Balance of Power II: The 1990 Edition* (Mindscape/Freeware), a strategy 'un-wargame' game in which the aim is to avoid the outbreak of hostilities. Players who spark nuclear conflict are greeted by a screen bearing the text: 'You have ignited a nuclear war. And no, there is no animated display of a mushroom cloud with parts of bodies flying through the air. We do not reward failure' (reproduced in Rouse 2001: 273). This was, of course, much easier to reproduce than spectacular images of destruction; an example of functionality serving moral imperative.

If interactivity is sometimes a bar to contemplative enjoyment of spectacle, it clearly offers much potential for the extension of the kind of impact-aesthetic offered by some films. Techniques such as hyper-rapid editing, unstable 'subjective' camerawork and the propelling of objects at high speed out towards the screen are often used in Hollywood action sequences to create a heightened impression of viewer proximity to, or participation in, the action. Impact that remains entirely vicarious in the cinema can become more literally and physically transmitted to the game-player, through the use of devices such as the vibrating 'dual-shock' mechanism available on the PlayStation. When the avatar is shot, injured or jumps from a height in *Die Hard Trilogy 2*, for example, the impact is felt in the hands of the player. How effective this is remains open to question. The vibration is hardly commensurate with the nature of some of the impact suffered by the avatar and lacks any sense of discrimination between one kind of impact and another. The form of impact offered by some Hollywood films through explosive editing and rapid camera movement is far more powerful, if viewed in the cinema or on domestic audio-visual equipment of a reasonably high standard. The fact remains, though, that the game offers a new dimension, an actual physical force imparted to the viewer, that is not available in the cinema,[6] or impact that has implications for the game-playing experience (causing injury, death or advancement of the avatar, for example).

More generally, a sense of assaultive impact and sensation can be found in combat sequences in games in which the player faces a range of antagonists, from the various kinds of bad guy faced in the *Die Hard Trilogy* games and *Max Payne* (some easier to tackle than others) to the more exotic beasts, including a tiger and a T-Rex, in the *Tomb Raider* series and the opponents faced in highly popular beat-'em-up games. In *Dino Crisis* (Capcom, 1999, a game influenced by the film *Jurassic Park* (1993)) the third-person avatar is subject to sudden attacks from dinosaurs, including one particularly spectacular assault by a T-Rex, the effect of which is to send the pulse racing. Limited scale and low fidelity of graphics reduce the audio-visual impact of such sequences to a level far below that achieved in the cinema, although the 'in your face' variety of impact is increased in a literal sense through the close proximity in which the player is often located to the screen (especially in the case of PC games). The nature of the experience is changed, however, and heightened in other respects, by the interactive dimension. This is a point at which the spectacular and particularly the *sensational* qualities of film and game appear to diverge more radically. Explosive spectacle in Hollywood films impacts *on* the viewer. For action-movie fans, part of the pleasure is one of being 'done to', as it is put by Barker & Brooks (1998: 146). Action-oriented games offer a similar pleasure of sensational impact, of things happening forcefully *to* the player, via the avatar, but one that requires a substantial reciprocal *response* from the player: a 'doing to' as well as being 'done to', an opportunity to engage with the source of sensational impact: to fight back, to attempt to negotiate difficult and potentially hazardous terrain, and so on. This can entail a frenzied response on the part of the player, as, for instance, in *Max Payne*, in which a difficult shoot-out might be re-attempted rapidly many times in succession in an extremely compressed burst of intense interactivity. If flames and fireball effects come out at the avatar and at the screen in one punishing sequence, in which Max has to be negotiated through a restaurant wracked by a series of explosions, the player has also to plunge him (repeatedly) *into* the inferno — in an active attempt to negotiate the threat — rather than just being assaulted by the jarring and camera-shaking impact.

Games have a variety of potential sources of appeal, including elements of narrative and various forms of audio-visual spectacle. The relative balance of appeal varies from one game, or one type of game, to another. Some invest relatively more highly than others in narrative, from the film-based mystery/ enigma-solving PC game *Blade Runner* (Westwood, 1997) to *Max Payne*. Others, such as the point-and-click game *Myst* and its sequels *Riven* (Cyan/Red Orb, 1997) and *Myst III: Exile* (Presto/Ubi Soft, 2001) are slower-moving than action-adventure-shooting games of the *Die Hard* trilogy or *Max Payne* variety, putting more emphasis on the leisurely exploration of lovingly rendered and detailed virtual landscapes. Higher-quality visuals tend to be associated with different game platforms at different moments in the ongoing development of rival technologies. At the time of writing, for example, the greater capacity of PCs and PC-based graphics technologies make PC games, in general, more likely to emphasise this variety of spectacle. New console systems such as the PlayStation 2 and Microsoft's X-Box have sought to redress the balance, with varying success (hence the emphasis on background visuals in commercials for *Gran Turismo 3* on PS2). PC games sought to regain their edge in 2002 with the launch of technologies such as nVidia's Geforce4. A mixture of elements of some kind is offered by many games. But one of the key pleasures and one, at least, of the defining characteristics of the medium, is the potential for an intense level of interactive engagement, a *testing* of the player, under pressure or against the stresses of frustration, of a kind that goes beyond the dimensions of narrative and spectacle.

How exactly this experience might be situated in the wider socio-cultural or media environment opens up a number of substantial issues that cannot be explored here other than in passing. The qualities offered by action-adventure-shooting games such as the *Die Hard* trilogies have something in common with, as well as extending, those sought by fans of the Hollywood action film: principally, an intensity of engagement (see Barker & Brooks 1998). Intensity is also one of the qualities identified by Richard Dyer (1992) in his attempt to explain the grounds of appeal of the 'classical' Hollywood musical, an account that can be extended to include more recent forms of spectacular production. Dyer suggests that pleasure created by such qualities can be understood in relation to the generally less intense or exciting realities of everyday life. This argument seems to map onto the gaming experience better in some respects than others, however: the frustrating aspect of games, when the player can spend a great deal of time achieving very little, seems uncomfortably *close* to some aspects of reality. A focus on experiences in which spectacle, sensation and intensity are favoured over other dimensions — such as those of narrative or 'depth' — is also found in various broad theories of contemporary Western media-centred culture, often under the label of the 'postmodern' (for a useful overview, see Darley 2000). As Andrew Darley suggests, however, many of these accounts are excessively sweeping and all-encompassing, failing as a result to pay close attention to the specific qualities offered by particular cultural forms such as film or the videogame in particular social-historical contexts.

More proximate analysis of games is found in the gender-based perspective taken by Henry Jenkins (1999). The appeal of action-adventure games to young American males in the late twentieth century, Jenkins suggests, might be understood in terms of the opportunities they offer for the rehearsal of

Burnill, Derek (2002) '"Oh, Grow Up 007": The Performance of Bond and Boyhood in Film and Videogames', in this collection.

Darley, Andrew (2000) *Visual Digital Culture: Surface Play and Spectacle in New Media Genres*. London: Routledge.

Dyer, Richard (1992) *Only Entertainment*. London: BFI.

Gamespot (2001) 'TenSpot: Best-Looking Games'. Available on-line at: http://gamespot.com/gamespot/stories/features/0,12059,2784321,00.html.

Jenkins, Henry (1999) 'Complete Freedom of Movement: Video Games as Gendered Play Spaces', in Justine Cassell & Henry Jenkins (eds) *From Barbie to Mortal Kombat: Gender and Computer Games*. Cambridge, Mass.: MIT Press, 262—97.

King, Geoff (2000) *Spectacular Narratives: Hollywood in the Age of the Blockbuster.* London: I.B. Tauris, 2000.

____ (2002) *New Hollywood Cinema: An Introduction*. London: I.B. Tauris.

Poole, Stephen (2000) *Trigger Happy: The Inner Life of Videogames*. London: Fourth Estate.

Rouse, Richard (2001) *Game Design: Theory and Practice.* Plano, Texas: Wordware Publishing.

chapter three

Spectacle of the Deathmatch: Character and Narrative in First-Person Shooters

jo bryce & jason rutter

Since the advent of the CD-ROM in PC gaming and Sony's PlayStation in the mid-1990s there has been a promise from the gaming industry that 'interactive movies' are just around the corner. Much of this was due to the CDs offering game designers hundreds of megabytes of storage previously unavailable at little cost. Until that point games had been stored on floppy disks or on chips in plastic cartridges. Sony's initial response to this development was to include music on their PlayStation CDs, but it was soon followed by the addition of full motion-video scenes to games intended to add value to the gaming experience and to exploit the storage capacities of the new consumer gaming medium. Games such as *Wing Commander III: Heart of the Tiger* (Origin/Electronic Arts, 1995) began to feature hurriedly filmed and badly acted scenes which introduced games, and provided context, plot and characterisation between gaming levels. This innovation carried novelty value but tended to interfere with the flow of gaming.

The difficulties of managing PC-based video content were claimed to be 'teething problems' and it was said that hardware and software would improve until high levels of interactivity were achieved. This would increasingly make the boundaries between films and games blurred, players being totally 'immersed' in the narrative as they played the new interactive films. The hype and excitement suggested that this new multimedia, hypertextual technology hybrid was to be the future of entertainment. As Richard Rouse (2000) points out, games developers were starting to develop 'movie envy'.

Links between the computer gaming and film industries exist on a number of levels. At the most superficial there is the crossover from games to films. Films such as *Super Mario Brothers* (1993), *Double Dragon: The Movie* (1993), *Street Fighter: The Movie* (1994), *Mortal Kombat* (1995), *Wing Commander* (1999), *Lara Croft: Tomb Raider* (2001), *Final Fantasy: The Spirits Within* (2001), *Resident Evil: Ground Zero* (2002) and *Duke Nukem: The Movie* (2002) are all based on computer games. Similarly, games have also provided the thematic starting point for films such as *Tron* (1982), *The Last Starfighter* (1984), *The Wizard* (1989), *Joysticks* (1993), *Brainscan* (1994) and *eXistenZ* (1999) (see Sullivan 2001).

There has also been a corresponding reverse crossover. Videogames based on film licenses are now relatively common and include titles from *Indiana Jones and the Infernal Machine* (Lucas Arts, 1999) and *Terminator: Future Shock* (Bethesda Softworks, 1995), to the strategy game *Starship Troopers* (Blue Tongue/Hasboro, 2001), and the excellent and wonderfully 'transtextuall'[1] (Genette, 1997, 1998) first-person shooter *Aliens vs. Predator* (Rebellion/Fox Interactive, 1999). George Lucas's *Star Wars: Episode I – The Phantom Menace* (1999) directly spawned at least four games on a variety of platforms,[2] most produced by Lucas Arts itself. This crossover is so prevalent that, according to Screen Digest/ELSPA (2000), more than 40 per cent of best selling games are based upon licensed themes. The link between film and games is further highlighted as computer games increasingly exist as video footage before they ever reach the retail shelves.

This chapter seeks to examine the convergence of cinema and computer games in terms of aspects of the design process and the orientation of the audience to the two forms of media. It looks specifically at the first-person shooter (FPS) and the way it draws increasingly on the cinematic spectacle of films such as *The Terminator* (1984) or *The Matrix* (1999) while maintaining an ethos of audience involvement and construction of the final text often found in independent or community film-making. It argues that while there may be some level of convergence between these two media in terms of technology and their production and marketing, there are still sufficient differences between the experience of viewing films and playing games to question the extent to which the realisation of the interactive movie is possible.

An examination of the evolution of the 3D FPS games is provided (using the highly successful and influential titles produced by id Software as an illustrative example) in order to build a contextual and historical backdrop to an analysis of the relationship between playing computer games and watching films. To facilitate such analysis, the chapter focuses on an examination of aspects of narrative, interactivity, spectacle, game aesthetics and author/audience distinctions.

The first-person shooter: a short game history

The FPS is fast approaching its first decade of existence. During its lifetime technical and creative innovations have allowed the development of more complex game narratives, game environments and varieties of gameplay, as well as an expansion in support for multiplayer and online gaming (for example, *Unreal Tournament* (Epic MegaGames & Digital Extremes/GT Interactive, 1999) and *Quake III Arena* (id Software/Activision, 1999)). Further, developments in the genre and game texts have facilitated new ways of gaming and an evolving sense of character, immersion and narrative development.

In any examination of recent developments and innovations in computer gaming, it is impossible to ignore the importance of a series of games developed by the Texas-based development company id Software. Although they no longer have a monopoly on the FPS genre, with developers such as Valve (*Half Life*, 1998), Interplay (*Descent*, 1994), Gathering of Developers (*Kiss Psycho Circus*, 2000) and Epic Games (*Unreal*, 2000) producing their own visions of the ultimate FPS computer game, the impact of id on PC gaming and developments in consumer computing is hard to overestimate.

The FPS story begins for the PC with id in 1992 when *Wolfenstein 3D* was released by Apogee and id Software. Although not truly 3D, this first FPS differed from previous games by providing the gamer with a vanishing-point perspective of the playing environment, directly mediated by player input.[3] Through their onscreen avatars players could negotiate a world that had similar physical rules to those of 'real life'. Movement in the *Wolfenstein 3D* game environment proceeded across the monitor in a similar manner to that of platform games, but also allowed movement up and down 'through' the screen. There were also corresponding changes in object size and resolution according to player movement around the game space. Since its release, *Wolfenstein 3D* has been viewed as the game that characterised a new format and since then a series of highly innovative FPS games have been developed. Each new game has contributed to a transformation of the format by offering increasingly complex narrative levels, supporting a variety of different gameplay features and contributing to the development of many online communities.

In 1993, id released a game that has become a legend among gamers everywhere: *Doom* (id Software, 1993).[4] Developments in game play allowed progression between different game levels through the finding of a 'key'. However, the greatest innovation was the utilisation of game graphics, sound and physics to create an atmospheric game environment. One of the reasons *Doom* was such a massive success was the sense of unease and anxiety created as the gamer's character travelled through deserted corridors. *Doom* was also the first FPS to support multiplayer options via Local Area Network (LAN) or modem connections. This allowed 'deathmatches' – violent and frantic games in which the aim is to score the greatest number of kills or 'frags' to win. Gamers could now compete against human opponents rather than just artificially intelligent adversaries as in previous games.

Given that John Romero, id's co-founder and lead designer, comes from a hobbyist programmer background in which there is an ethos of sharing code within the gaming community (see Laidlaw 1996), it is not surprising that *Doom* was released initially as a shareware product available on the internet as a free download or for a small fee from retailers. When *Doom* was released the games development and publishing industry was increasingly establishing itself as a professionalised business and building up credibility after the mid-1980s crash of the games market. However, the method of initial release for *Doom* exploited new methods of distribution and user involvement that were essential to market success. It demonstrated that although a rapidly growing industry, games dev-elopment and distribution was a business that could not be divorced from the interests and activities of gamers. It marked the continued blurring of boundaries between producer and consumer in the gaming community. Later, id went even further when it released the source code for *Doom* that enabled players to modify the game to suit their own tastes. Such practices, as well as the game itself, practically guaranteed the commercial success of *Doom II: Hell on Earth* (id Software/GT Interactive, 1994) when it was released as a retail product.

id Software went a step further with the release of *Quake* in 1996. This game marked the development of an impressive new graphics engine, which produced a fully 3D-rendered game environment but placed significant demands on many home PCs. The overall look and playability of this game, together with its support for up to 16 players competing against each other, quickly established *Quake* as the benchmark FPS. It also facilitated web-based gaming for up to eight players and allowed access to the Quakeworld network. This, together with the customisability of the game controls and the ability to send messages to other players during the game, contributed to the overwhelming popularity of the game, as highlighted by the growth of online communities of fans and modifiers of the *Quake* series. This community grew even richer when id released the Quake C language that allowed players even greater power to change the game by altering existing levels and creating new ones.

While *Quake* was technically innovative, it was the sequel, *Quake II* (id Software/Activision, 1997), that marked a break from the format of previous FPS games. The game offered a progression from the linear gameplay that characterised its predecessors to a more open level structure. Another important development in *Quake II* was the variety of models and game characters available to players. The game provided choice between male and female characters and allowed the application of 'skins', permitting gamers to customise existing characters, for example, into those from other games, film, televison or real life. The online option was improved by the ability to use *Gamespy*, a piece of software used to locate servers supporting *Quake* gaming, the names of players using the servers and the ping rate at any given time.

Drawing on the successful format of the first two games in the series, *Quake III* (2000) is largely characterised by improvements to graphic representation of the game environment, game physics and facilities for online and multiplayer gaming. While previous versions of *Quake* have been converted for use on gaming consoles, the difference in the port of *Quake III* to SEGA's Dreamcast and the Sony PlayStation is the development of facilities for online gaming that aim to be compatible with PC gamers.

Throughout the ten-year history of this format the greater sophistication of graphics, narrative, and gameplay have created conditions that increasingly allow the gamer to feel part of the unfolding and progressively spectacular narrative. This format has also become particularly important to the development of both multiplayer and online gaming.

Game aesthetics

In some respects it is possible to claim that games are becoming more 'cinematic'. Links at the level of game design and development suggest some level of confluence between game and film aesthetics. In the following sections computer games are considered in relation to narrative, realist cinema and Hollywood blockbuster films, through an examination of spectacle, aesthetics, narrative and interactivity.

The production of spectacle has a long history in popular entertainment, contemporary forms having roots in the eighteenth and nineteenth centuries.[5] Andrew Darley describes the spectacle of this period as a form of popular entertainment in which the 'emphasis was on performances which were designed to elicit intense and instantaneous visual pleasure, the production of image and action which would excite, astound and astonish the audience' (2000: 40). Spectacular entertainment aimed to provide a visceral thrill, something highly physical and although many areas of film have developed a greater emphasis on the conventions of story, plot and characterisation, the entertainment power of spectacle is still clearly visible in many large-scale, mainstream films.

Although narrative has asserted itself a central position in contemporary cinema it has been challenged to some extent within the Hollywood blockbuster – as an important part of contemporary cinematic entertainment (see Darley 2000: 56). For films such as *Terminator 2* (1991), *Jurassic Park* (1993), *Independence Day* (1996), *Con Air* (1997) or numerous other blockbusting successes, it is not character development, introspection and social discourse which is most prominent in the film but the size, frequency and breath-taking excitement of the on-screen spectacle.

There are historical similarities in the genesis of both film and computer games in that both media have moved from the status of illegitimate offspring of other forms of art (whose origin owes more to technology than art) to being respectable and economically important forms of entertainment in their own right. For both media the technology allows the placement of moving images onto a screen and its continued development has made increasingly bold and believably realistic spectacle possible.

Through the introduction of the CD as a medium for storing gaming software, games producers were able to include film sequences in games in an attempt to add context, narrative and spectacle. The fashion for these full motion video (FMV) bridging sequences soon waned and now games like *Half-Life* (Valve/Sierra, 2000) put exposition within the game itself rather than between levels. Similarly, third-person shooters (TPS) such as *Tomb Raider: The Last Revelation* (Core/Eidos, 1999) attempt to blend narrative development with the gaming action, as does *Max Payne* (Remedy/GodGames, 2001) with its combination of graphic novel and Mickey Spillane/Mike Hammer-style approach. Indeed much effort has been put into minimizing the high visibility of level changes, so that these games, like television, have a sense of *flow*.[6] Rather than having the episodic experience of level-orientated game structure, which finishes each level with a boss before loading the next part of the game, these games aim for more seamless collection of elements. These games are less like an interactive movie, in which the film stops as plot decisions are made at marked crossroads, but the development of character and causality are more effectively knitted into game play, improving the experience of the games' narrative. Increasingly, the FPS (and its off-shoot, the TPS) is attempting to create an immersive experience in which the gamer feels involved on a more or less continuous basis.

To heighten this effect, games have begun to borrow heavily from cinematic styles and aesthetics. *Max Payne* uses the vocabulary of film noir as well as the action thriller *Dirty Harry* (1971) and the work of John Woo. It includes effects drawn from the work of the latter such as the ability to invoke slow motion action sequences at the press of a mouse button. Covering the game's exhibition at E3, *Gamespot* pointed out that the development team had implemented

> a very movie-like technique that involves action sequences (usually featuring guns) being slowed down. Jump sideways while firing a gun and the sequence goes into slow-mo while you're in the air — bullets pumping, muzzle flashing and the bad guy doing the dance of death as the lead bites him. Then you hit the ground and the pace instantly picks up again. (Allen 2001)

This movement into 'bullet time' allows gamers more than the joy of the cinematic spectacle and the 'shoot dodging' manoeuvre rapidly becomes an essential part of the game play in the trickiest of confrontations. Similarly id's sequel, *Return to Castle Wolfenstein* (Gray Matter/Activision, 2002), draws inspiration from World War II propaganda films and Hollywood movies including *The Dirty Dozen* (1967).

With the increased borrowing from cinematic technique, games have experimented with differences in the use of perspective and point of view. Players of FPSs have a proxy view of the gaming world from behind the eyes of their onscreen characters rather than watching them travel, as would be the case in a platform game or a TPS. These contrasting perspectives play as an important a role in games as in films, offering different relationships between player and character. The decision of whether to employ a first-person or third-person perspective alters factors such as whether we watch a more distanced character within a developing narrative or play from within a character with whom we have a more immediate relationship.

In the *Quake* series our perspective is that of our gaming character. It has a film parallel in the early scenes of *The Terminator* in which the audience sometimes sees the world through the eyes of Arnold Schwarzenegger's cyborg as he explores his new surroundings and acquires clothes, shades, motorcycle and weapons. It is the perspective of the combatant that is given preference here: gamers are given the illusion of inhabiting the same space as the avatar and see what they see. During *Quake* there are no panning or aerial shots, no cuts to close ups or reverse shots from the perspective of the enemy. Instead, the view remains solidly first-person. This never-changing perspective heightens the sense of 'being there' and immersion in the gaming narrative.

Quake has spectacular delights (mostly concerning violence and high-speed action) but these are not the same as those offered to the gamer by the third-person perspective on Lara Croft in the *Tomb Raider* series. *Tomb Raider* allows the gamer to look upon Croft, enjoying the rendered spectacle of improbable agility and impossible figure. The gamer is in the position of both being in control of the onscreen avatar and able to watch it. This perspective permits a highly sexualised focus on the female form that differs from the way Max Payne is presented, despite the fact that both are experienced in the third person. As gamers we bring to each of these characters a set of scripts and semiotic encoding that help us understand who they are, their role and their motivations. These, of course, are character specific, and are drawn from our own literacies in other forms of culture whether they be film, comic book, novels, advertising or whatever. This difference in gaze and the objectification it encourages means the gamers watch and control Croft and Payne rather than 'sit inside' on the screen as they might with their own character in *Quake*.

Decisions about character and gamer's perspective and other basic tools of cinematography in games have been accompanied by the growing maturity of the use of sound and music in this genre.[7] Again, the origins of the use of sound and music can be traced back to *Doom*. Unlike its gaming predecessors, *Doom* did not just have electronic sound effects such as the feedback beeps found in *Pong* (Atari, 1974) or the threatening 'Dum, dum, dum, dum' of *Space Invaders*. With its atmospheric rumblings and the slow build up of tension in the music by Bobby Prince,[8] *Doom* was effectively the first major computer game to have a film-like soundtrack. This soundtrack was integral to the accumulation of tension for players travelling the eerie mazes of the game, constantly awaiting attack. As well as music, the game featured low breathing sounds, suggesting that enemies waited around every corner. id further raised the standard with *Quake* by commissioning Trent Reznor from Nine Inch Nails to produce the music and sound effects. More recently, David Bowie, along with Reeves Gabrels, has written gaming music through his involvement with *Omikron* (Quantic Dream/ Eidos, 1999).

The utilisation of graphic and audio production techniques in the creation of atmospheric game environments adds to the visceral reaction and to the stimulation provided by the spectacle presented by the game. The use of complex modelling and rendering technologies, similar to those used to create computer generated effects in action movies, adds visual excitement to the game environment and illustrates how aesthetic techniques from one medium may cross over to inform production in the other.

The continuing development of graphic sophistication and life-likeness has been fundamental to games production, and visual realism has been claimed to be an important marker of the success of computer games (see Darley 2000: 29–30). This includes the attempt to create more life-like game environments and characters. A specialism in its own right, game physics is increasingly sophisticated and vital in order to make objects and the physical characteristics of game characters behave in a realistic manner. Characters' hair, clothes and body parts now sway, move or bounce in life-like fashion or indeed in a fetishised manner that potentially solicits voyeurism.[9] Given such developments, it is no surprise that most of the innovations in *Quake III* centre not around changes in gameplay but on improving the graphics engine. This enabled the game to display curved objects in a less 'blocky' fashion and to allow fog, fire and water effects to be used to heighten the atmosphere in the game's arena and to allow game designers to control these in real time.

Although both reviewers and gamers often comment on the realism of gaming graphics and the spectacle they create, there is a gaming trade-off: increases in graphics quality mean higher demands on the gaming hardware and, generally, slower gaming. But how important is realism in gaming? Anna Warm (2000) found that playability and pace were more important to gamers' enjoyment than realism or stunning graphics. Indeed the notion of realism is a problematic one at the best of times: are we really supposed to consider the characters, settings and narratives of games as 'real' as those of science fiction, period drama or a soap opera?[10] Demands for realism in game environments are likely to be secondary to the requirement for spectacle as the backdrop for competitive gameplay.

While the notion of realism in games is complex, as it is elsewhere, it is possible to accept as 'real' the experience of gaming and the creative activities associated with it. This is why it is important not only to explore the connections between computer gaming and film through textual comparisons or industry alliances, but also to look at gamers and their active role in experiencing, creating and recreating gaming texts. This approach enables us to see how aspects of FPS games have encouraged a new type of player/audience involvement, and how technological and textual developments have facilitated and encouraged gamers to create their own narratives, characters and gaming communities.

Game narratives and gamers as authors

One important issue to consider when examining the convergence of film and games is the extent to which computer games have narrative structures comparable with those of films. The development of game narratives can be traced in relation to the development of FPS games. At its most basic level, the aim of *Wolfenstein 3D* (and the FPS games that followed) was not particularly different from that of previous games: moving around a virtual space, killing enemies and avoiding being killed. This basic action-narrative can be traced back all the way to the very first distributed computer game, *Spacewar*, created by Steve Russell in 1961. Although there were elements familiar to platform games such as the collection of items for points (in this case Nazi gold), what made *Wolfenstein* so different was that, although somewhat crude by today's standards, the world looked 'real': when you shot people they would recoil and splatter blood. Further, you would be faced by enemies with a referent in the real world; that is they were not imagined spacecraft, aliens, or geometric oddities like the ghosts of *Pac-Man* (Namco, 1980) but Nazi soldiers, their dogs and a fierce collection of weapons.[11]

But more than this, *Wolfenstein* had a story. The events had a context and the gamer played a real-time role in moving the narrative towards its dénouement. According to publicity on the 3D Realms' web site:

> You're William J. 'B.J.' Blazkowicz, the Allies' bad boy of espionage and a terminal action seeker. Your mission was to infiltrate the Nazi fortress Castle Hollehammer and find the plans for Operation Eisenfaust, the Nazi's blueprint for building the perfect army. Rumors are that deep within the castle the diabolical Dr. Schabbs has perfected a technique for building a fierce army from the bodies of the dead. It's so far removed from reality that it would seem silly if it wasn't so sick. But what if it were true?

The release of *Half-Life* in 1998 represented a quantum leap in narrative for FPS games by providing a complex plot and increased depth of game characters. Here the gamer does not just take part and develop the narrative by moving through walled mazes and shooting pretty much anything that moves: the main character has a history and personality which affect his progress and the final outcome. The script for *Half-Life* came from the science fiction novelist Marc Laidlaw, one of the authors featured in Bruce Sterling's landmark cyberpunk anthology, *Mirrorshades* (1986), author of *Dad's Nuke* (1986) and *Kalifornia* (1992).[12] Influenced heavily by playing the free-form adventure game *Myst* (Cyan/Broderbund, 1994) as well as *Doom*, Laidlaw was intent on realising the storytelling potential of the FPS. The role created by Laidlaw for the gamer was one that attempts to 'make a difference in Gordon Freeman's life', a task which 'deepened their involvement in the game instead of booting them out of it' (Bergman 1999). Unlike the protagonists in *Quake* and *Doom*, Freeman, the central character in *Half-Life*, is not a product of the John Wayne/Sylvester Stallone mould of action hero but rather a (fairly) run-of-the-mill assistant in a science lab. He is the accidental hero who battles not just with aliens but rival colleagues who are out to save their own lives at any cost.

The standard set by the *Half-Life* narrative, and the involvement of gamers with the characters and contexts of the game, is further demonstrated by the intriguing official add-ons that have become available to the main game. *Opposing Force* (Gearbox/Sierra, 1999) allows the player to take the role of a soldier sent into the lab to eliminate Freeman, while *Counter-Strike* allows you to choose to play either the part of a terrorist organisation or the anti-terrorist squad sent to stop the alien invasion.

Game narratives such as those of *Wolfenstein* and *Half-Life* provide a context for the game and a rationale for game play (see Darley 2000: 150—5), offering an indication of the manner in which computer gaming has started to mature as a creative industry. If games ever were *solely* about 'someone getting killed, finding out why someone was killed, or taking over the world' (Subrahmanyam & Greenfield 1998: 51), to maintain that this is still the case either underestimates the craft of games production and active gaming, or demonstrates a lack of familiarity with this gaming genre. Earlier games often had some sort of implied narrative associated with them; for example, *Space Invaders* makes no sense without the understanding that the gamer plays the role of defender against the attacking alien hordes.

There are, however, a number of fundamental differences between the narrative texts of computer games and those of cinema. It has been claimed that, because of the importance of spectacle in computer games, narrative content is 'basic in the extreme', secondary to game play and the rendering of the game environment (Darley 2000: 150). To a greater extent, the narrative content of games is comparable with that of the Hollywood blockbuster format, but the issue of interactivity and the performative nature of the engagement entailed with computer games suggests that game narratives might have a function different from those of contemporary cinema.

Recent developments have also allowed a move away from the linear progression in narrative through various levels that characterized early FPS games. As already mentioned, *Quake II* allows players to return to previous levels in order to complete aspects of subsequent missions and the development of more complex and non-linear game narratives have become essential to the experience of FPS gaming. This is also apparent in the third-person *Tomb Raider* series, where puzzle solving is crucial to progression in the game, and also in the latest breed of cross-format games, such as *Deus Ex* (Ion Storm/Eidos, 2000) that combine traits from the FPS as well as role-playing and strategy games.

In films, the narrative progresses without the input of the audience member, whereas in games the player is crucial to the progression of the narrative and spectacle (see Darley 2000: 56). While games such as *Duke Nukem 3D* may use wisecracking or foot tapping characters to mark non-action, these highlight the fact that the game is not continuing and are, therefore, an interruption to game narrative and spectacle. Lack of action in a game of *Quake III* may lead to a fairly rapid termination of your involvement in the game as you are fragged either by your opponent or the computer, but the game will not normally continue during periods where the player is not actively involved. If a spectator/player stops playing a computer game, the game itself usually stops.[13]

This contrasts with the experience of watching a film in a cinema or broadcast television at home. The spectator of a sports match on television or the cinemagoer finds that the programme or film continues if they leave their viewing location. Goals or points may be scored in a sports match, players may be injured or the game might be won or lost during the spectator's absence; in film, crucial aspects of the plot may be revealed.[14] The difference between film and games is not only that the audience makes the spectacular happen in games but that they can make the spectacle itself.

The difference in narrative structure and content between computer games and films relates to the ability of gamers to actively engage in the modification of the game narrative and environments. Games such as *Half-Life, Unreal* and *Quake* have followed the tradition started by *Doom* of allowing gamers to create their own levels, characters and inventories for the games. In id games prior to *Doom* there had been a large amount of compression of files which made them harder to manipulate. This was changed for *Doom* and editors became readily available so that anyone with the time, inclination and dedication could create a new text for the game.

Such game modifications, or 'mods', allow the creation of entirely new texts around the basic FPS engine provided as part of the official game. Player-authors can experiment with the inclusion of new weapons in the game, from crossbows and grappling hooks to complete Jedi Knight or World War Two arsenals. The ability to create 'skins' allows gamers to bring in characters from other texts. Like the literature of sci-fi fans, creating narratives which experiment with the meeting of characters from different television series (Jenkins), mod authors have brought into their Quake worlds characters from *The Matrix*, Norse mythology, *South Park*, even *Wolfenstein 3D* or their own virtual clones.[15] Mod tools also allow player-authors to alter games physics so that 'rocket jumping' (the combination of jumping and firing a rocket launcher at the ground at the same time) can be finely tuned, or that items to be picked up have real weight that slows the player down.

The ability to alter characters, environment and events within texts suggests that gamers can become producers in addition to being consumers of the game. They not only participate in the gaming narrative but can also take control over its setting, characters and physical rules. This is not merely a matter of tinkering with the original product or playing around with authorial intention but, in the hands of a talented mod developer, a way of creating a substantially different text that can be distributed uncensored directly to a new audience. As such, we can argue that it marks a development in gaming that has more similarities to auteurism than to the complex hierarchies of Hollywood film-making. Indeed, computer gaming has a long tradition of refusing to establish a clear line between author and audience. Even influential gaming companies such as Eidos are still not too distant from their histories as bedroom programmers. The growth of the gaming market, the level of money involved in production and the growing professionalisation of computer gaming has encouraged the creation of a produce/consumer divide but there is still an overlap between game producers and consumers.[16] The difficulty in distinguishing the player from the producer continues today. Players are used as testers, bug finders and generators of wish lists for development companies; this, plus the reliance on core gamers as agenda setters for gaming purchases, means player input is vastly important to the industry.

This highlights a difference between computer game players and film audiences as they are often understood. Film audiences have a history of being viewed as gatherings of passive individuals who sit, in a darkened cinema, as the light and sound of the cinema projection pours over them. In this environment audience members are 'passive' recipients of the narrative of the film:

> Under the regime of the culture industry ... the film leaves no room for imagination or reflection on the part of its viewers ... the film forces its victims to equate it directly with reality. (Adorno & Horkheimer 1977: 353—4)

However, since the work of the Birmingham Centre for Study of Contemporary Cultural Studies in the mid-1980s (see, for example Morley 1986; Radway 1987), and work influenced by and built upon it (for example Ang 1982; Jenkins 1992; Stacey 1994; Abercrombie & Longhurst 1998), there is now little real doubt abou the active nature of media audiences, including those of television and film.

Ideas concerning audiences as producers are not specifically new (see Longhurst 1995), but the computer gaming industry provides a very interesting and advanced example of this. As we have seen, games such as *Doom*, *Quake* and *Half-Life* represent only the start of the text's life and are not hermetically sealed entities. A similar, if more limited, approach to narrative has been seen in playfully postmodern films such as *Wayne's World* (1992), the text of which presents alternative conclusions but refuses to establish if any is definitive (see Rutter 1998). However, the FPS games considered here surpass this interaction through an even greater allegiance to a transtextual approach to reading and recreation.

As the previous discussion has shown, game players or audiences[17] are more actively engaged than film viewers in both the narrative and other events within the game environment. The ability to modify both of these aspects of a computer-based game shows a level of interaction with the text that is not provided by traditional cinema or Hollywood blockbuster movies.

Conclusions

This chapter has examined the extent to which FPS games utilise the production and aesthetic techniques of cinema to create a sense of narrative and spectacle. It has argued that although the age of interactive movies has not arrived there is some level of convergence between computer games, specifically in the FPS format, and Hollywood blockbuster movies such as *The Matrix* and *Terminator 2*. Further, it has suggested that these similarities are to be found primarily in the creation and manipulation of aesthetics and narrative in games, along with audience/player involvement.

The similarity between these two forms of popular entertainment lies in the privileging of spectacle over narrative and the importance placed upon physical rather than intellectual responses. While we can see that games developers are increasingly recognizing the potential of narrative to enrich game play this remains largely a non-technical innovation. Indeed, while both blockbuster film and FPS games have narrative structures of varying complexity, it is difficult to claim that these are grossly similar to those of realist and emotional-realist cinema. In spectacular media narrative offers a brief rationale on which to hang visceral pleasures rather than the driving engine of the text.

The heralding of interactive films as the future of popular entertainment has become a little stale as it appears that the development of such media has not been realised yet and there is a major question as to whether problems such as negotiating flow and interactivity will be successfully solved in the future. However, the increasing alliances between gaming and media companies (along with the embodiment of the two in organisations such as Disney and Lucas Arts), and the current realignment of computer and video games as 'leisure software' and 'interactive entertainment', indicate that the industry itself sees a viable future enterprise in interactive media.

What this future may be remains to be seen, but it is worth hypothesising that, rather than becoming part of an affiliation with narrative cinema, the future of computer gaming lies with its borrowing from, and developing of, the cinema of spectacle. However, what gaming continues to offer that Hollywood cannot is the intimate sense of the consumer as producer. In gaming, texts can be technologically and narratively left open so that gamers can create and manipulate their own add-ons and modifications. This happens in a way not available to Hollywood film-making but perhaps has echoes in the alternative form of cinematic production in which production and consumption are not so distant.

It is the interactivity and active participation in the game environment and creation of the game text and game community that distinguishes computer games from most films. This, along with gaming's requirement for control and kinaesthetic skills, link it closely to the visceral thrills of the spectacular forms of popular entertainment since the late nineteenth century and, ironically, marks gamers themselves — rather than any technical, industrial or market feature — as the main point of difference between film and computer games.

Of course, what these gamers will bring to cinema as it develops remain to be seen.

notes

1 Gérard Genette describes transtextuality as 'all that sets the text in a relationship, whether obvious or concealed, with other texts' (1998: 8–12). He presents a five-element taxonomy for understanding the way texts, such as books, refer to, quote from and comment on other texts. As such it is similar to — but more encompassing than — the more commonly used idea of intertextuality.

2 *Star Wars Episode 1: Jedi Power Battles* (Dreamcast, PlayStation — LucasArts, 2000); *Star Wars Episode I Racer* (Game Boy Color, PC, Dreamcast, N64 — LucasArts/Activision, 1999); *Star Wars: Episode 1: The Phantom Menace* (PC — LucasArts/Activision, 1999) and *Star Wars Episode 1: Battle for Naboo* (N64 — Factor 5/LucasArts, 2001).

3 Although *Wolfenstein 3D* was successful and influential, the title for first 3D FPS arguably goes to one of 'the lost games of id', *Catacomb 3D* (id Software/Softdisk, 1991), a fairly slow EGA (as opposed to VGA) game which is reminiscent of id's later game *Heretic* (Raven/id Software, 1994). The first 'true' 3D game for the PC was *Descent.* (Parallax/Interplay, 1994). Beyond the PC, Atari's arcade game *Battlezone* (Atari, 1980) was probably the first 3D game and FPS precedents are found in *3D Monster Maze* (J K Greye, 1981) on the Sinclair ZX81, along with *Dungeon Master* (FTL/FTL, 1989) and *Bloodwych* (Image Works/Mirrorsoft, 1990) for the Atari ST.

4 *Doom* is often quoted as the most successful computer game of all time but this is a hotly contested issue. The *Command & Conquer* (Westwood Studios, 1995) series is listed by the *Guinness Book of Records* as having sold over 10 million copies, however *Myst* (and its sequel, *Riven*) have sold a similar amount and the multi-platform *FIFA Soccer* series from EA has sold 16 million copies. This pales when compared to Nintendo's *Super*

Mario Brothers (over 40 million copies) and the number of PCs that have *Solitaire* installed upon them. *Doom* is credited with 2 million copies sold but it is estimated that something in the region of 20 million copies of the shareware version have been installed worldwide.

5 See Darley 2000 for a more detailed discussion of the importance of spectacle in early forms of popular entertainment.

6 Raymond Williams uses the term 'flow' to describe the manner in which rather than being a collection of discrete units (programmes, adverts, announcements, and so on), television is made up of *planned flow*. That is, items have a sequence and place within the onward rolling of continuous broadcasting (Williams 1975: 86).

7 The ability to change from first to third person perspective or alter viewing position is similar to camera view options beginning to be offered in other domestic digital technologies such as football broadcast on some digital TV services and recent pornographic films on DVD.

8 A collection of Bobby Prince's music from *Doom* can be found at: http://doomworld.com/music/index.shtml.

9 The *Dead or Alive* (Tecmo, 1997) series of beat-'em-ups featured the 'breast physics engine' which produced highly stylised and sexualised movements of female characters.

10 See Abercrombie (1996) and Ang (1982) for discussions of 'reality' in television programmes.

11 Even today *Wolfenstein 3D* is unavailable in Germany because of its narrative setting and content.

12 This is not linked in any way to the 1993 film of the same name directed by Dominic Sena.

13 This does not necessarily apply to multiplayer games such as online versions of *Quake III*. This is why the convention has been established that if a player's character stands facing a wall motionless they are recognised as being currently out of play. To kill such a player is considered within the *Quake* online gaming community as 'unsporting'.

14 The ability to time shift viewing is commonly facilitated through videoing television programmes and watching them at a convenient time. Video permits rudimentary pausing, replay, and fast forwarding, the quality of which is being built upon with digital systems such as TiVo.

15 The company 3Q is beginning to provide photo booth-style facilities which take three dimensional pictures of gamers and use the image to create models which are burned onto CD as personalised skins for use in games such as *Quake III* and *Unreal*.

16 Organisations such as the CyberAthletes Professional League now attract sufficient sponsorship and advertising to permit a handful of world-class gamers to live quite well off their skills.

17 Research undertaken by the authors has demonstrated that vital to much computer gaming is the experience of playing as part of a group. As such, there is often an audience for individual games as well as the active players. This applies to domestic gaming as well as international competitions.

citations

3D Realms www.3drealms.com/wolf3d/

Abercrombie, Nicholas (1996) *Television and Society*. Cambridge: Polity.

Abercrombie, Nicholas and Brian Longhurst (1998) *Audiences*. London: Sage.

Adorno, Theodor and Max Horkheimer (1977) 'The Cultural Industry: Enlightenment as mass Deception', in James Curran and Michael Gurevitch (eds) *Mass Media and Society*. London: Edward Arnold, 1977, 349—83.

Allen, Mike (2001) 'Max Payne First Impressions', Gamespot. Available on-line at: http://www.gamespot.co.uk/stories/news/0,2160,2087148,00.html.

Ang, Ien (1982) *Watching Dallas: Soap Opera and the Melodramatic Imagination*. London: Methuen.

Bergman, Jason (1999) 'Writing the Game' interview with Marc Laidlaw, *Looneygames*, 1.34. Available on-line at: http://www.loonygames.com/content/1.34/feat/

Darley, Andrew (2000) *Visual Digital Culture: Surface Pay and Spectacle in New Media Genre*. London: Routledge.

Genette, Gérard (1997) *Paratexts: Thresholds of Interpretation*. Trans. Jane E Lewin. Cambridge: Cambridge University Press.

___ (1998) *Palimpsests: Literature in the Second Degree*. University of Nebraska Press.

Jenkins, Henry (1992) *Textual Poachers: Television Fans and Participatory Culture*. London: Routledge.

Laidlaw, Marc (1996) 'The Egos at Id', *Wired*, 4.08. Available on-line at: http:www.wired.com/wired/archive/4.08/id.html.

Longhurst, Brian (1995) *Popular Music and Society*. Cambridge: Polity.

Morley, David (1986) *Family Television: Culture, Power and Domestic Leisure*. London: Comedia.

Morris, Sue (1999) 'Online Gaming Culture: An examination of emerging forms of production and participation in first-person-shooter multiplayer gaming', GameGirlz. Available on-line at: http://www.gamegirlz.com/articles/gameculture.shtml.

Radway, Janice (1987) *Reading the Romance: Women, Patriarchy, and Popular Literature*. London: Verso.

Rouse, Richard (2000) 'Computer Games, Not Computer Movies', *Gaming & Graphics*, 34.4. Available on-line at: http://www.paranoidproductions.com/gamingandgraphics/gg11_00.html

Rutter, Jason (1998) 'Stepping into *Wayne's World*: Exploring Postmodern Comedy', in Arthur Asa Berger (ed.) *The Postmodern Presence: Readings on Postmodernism in American Culture and society*. Walnut Creek, CA: Alta Mira, 112—24.

Screen Digest/ELSPA (2000) 'Interactive leisure software: New platforms, new opportunities', ELSPA.

Stacey, Jackie (1994) *Star Gazing: Hollywood Cinema and Female Spectatorship*. London: Routledge.

Subrahmanyam, Kaveri & Patricia M. Greenfield (1998) 'Computer Games for Girls: What Makes Them Play?', in Justine Cassell & Henry Jenkins (eds) *From Barbie to Mortal Combat: Gender and Computer Games*. Cambridge, MA: MIT, 46—67.

Sullivan, Kevin (2001) 'The Adaptation Games'. Available on-line at: http://www.myvideogames.com/features/feature59.asp.

Warm, Anna (2000) 'What makes a video game enjoyable?' Paper presented at the British Psychological Society, Social Psychology Section, Nottingham Trent University, UK.

Williams, Raymond (1974) *Television: Technology and Cultural Form*. London: Fontana.

chapter four

First-Person Shooters — A Game Apparatus

sue morris

While an ever-increasing body of academic research on computer games and their surrounding cultures is beginning to emerge, much of the basic analysis of how players actually interact with games and within gaming environments has yet to be undertaken. This essay sets out to explore the operations of subjectivity in relation to one genre of computer game — the first-person shooter (FPS) — through the identification of the game 'apparatus'.

The model of the cinematic apparatus is a concept that has proven useful in the study of film, recognising as it does the interconnected technical, environmental, textual, psychological and social processes involved in the cinema-viewing situation. For psychoanalytic film theory, the power of the cinema lies not in its ability to reproduce reality, but because the conditions of the cinematic apparatus allow one to suspend disbelief: 'it is the apparatus that creates the illusion, and not the degree of fidelity with the Real' (Baudry 1980: 47). The term 'apparatus' is a useful one, describing as it does the intersecting processes involved in audience interaction with a media form; it translates readily to an exploration of the kinds of subject positions offered by other media.

I will also be drawing on some models of the operations of subjectivity that have been identified in studies of film and television. From the outset, it is important to emphasise that film, television and computer or video games are completely distinct and different media — both as textual systems and in terms of their mechanisms of engagement. My goal here is not one of applying film and television theory directly to computer games, but rather to see how some of the concepts developed in the study of other media may assist in an exploration of this relatively new and unexplored medium.

The games

This analysis will focus on the scenario surrounding the 'computer game' in the purest sense of the term — that of a single person playing at a computer screen using mouse and keyboard. Although any one game text may be available on several game platforms (for example, PC, Dreamcast, GameBoy), each platform has its own technical, environmental and social conditions of play, and to examine them all here would introduce too many variables to take into account in a analysis of this size. Here I will be drawing examples from the FPS games *Quake* (id Software, 1996), *Quake II* (id Software/Activision, 1997), *Quake III Arena* (id Software/Activision, 1999), *Unreal Tournament* (Epic MegaGames & Digital Extremes/GT Interactive, 1999) and *Half-Life* (Valve/Sierra, 1999).

The scenario of the typical FPS game goes something like this: you find yourself, usually unintentionally, in a strange, hostile place, unarmed and vulnerable. (The hostile quality of the environment is essential to the shooter genre; otherwise there is not much for the player to do besides solve the occasional puzzle and admire the scenery, à la *Myst* (Cyan/Broderbund, 1993).) You must explore the place to find weapons and other useful items, moving

Figure 9 A typical FPS composition: the *Quake III Arena* (id Software/Activision, 1999) screenshot, showing current weapon (rocket launcher), health (69) and ammunition (rockets, 9)

Figure 10 Single player *Half-Life* (Valve/Sierra, 1999): player (holding gun) faces concerned scientist in foreground, mutant alien invader in background.

through the many game arenas or levels on some form of quest. In the process you must fight and/or avoid many enemies or monsters. The retail version of *Half-Life* describes the game thus:

> Just another day at the office. Or so you thought ... until your experiment blew up in your face. Now, with aliens coming through the walls, a military death squad killing everything in sight, and your colleagues in bits and pieces, you're scrambling to stay alive. Where should you go? Who can you trust? And can you figure it all out before they scrape you into a body bag?

This narrative-based interaction with the game software is called the 'single-player game', played as it is by one person against the computer software.

FPS games also have the capacity for multiplayer games, played either over a Local Area Network (LAN) connection between computers in the same physical location, or over the Internet, in which case a dedicated machine, usually at an Internet service provider (ISP),[1] university or other bandwidth-rich location, acts as a server. Multiplayer games may be 'deathmatches', in which the players fight against each other to score the highest number of kills or *frags,* or any of a variety of mods (modifications of the original game code) that often involve some form of team-based competition, such as Capture the Flag (CTF), which is somewhat like a football match with rocket launchers, or *Half-Life: Counter-Strike,* in which players are divided into teams of terrorists and counter-terrorists who must either carry out, or defend against, a variety of missions. Team mods can be quite complicated, involving different character classes and advanced strategy requiring complex cooperation and communication between team members.

In multiplayer games, the game space is physically located in software running on the server machine, but is experienced by the player as a game arena consisting of a 3D-rendered game arena or map in which all the players meet and interact. When not actively playing, game players may spectate, either by following an active player or by moving freely around the level, as if flying through the 3D space. In the multiplayer game, the characterisation and narrative aspects of the single player game are greatly minimised; in their place is a social environment formed at the intersection of the text of the game, the specific rules of whichever game mod the server may be running and the presence of other human participants, who may communicate with each other during the game by typing.

Multiplayer is by far the most common mode of FPS gaming; the single-player game may be played through once or twice (if at all), but gamers will play the multiplayer version regularly for months or years.[2] Although I will be referring to both multiplayer and single-player forms of play, I will be focusing more on the multiplayer gaming experience, not only because it is the most dominant

Figure 11 .*Quake III Arena* (id Software/Activision, 1999) deathmatch screenshot showing game event information and player chat in top left corner.

form of play, but also because the social dimensions of multiplayer gaming have influences over game/player interactions in both single-player and multiplayer situations.

Apparatus

The cinematic apparatus is seen as comprising the technical basis of film (the specific effects of equipment including camera, lighting, film, projection); the conditions of film viewing (darkened theatre, immobility, light projected from behind onto the screen facing the viewer); the film itself as a text; and the psychological processes inherent in the act of spectatorship, which place the spectator at the centre of the process (Baudry 1980). To analyse the first-person shooter game in terms of its apparatus, I will adapt these basic categories of the cinematic apparatus, distinguishing between the *technical basis* of computer games, the *conditions of game playing*, the *game itself as a text*, and the *psychological processes* at work in the game player.

By the term *game text* I am referring to the manifestations of the game software itself as purchased on the CD-ROM: visual images, characterisation, narrative and the code-driven rules and general organisation of gameplay; basically all the media the player accesses in terms of the game itself. The term *game space* refers to the computer-generated environment seen on the computer screen and heard through the PC speakers or headphones, and is also understood conceptually by the player as the environment one 'enters' when playing the game. I use the terms *player* and *gamer*, which would seem to be interchangeable, but there is a subtle difference. 'Player' describes a person engaged in the act of playing (analogous to 'spectator' in regards to cinema). The term 'gamer' implies the adoption of a subjective positioning based on gaming practices. Functionally it tends to mean that the person plays games regularly, has developed a respectable degree of proficiency at them and is party to a certain degree of shared knowledge held by those who identify as gamers (to continue the film analogy this would be equivalent of a 'film buff').

Technical basis

FPS games create a 3D-rendered environment on the computer screen that is seen by players from a first-person point of view as they 'move around' the 3D world (as opposed to third-person shooter games, such as *Tomb Raider*, in which the player controls a character that is visible on-screen). Unlike games such as *Myst*, which use pre-rendered still images, and therefore restrict the player to a particular point of view, there are no limitations on the viewing positions a player may adopt, apart from the physics enforced by the game engine (for example, simulated gravity). The player controls his/her movement and actions in the game using (most commonly) a keyboard and mouse.

The most common situation for computer game playing is that of a single person sitting at a desk or table in front of a PC. The PC screen is at eye level with the player, and shares virtually the same technical basis as television: an image on a screen that emits light in the direction of the viewer. However the computer screen is much closer — 30 to 60cm from the player's eyes — so, as in the cinema, most of the player's visual field is taken up by the image on the screen. Unlike cinema viewers, game players may not be in ambient darkness, but the screen image is their primary visual focus while playing, and the game itself demands their full attention and participation.

Conditions of game playing

The setting for most computer game-playing, like that of television viewing, is in the home — either in a private space (office, bedroom) or shared (living room). But most frequently the player is drawn away to some sort of enclave to minimise distractions from and disruptions to the surrounding environment. Multiplayer FPS games are also played at LAN meetings where groups of players take their computers to play over a LAN connection. These may range from small gatherings at one person's home, to regular meetings of a few hundred players, to large annual events such as QuakeCon, which attracts more than 3,000 gamers. Whether at home or at a LAN meeting, gaming often takes place in some sort of dedicated location.

A major consideration in the choice of location is sound. Because of both the player's need to be able to concentrate on sound within the game, and the tolerance of other persons to the noise generated by the game, it often becomes necessary for the player to wear headphones. Unless they have a separate room for gaming, players must create their own dedicated sonic space, which, not surprisingly, increases the immersiveness of the gaming experience.

Kinaesthetically, gamer-players are in a curious situation: immobilised yet highly active. They are immobile in terms of physical location; they stay sitting in a chair at the PC. There is no option for them to move out of this position and still be in full control of the game. Any deliberate movements they make are related to the game. Both hands are occupied: one clicking and moving a mouse or trackball, the other tapping the keys of the keyboard. Very little in the way of physical activity involving the hands may be carried out during the game without adversely affecting the player's performance. Even the 'immobile' cinema viewer is able to drink, eat or make any physical movement that does not require them to leave their seat. For gamers to carry out any of these activities, they must pause the game (if single player) or, if playing a multiplayer game where 'pausing' is impossible (because the game continues with or without their input), either leave the active arena and spectate, find a quiet corner (in the game map) where their chances of being seen by an enemy are low, or just stop playing if they are willing to forfeit their performance in the game. It is worth noting that a broad range of player participation is possible in multiplayer games. Players may play solidly for hours on end, or play a level or two before taking a break for a cup of tea or a cigarette; or maybe just join a game server and chat with friends. Successful playing of the game requires a committed focus from the player, however, and it is this mode of play that is the basis of the argument of this chapter.

Although largely immobilised at the PC, players are engaged in much bodily movement, not just controlling the game, but also in response to it. FPS players often move in response to the activity of their avatar on-screen, in a kind of unconscious force-feedback relationship with the on-screen action. Their upper body may tilt and lean as they swerve to avoid projectiles or turn corners in the game, or they may physically jolt when receiving a sudden fright. Laidlaw describes an FPS player as:

> That typically teenage, typically male soul who appears to outsiders to be caught in a sort of spastic fugue as he leans close to his computer, oblivious to other stimuli, twitching and gasping and attempting to see around the edges of the monitor. Occasionally he jumps out of his seat as if someone invisible had come up from behind and jabbed him. (1996: 126)

Another involuntary physical reaction to computer game play occurs in the form of a systemic adrenergic response, in which heart rate, blood pressure and breathing rate are increased (see Ballard & Wiest 1996; Lundberg *et al.* 1991). FPS players frequently use the term 'adrenaline rush' to describe the experience (for example, Laidlaw 1996: 122). While this occurs in both single and multiplayer games, it is likely to be stronger amid the increased pace, unpredictability and competitive stress of multiplayer gaming. These unconscious physiological responses, in which on-screen events initiate a physical reaction in the player's body, provide a bodily reinforcement of the player's perception of embodiment within the game space.

The skilled player's hand movements controlling the keyboard and mouse also become unconscious to a degree. Some manoeuvres require a complex sequence of keystrokes and mouse movements to be performed. These are analysed, designed, memorised and practised, but beyond this they are internalised, to the point at which individual moves are not carried out consciously and individually, but are absorbed into the player's style of playing (just as a trained dancer performs a pirouette from 'muscle memory', rather than a conscious awareness of the series of twists, elevations and arm movements that make up the manoeuvre). To achieve mastery of the game, conscious playing is not enough; players must be able to 'think with their fingers' to the point at which the player feels like an extension of the game or the game feels like an extension of the player (Turkle 1984: 85). In this respect games can create an escapist, meditative state in which intense concentration creates a zone of awareness or 'flow' into which everyday thoughts and concerns do not intrude (see Csikszentmihalyi 1990).

The computer game as text

The game player, like the film viewer, is involved in a single text: the game itself. However, FPS game players have a much higher level of engagement with that one text. Although one of the qualities of a successful single-player game is the creation of an evocative sense of the game as a real space, players do not necessarily get to know the spaces well; gameplay is organised around moving through one map to the next. In multiplayer gaming, however, players get to know game levels extremely well, even to the point of being able to navigate them blindfolded (see Zain 1999). Knowing a level is essential to the competitive player: where each weapon may be found, where and when ammunition, health and special items respawn, which weapons are most effective in certain areas, or the timing needed for specific manoeuvres. As well as being useful to the player, this familiarity leads to an increased perception of the game space as a real place: everything is familiar, it is a 'place' to which the gamer can go and find everything as s/he expects it, the only variations being in the presence and actions of the other players.

The temporal setting of the game is very much in the present, but it is a dislocated present. There is a sense of immediacy in the gaming experience provided by the interactivity. Every action gets immediate feedback (whether from the game software itself or server/player information from an online connection). But the gamer's experience of real time is significantly modified; hours can pass very quickly. Although this effect is common to many experiences requiring intense concentration and involvement, in the game it increases the 'otherworldliness' of the game-space, as it appears to have temporal rules of its own, like those of a dream.

Sound in games operates on a number of levels. As in the cinema, sound effects are used to provide an audio complement to action on the screen (when a weapon is fired, the vision is accompanied by the appropriate sound effect) and to create a sense of a real physical space (wind is heard whooshing around an outdoors area, a pit of steaming lava bubbles and hisses). However, unlike the principle uses of sound in film (see Ellis 1992: 128–9), game sound does not rely upon the visual image as its primary referent. Although players can only see 90–120 degrees of their environment at any one time,[3] they get sonic information from the full 360 degrees of their surroundings (as in real life). They hear the impact of someone jumping down an adjacent elevator shaft, or a box of ammunition respawning behind them. The stereo sound of 3D games provides accurate directionality and volume attenuation over distance, creating a realistic sense of events occurring in a surrounding environment (see Prince 2001).

Sound is highly important to players, less for aesthetic reasons than as a carrier of information. All game events have an associated sound effect, and experienced players learn to recognise these and make strategic use of them. The sound of respawning ammunition, weapons or armour, the footsteps heralding the approach of another player and the sound effects of weapons, all provide the player with essential information that can be obtained much faster and over a greater distance than if the player were relying upon visual input. For this reason, many players (and all players in official competitions) wear headphones not only to create an immersive sonic space, but also to make use of the directional qualities of sound. The ability to use this sonic information well is one of the qualities that divides expert players from the rest.[4]

Psychological processes

For psychoanalytic film theory, the significance of the cinematic apparatus lies in its creation of a dream state. Whereas for Freud the dream is a 'normal hallucinatory psychosis', film is seen as creating 'an artificial psychosis without offering the dreamer the possibility of exercising any kind of immediate control' (Stam *et al.* 1992: 144). This dreamlike state is seen as allowing the film viewer to experience primary cinematic identification: the cinematic subject's unconscious identification with the act of looking, with the invisible seeing agency of the film itself, which functions as a transcendental subject, 'a pure and all-seeing invisible subject' (Metz 1982: 97).

Elements of the game apparatus can be seen to be contributing to an immersive, dreamlike state using similar mechanisms to those of cinema. Because of its proximity to the player, the computer screen, while much smaller than the cinema screen, takes up a corresponding amount of the player's visual field. Sound is immersive, as in cinema; it dominates any environmental sound and is made more enveloping with the use of headphones. Playing generally occurs in a space that is (temporarily or permanently) dedicated to gaming, whether a solitary location in the home or at a LAN meeting. The attention level of players is high and they are engaged with, and highly focused on, a single text.

However, unlike Baudry's spectator/dreamer, the game-player has a very high degree of control over the on-screen events — this is essential to the game, and antithetical to the dream. While this sense of control can be seen to lessen the dream-like qualities of the medium, and hence primary identification in the cinematic sense, other mechanisms within the FPS game increase the player's sense of immersion and identification within the game. Unlike the notion of primary cinematic identification, which relies upon a theoretical identification with a transcendental subject or mechanisms of 'suture' which draw the spectator into the interplay of looks between characters (Stam *et al.* 1992: 169), primary identification in the FPS game is established more directly through the constant first-person point of view, the player's own sense of agency and experience of interactivity.

First-person point-of-view is used very successfully in games, not just in first-person shooters but also in adventure/puzzle games such as *Myst* or *Riven* (Cyan/red Orb, 1997), to create a sense of the player's embodiment within the game space, and is recognised by game designers as contributing to a more visceral game experience because of the sense of immersion created (see Clarke-Willson 1998: 230). If primary identification is the cinematic subject's identification with the act of looking, then the FPS player is unequivocally the one doing the looking. He or she is invisible in the game, just as one's own body is mostly invisible from one's point of view in real life. The player is placed in the scene not only by the first-person point of view but also by his or her total control over this point of view.

In film, the enunciative position of the 'producer of the fiction' is internalised and naturalised by the viewer as his/her own viewing position — even though this is constituted industrially from the position of the camera and, by relay, the director. In the game, players can see themselves as producers of the fiction (despite the authorial stamp of the game's programmers and designers on the game's engine and graphics) because of their active role in the game. The design and user interface of FPS games also contribute to this. Players may type in console commands during play to change settings in the game, and the 'open source' nature of the game code allows players to make their own models, maps, skins and mods, which many do.[5] So FPS players may experience themselves as 'producers of the fiction' both figuratively, and to some degree, literally.

Sherry Turkle refers to computer games as 'something you do, something you do to your head, a world that you enter, and, to a certain extent, they are something you "become"' (1984: 65–7). William Bricken describes virtual reality as inclusive; by placing 'the participant inside information' it shifts the participant 'from a feeling of viewing a picture to a feeling of being in a place ... from being observers to having experiences, from interfacing with a display to inhabiting an environment' (quoted in Calcutt 1999: 133). Although games do not (currently) completely surround the player with images of the virtual environment, as is the goal of fully immersive VR systems, the FPS game apparatus creates an existential sense of the game space as a place where they have *been*. Gamer 'LadyICE' describes the FPS experience:

> I have played a lot of different genres ... and have always found that I prefer First Person Shooters. Why? I think it boils down to the fact that I actually feel like I'm 'in' the game – in total control of my character. (quoted in Wong 2001)

Although one common quality of both the film and the dream is the participant's lack of control over the images they are seeing, in the game the level of control possessed by the player contributes to their sense of being *in* that virtual space. One experienced gamer of my acquaintance reported passing the time during a uncomfortable, hour-long medical procedure by mentally playing his favourite *Quake* level from memory, a process through which he managed to 'remove' himself to some degree from the physical pain he was experiencing in real life. When describing their in-game experiences, gamers speak in the first person, displaying a sense of their presence within the game space. The following example is typical:

> This flag carrier had our flag and had evaded us for some time on q3wctf2. So I decided to check the red armour room where the teleporter is, because, frankly, I hide there all the time when I have the flag! I stand at the doorway, but can't see anything. So I shoot a few rockets at the teleporter and wouldn't ya know... he was there all the time. ([EvEm]_Xtro 2000)

From this it can be seen that FPS players report a sense of immersion and primary identification far greater than that established in relation to other screen media. If film has 'the gaze' and television has the viewer's 'glance' (Flitterman-Lewis 1992: 217), then FPS games have the penetrating 'stare'.

The following table summarises the respective apparatus elements of film, television and FPS computer games. The elements of the computer game apparatus that contribute to the player's sense of immersion in the game space are marked in bold. Again I am not implying that there is any continuity between these qualities in film, television and games, but rather that these are elements that can be identified in each medium to varying degrees. Any such chart is, inevitably, schematic and risks some oversimplification in order to draw out certain prevailing tendencies.

Elements of Apparatus	Cinema	Television	Computer Game
Technical basis			
Screen distance	Far	Medium/close	Very close
Light projection	From behind	Towards viewer	Towards viewer
Image quality	Solid image	Interlaced	Interlaced
Sound	Immersive	Used to get viewer's attention	Immersive
Conditions of viewing			
Place	Public	Domestic	Domestic
Physical proximity to others	Close	Solitary or with others	Mostly solitary
Environmental sound	Silence	Distractions	Dominated by game sound
View	Up	Down/eye level	Eye level
Ambient lighting	Dark	Dark or light	Dark or light
Image vs spectator size	Image larger	Image smaller	Image smaller
Attention of viewer	Involved	Distracted	Highly involved
Access – to technology	Restricted	Available	Available
Social context	Event – 'Let's go to the movies'	Event or diversion – 'What's on TV?'	Event – 'Let's play'

On-screen text			
Time	Edited/ condensed	Condensed/real	Real-time but with warped sense of time
Temporal location	Distanced in time	Present	Present
Number of texts	Single	Potential for many	Single
Access – to text of choice	Restricted	Restricted (more available with video)	Available
Authorial presence	Present	Mostly absent	Player contributes to text
Point of view	Varied	Varied	First-person
Textual commitment	Focused	Diversion	Focused
Mental machinery of spectatorship			
Primary identification	Strong	Varied	Very strong
Secondary identification	Strong	Strong	Little
Absorption	Viewer is absorbed	Viewer absorbs	Player is absorbed
Sense of responsibility for on-screen action	Low	Low (but increased by socialisation of viewing subject)	High
Mechanism of engagement	Viewer absorbed into gaze	Addresses viewer	Player enters game space

Table 1: Apparatus elements in cinema, television and the FPS computer game

Social subjects

Because of the differences between the cinematic apparatus and that of television, psychoanalytic film theory has not been considered very useful in the study of television (see Feuer 1986: 102; Fiske 1987: 226). Television viewers are also considered to be 'social subjects' because of the home-based viewing location, their increased sense of responsibility for what they view on-screen, and the way they feel themselves to be addressed personally by televisual texts, all of which draw on the viewer's everyday subjective positionings (see Fiske 1987: 62). Althusser's notion of 'interpellation' refers to the way that discourse hails the (model) addressee, and how, by responding, we accept the discourse's definition of 'us', adopting the position proposed for us by the discourse (1971: 132–4). For example, much of television addresses the viewer as a family member: many popular programs are structured around the family unit, sit-coms are created by variations on the 'normal' family, and traditional television program scheduling is based upon the daily routine of the 'typical' family (see Ellis 1992: 164–5; Fiske 1987: 56–8).

Primary identification as established in FPS games is so strong that gamers may not be aware of the textual and social influences affecting their gaming subjectivity. It is easy to believe it is just 'me playing this game', but the gaming subject is strongly affected by interpellation from the game text itself and social influences, both intraludic (experienced during gameplay) and extraludic (the wider body of textual and social manifestations of the gaming community).

Social influences from the game text

In single-player FPS games the player is required to adopt some degree of characterisation and address as the text's protagonist, from the minimal (the unnamed space marine of *Quake II*, addressed by the game as 'you') to the more definite (*Half-Life*'s Gordon Freeman, addressed as 'Gordon'). In a multiplayer game, direct characterisation is absent. Instead players must choose a name and a model to represent themselves. Names used by players are either taken from fictional characters (for example, 'Dr Evil', 'Cartman', 'Trinity') or are invented by players and range from the aggressively themed ('xTerMin8R') to the whimsical ('ThindyBrady'), but frequently indicate a subjective positioning dictated by the fighting nature of the game itself, for example 'Armageddon', 'Hellbitch', 'CopKiller'. Many clan names also follow this theme, examples including the Australian clans 'War' and 'Carnage' and the North American female clans 'PMS (Psycho Men Slayers)' and 'Violent Femmes'.

The way players choose identities based upon, or influenced by, the game text itself takes Althusser's concept of interpellation a step beyond that which has been recognised in regard to either film or television by actively constructing gaming identities influenced by that text. Gamers also use their game names in online chat environments and in real-life social environments with other gamers, such as LAN meetings, where they rarely refer to each other by their given names. For many players their game name also functions as their general online name — in their email address, for example — and forms an important part of their identification as 'gamers'. While gaming is only one influence on their subjectivity, and not its principle source of definition, it joins other more widely acknowledged aspects of subjectivity — such as race and gender — in a player's 'structure of accessed identifications' (Hartley 1983: 69–70).

Communication within the game-space is also influenced by the game text itself. 'Trash talk' and taunting within multiplayer games can be seen as the result of the 'attitude' displayed in FPS games since the inception of the genre. In *Wolfenstein 3D* (Apogee/id Software, 1992), players have a choice of four levels of difficulty: 'Can I play, Daddy?', 'Don't hurt me', 'Bring 'em on!' and 'I am Death incarnate'. *Duke Nukem 3D* (3D Realms/GT Interactive, 1996) was influential because of the Duke character's trash talk, with quotes taken from and influenced by Bruce Campbell's satirical action hero character 'Ash' in the *Evil Dead* movies ('Come get some'; 'Hail to the king, baby'). Multiplayer *Quake* carried this further with aggressive or humorous but often puerile 'kill' messages (for example, 'Player1 tears Player2 a new one') and by taunting players for being cowardly when they attempted to quit the game.

Player communication in multiplayer games sometimes takes on an element of the aggressive quality of the game's pre-programmed statements. Players taunt each other, usually good-naturedly and with humour, but not always. Taunting has become so much a part of the ethos of FPS games that *Unreal Tournament* includes automatic taunting (even by bots),[6] in which a player who has been killed will receive an insulting message generated by the game software such as 'Die, bitch!' or 'Try turning the safety off'. This tone of address has also been carried over into gaming magazines and the many web pages devoted to such games; an air of tongue-in-cheek bravado pervades many of these secondary gaming texts.

Social rules of the game

In computer games, the rules as enforced by the game software are black-and-white: a manoeuvre is either possible or it is not; a shot either hits a defined target area or it misses. Unlike in physical sports, there is no opportunity to enter a debate with the line judges. Because the rules enforced by the game software itself are so clearly defined, the player is ostensibly freed from making any moral choices in the game — anything that is possible is permissible. One phenomenon observed in multiplayer gaming is the development of social rules and restraints, however, in which certain actions are considered to be unsporting or forms of cheating even though they are well within the possibilities of the game. These may relate to weapons used, gameplay strategies or just general social behaviour.

In multiplayer *Quake II*, for example, a player who uses the game's strongest weapon, the BFG, will often be abused by other players. The rationalisation is that, because the BFG inflicts damage over a wide area, it does not require great skill to use effectively and spoils the game by allowing easy kills. Another weapon, the hyperblaster, is considered unfair to other players because the graphics it generates are considered to cause inconvenient delays or lag. One strategy that has been highly controversial in deathmatch games is 'camping' — the practice of staying in one strategically advantageous area and amassing frags. While it is a very efficient and logical way of playing (considering that the goal is to score as many frags as possible), it is considered generally to be unfair because of the advantage achieved by the camping player: running around in the general mêlée is somehow considered to be more honourable. If a player is camping, other players will begin to complain and abuse them, and sometimes join together to eliminate the camper and return some balance to the game.[7]

While these conventions are developed and enforced socially, and often appear in online strategy guides, some may be enforced institutionally. Some game server administrators 'turn off' the BFG, so the weapon does not appear in the game at all. Servers may run anti-camping algorithms, which detect when a player has spent too much time in the one location (see Ownby 2001).

The gaming community

Once players are playing online, they are, to varying degrees, drawn into the gaming community. Although it is now possible to buy a game such as *Quake III Arena* or *Half-Life: Counter-Strike* and connect straight to an internet game, all players will at some stage need to make use of the vast amount of resources available for players online; to download upgrades and to obtain information on strategy and customisation. Such resources are indispensable to gamers who wish to achieve proficiency. They also provide a source of interest, education and contact with the gaming community beyond the playing experience itself. Involvement in the online culture, not just through playing the game, but also through web-pages (including discussion forums), mail-lists, Internet Relay Chat (IRC) channels and real-time chat programs, contributes further social influences to the formation of the gaming subject.

Conclusion

Here I have been able to show how a computer game may be analysed in terms of its 'apparatus' by examining the various technical, textual, environmental, psychological and social aspects of the playing of a FPS computer game. I have demonstrated ways in which the FPS game apparatus creates for the player a highly immersive media experience, in which a first-person point-of-view, player agency and the operations of interactivity combine to create a sense of primary identification greater than that of cinema. To rephrase Baudry, the FPS computer game can be seen as offering *an artificial psychosis that gives the player the illusion of full control.*

I have also been able to explore some of the social influences on gaming subjectivity, in which players are influenced by their address by the game text itself, intertextual sources from other media and secondary gaming texts and the wider socio-cultural context of gaming practices. Identification of these mechanisms of player engagment with, and use of, the medium can shed new light on discussion of some of the current issues surrounding FPS games and contribute to a wider body of work addressing gaming practices and communities.

notes

1   At the time of writing there are over 20,000 FPS game servers worldwide, with some

70,000 players logged on at any one time. *Half-Life* is currently the most popular game by far, due to the highly successful mod *Counter-Strike,* and accounts for two-thirds of the players and servers (*Gamespy*).

2 Game development practices have shifted in recognition of this. *Quake III Arena* (1999) was released as a multiplayer-only game, a narrative-based single player version was not developed. The *Half-Life* multiplayer mod *Counter-Strike* was sold on CD-ROM as a separate title, unlike previous game mods that were available as a free online download.

3 The field of view setting in FPS games is customisable — settings between 90-120° are the most popular.

4 For further examples of the high degree of importance gamers place on sound, see Fong 2000.

5 The creative contributions of gamers are a very important facet of the FPS scene. In a 1999 survey I did of FPS gamers, three-quarters of gamers surveyed had completed some sort of creative project associated with their gaming practices. See Morris 1999.

6 Computer generated players designed for deathmatch practice and for creating a multiplayer game experience for a single player.

7 For a satirical yet accurate list of some of the social conventions attached to *Quake II,* see O'Keefe 2001.

citations

[EvEm]_Xtro 'I Can SeeYouuuu!' (2000) *Evil Empire Gaming.* 10 July. Available on-line at: http://evem.org.au/clan.nsf/docs/200007102013431.

Althusser, Louis (1971) 'Ideology and Ideological State Apparatuses,' *Lenin and Philosophy and Other Essays.* Trans. Ben Brewster. New York: Monthly Review, 127—86.

Ballard, Mary E., & J. Rose Wiest (1996) 'Mortal Kombat (tm): The Effects of Violent Videogame Play on Males' Hostility and Cardiovascular Responding', *Journal of Applied Social Psychology,* 26, 717—30.

Baudry, Jean-Louis. 'The Apparatus', in Theresa Hak Kyung Cha (ed.) (1980) *Apparatus, Cinematographic Apparatus: Selected Writings.* New York: Tanam, 41—62.

___ 'Ideological Effects of the Basic Cinematic Apparatus.' in Theresa Hak Kyung Cha (ed.) (1980) *Apparatus, Cinematographic Apparatus: Selected Writings.* New York: Tanam, 25—37.

Calcutt, Andrew (1999) *White Noise: An A—Z of the Contradictions in Cyberculture.* Houndmills: Macmillan.

Cha, Theresa Hak Kyung (ed.) (1980) *Apparatus, Cinematographic Apparatus: Selected Writings.* New York: Tanam.

Clarke-Willson, Stephen (1998) 'Applying Game Design to Virtual Environments', in Clark Dodsworth Jr. (ed.) *Digital Illusion: Entertaining the Future with High Technology.* SIGGRAPH series. New York: ACM, 229—39.

Csikszentmihalyi, Mihaly (1990) *Flow: The Psychology of Optimal Experience.* New York: Harper Perennial.

Ellis, John (1992) *Visible Fictions.* London: Routledge.

Fiske, John (1987) *Television Culture.* London: Methuen.

Flitterman-Lewis, Sandy (1992) 'Psychoanalysis, Film and Television', in Robert C. Allen (ed.) *Channels of Discourse, Reassembled: Television and Contemporary Criticism*. 2nd rev. edn. Chapel Hill: University of North Carolina Press, 203—46.

Feuer, Jane (1986) 'Narrative Form in American Network Television', in Colin MacCabe (ed.) *High Theory/Low Culture*. Manchester: Manchester University Press, 101—14.

Fong, Dennis (2000) ('Thresh') 'Knowing Sounds', *Thresh's Quake Bible*. Available on-line at: http://www.gamersx.com/bibles/quake/subsections/techniques/adv-sounds.asp.

GameSpy Live Stats Page (2001) 14 Sept 2001. Available on-line at: http://www.gamespy.com/stats.

Hartley, John (1983) 'Television and the Power of Dirt', in *Australian Journal of Cultural Studies*, 1, 2, 62—82.

Laidlaw, Mark (1996) 'The Egos at id', *Wired*, 4. 08, 122—7; 186—9.

Lundberg, U., B. Rasch and O. Westermark (1991) 'Physiological Reactivity and Type A Behaviour in Preschool Children: A Longitudinal Study', *Behavioral Medicine*, 17, 4, 149—57.

Metz, Christian (1982) *The Imaginary Signifier: Psychoanalysis and the Cinema*. Trans. C. Britton, A. Williams, B. Brewster and A Guzzetti. Bloomington: Indiana University Press.

Morris, Sue (1999) 'Online Gaming Culture.' *Game-Culture*. June. Available on-line at: http://www.game-culture.com/articles/onlinegaming.html.

O'Keefe, Paul (2001) 'Strategies: 25 Tips for Multiplayer Quake', Lamerkatz. 14 Sept. Available on-line at: http://www.lamerkatz.com/strategies/25tips.shtml.

Ownby, Matt (1999) *Balance of Power*. Available on-line at: http://www.planetquake.com/bop/bop.html.

Prince, Bobby (1997) 'Tricks and Techniques for Sound Effect Design.' *Gamasutra*. August. Available on-line at: http://www.gamasutra.com/features/sound_and_music/081997/sound_effect.htm.

Stam, Robert, Robert Burgoyne and Sandy Flitterman-Lewis (1992) *New Vocabularies in Film Semiotics*. London: Routledge.

Turkle, Sherry (1984) *The Second Self: Computers and the Human Spirit*. New York: Simon and Schuster.

Wong, Chin ('Frosty') (2001) 'HellChick and LadyICE Interview.' *GamersOrb*. 4 June. Available on-line at: http://www.gamersorb.com/main/interviews/go_int_hcli.shtml.

Zain, Adrian ('Zeeko') (1999) 'The Things We Do', *Singnet Dominion*. 2 April. Available on-line at: http://gaming.singnet.com.sg/ttwd.html.

chapter five

Vision and Virtuality: The Construction of Narrative Space in Film and Computer Games

wee liang tong & marcus cheng chye tan

Visualisation and virtuality

Human experience is now, more than ever, saturated with the mediation of various forms of visual interfaces ranging from advertising posters to television programmes, mass-consumed Hollywood films and computer games. There is, as Nicholas Mirzoeff describes in his introductory chapter to the *Visual Culture Reader*, a prevalent tendency 'to picture or visualise experience' (1999: 6). The study of visual culture entails an awareness of the fact that 'visual culture is concerned with visual events in which information, meaning or pleasure is sought by the consumer in an *interface* with visual technology' (1999: 3). There is, hence, a need to investigate how visual content is framed and presented by the technical apparatus in question. Given the level of graphics realism of which the latest computer games are capable, it is necessary to question how the emphasis and employment of digital graphics interfaces re-defines our experience and understanding of visual narrative as it is re-mediated in computer games.

With the greater degree of autonomy that recent 3D computer games begin to offer in terms of camera movement and perspective, the gamer is often invited to take an active role in the framing and composition of the game *mise-en-scène*. This process of visualisation is also an act of narrativisation, as both framing and composition of on-screen figures and objects take place in real-time. The visualisation of the game, as it unfolds in real-time and in a virtual 3D space (rendered by advanced graphics engines and cards), not only generates an immersive gaming experience but also fosters the construction of a distinct form of visual narrative. Game narrative is, then, a visual narrative that is composed of certain cinematic techniques akin to, though not directly equated with, continuous filming. This 'filming' without cutting and editing departs from rules of conventional cinema as a result of the simulation of three-dimensional space. Playing the game resembles watching a film, in some respects, but difference lies in the levels of interactivity offered by the game, between the gamer and the game-environment. The crucial sense of real-time continuity demanded by a 3D game prohibits it from employing cinematic techniques of editing (other than those evidenced in cinematic cut-scenes or in changes in fixed camera positions that occur during interactive gameplay in some in third-person shooters, such as *Resident Evil* (Capcom 1999)). With reference to Stephen Heath's theory of narrative space in film (1981), this essay will attempt to delineate the ways in which particular PC games have developed a distinct form of visual narrative. To what extent is this film-like aspect of the game also a form of visual expression of the game action, a narrativisation of the game as it is played?

The status of narrative in computer games

In *Visual Digital Culture*, Andrew Darley (2000) brings to attention a need to further explore the possible ways in which interactivity and visual interface, in computer games, may affect the construction of narrative coherence. Darley points out that the digitisation of images in film and games alike has led to new technical and aesthetic possibilities that have yet to mature. With regards to computer games, digital visual images have been manipulated mainly for the purposes of creating a form of vicarious kinaesthesia (see Darley 2000: 155, 194), directed to impress the gamer and encourage him/her to play on. As the game attempts to create a sense of a 'peculiar pretended residency or vicarious sense of presence in a fictional world' (2000: 152) the formation of a sophisticated and meaningful narrative becomes compromised. To put it simply, the sense of narrative continuity and coherence becomes secondary and subordinated to the simulation of an immersive virtual environment. In Darley's opinion, this vicarious kinaesthesia, which appeals predominantly to the sensory pleasures of sight and sound, limits the gamer's immediate attention to objects that are close at hand. Any form of game narrative can therefore only be developed in the strictly sequential, real time unfolding of the game. As 'surface play', computer games engage the player superficially in terms of immediate reflex actions and through the performance of largely instrumental or functional tasks. Games thus suffer from what Darley describes as the 'fragmented character of [the] story passage' (2000: 152). Games might, at times, incorporate engaging storylines but even these are often fragmented by the demands of the game programming. The explicitly goal-oriented nature of games tends to generate a prescribed path, concluding in a predetermined fashion. The gamer must complete tasks in a particular manner or sequence before proceeding (or completing the game). Any form of narrative that is interwoven into the game becomes subordinated to the linear logic of the game sequence. As a consequence:

99

> The space for reading or meaning-making in the traditional sense is radically reduced in computer games and simulation rides. In this sense the much maligned 'passive' spectators of conventional cinema might be said to be far more active than their counterparts in the newer forms. (Darley 2000: 164)

While recognising the technical advancement of games as evidenced in the extensive employment and manipulation of digital image interfaces, Darley believes that games have not, and perhaps cannot, match forms such as film in the construction of strong and meaningful narratives. Accordingly, a movie can engage the viewer 'at a poetic level (form and style), [in] a more profound aspect of semiotic dimension and semantic depth' (2000: 164). Measured against the yardstick of a generally literary poetics, games are regarded as lacking in 'semantic engagement' compared with more established media such as film.

Producing a game story is, however, not equivalent to writing/reading a novel or making/watching a film, as Ben Sawyer, Alex Dunne and Tor Berg suggest:

> Every great game story is driven by the game play. *The story emerges from the game; the game doesn't emerge from the story.* ... The very notion of interactivity means that the decision and skills of the player will move the story in a certain direction. Thus, *the game becomes the interface for the story.* The player interacts with the game, which then results in the game presenting the actual underlying story back to the player. (1998: 112; emphasis in original)

A game, according to Sawyer, Dunne and Berg, produces a particular story specific to its own terms. As such, the nature of the story that emerges from the game would not conform neatly to the kinds of literary-poetical forms and styles to which Darley alludes. The conveyance of the game-story would be different from the way a novel or a film narrativises its story, due in no small part to the active participation required of the gamer in affecting the process and outcome of the course of the game in its entirety.

A more worthwhile venture might be the analysis of the ways in which games, with their heavy reliance on visualisation, construct a distinct sense of spatial and narrative coherence, specifically; a visual rather than literary narrative structure. The tools by which the sense of immersion and interactivity are produced in computer games can be seen as *constitutive of* the general framework of a distinctively visual narrative unity rather than be regarded as interruptive elements. The digital rendition of a virtual 3D environment is one such tool.

A critical understanding of the process of visualisation in current PC games requires an engagement with, and comprehension of, 3D technology and its ability to construct virtual spaces. Computer graphics can present 3D objects that appear to possess qualities of solid extensions in space, which therefore acquire a higher degree of 'realism'. The sense of immersion in a virtual world, where laws of physics are applied (or rather, simulated), creates in the gamer an acute awareness of space and spatiality of the game environment. Darley's insightful analysis of videogames does not appear to give sufficient attention to the increasing reliance of games on 3D graphics, a factor that can affect the relations between gamer and game. Darley's examination of *Quake* (id Software, 1996) convincingly exposes the game's threadbare narrative content and its heavy emphasis on the immediate sensory excitement. *Quake* fails to generate any narrative depth because the avatar and the enemies are stereotypes without complex personalities; conflicts and motives are starkly defined without ambiguity and the gamer's range of actions in this world is greatly limited to the parameters of the game programme. While Darley's analysis might be consistent with a game such as *Quake*, which was among the first generation of PC-based games to incorporate 3D graphics, the current preoccupation with generating virtual realism in PC gaming necessitates a reassessment of the situation. As the environment and the characters are invested with richer visual details and textures, the gamer can find aspects to relate to in the game environment, features that have meaning beyond the functional need to complete the game quest. Coupled with the ability to control the simulated camera view, such details not only serve an aesthetic appeal but also provide the gamer some (minimal) measure of constructing the fictional narrative space.

Narrativity and narrative space

Although first published in 1976, a full decade before computer games began to capture the popular imagination, Stephen Heath's seminal essay 'Narrative Space' contains insights that assist in the study of the construction of narrative space in games. Through the analysis of specific film-making techniques – such as editing, close-ups, the use of off-screen space and eye-line matches – Heath argues that film narrative is the result of an active re-constitution, by the viewer, of the various gaps and spaces exposed by these formal aspects of the film-making process. Many games today aspire to be 'cinematic' in their presentation by establishing a game environment (and storyline) based on popular Hollywood genres and titles, and incorporating elaborate cut-scenes which are, in effect, mini-movies in themselves. This sense of a cinematic presentation extends further in games that allow the gamer considerable control and direction of the virtual camera. Playing the game thus becomes almost synonymous with directing a movie.

Space, according to Heath, is not a detached empirical given that the camera merely captures on film. Objects captured on film take on a significance that goes beyond the recording of their physical extension in reality, because of the way the view is framed and edited. The presentation of cinematic space is a process of selective framings and editing that produce 'gaps' or jumps in the continuity of the flow of images. What is required, on the spectator's part, is to actively interweave these distinct and fragmented visualisation of spaces into a coherent notion of place.

> The film poses an image, not immediate or neutral, but posed, framed and centred. Perspective-system images bind the spectator in place,

> the suturing central position that is the sense of the image, that sets its scene (in place, the spectator completes the image as its subject). ... What moves in film, finally, is the spectator, immobile in front of the screen. Film is the regulation of that movement, the individual as subject held in a shifting and placing of desire, energy, contradiction, in a perpetual re-totalisation of the imaginary (the set scene of image and subject). This is the investment of film in narrativisation; and crucially for a coherent space, the unity of place for vision. (1981: 53)

In Heath's opinion, the centrality of vision is crucial in the construction of narrative space. The desire for a centrality of vision drives the viewing subject to suture disparate spaces and images together into a meaningful narrative sequence. Narrativisation, in Heath's opinion, is not simply the telling of the story or the unfolding of the plot, but rather, a holistic form of interpretative response.

> Narrative makes the join of symbolic and imaginary, process and reflection. That making, the elaboration of the narrative, may be called narrativisation: the narrative is the close, *the fiction of the film ultimately rendered*; narrativisation is the rendering, the movement to the narrative in the film, of the film to the narrative. (1981: 122, emphasis in original)

Film narrative is comprised of a series of editing cuts, sequencing gaps and spatial ambiguities. A narrative thus refers not just to a pre-established storyline or plot, nor does it only include the sequence of actions that transpires in a film, or for that matter, a game (the 'moves' or actions that the gamer executes). What Heath describes as 'narrative' might be better expressed as 'filmic fiction' (and Heath qualifies it as such in the citation above), a fiction constructed by the specific techniques of film-making. Heath's theory opens up possibilities for the examination of narrative space in computer games. Narrative is understood not only in terms of the unfolding of a series of actions and events on-screen, but it also relates to the way the visual images are framed, positioned and, in the case of film, edited. These stylistic techniques open up a fictional space where the organisation of visual space contributes significantly to the narrativisation of a film.

Cut-scenes and narrative space

A recent game that aspires very much to present itself in a cinematic fashion, while providing a rich and interactive gameplay environment with a strong narrative, is *No One Lives Forever* (*NOLF*) (Monolith/Fox Interactive, 2000). *NOLF* belongs to the highly popular first-person-shooter (FPS) genre. In such games, the gamer assumes control of a character from the first-person camera perspective. In the case of *NOLF*, the interface places the gamer in direct control of the protagonist, UNITY agent Cate Archer. Such a window of perspective creates a strong sense of immersiveness, as the gamer's view equates with that seen through the eyes of the character. To further simulate the experience of being in a spy movie, *NOLF* borrows extensively from popular spy films. The title itself is an explicit play on popular James Bond titles such as *Tomorrow Never Dies* (1997) and *You Only Live Twice* (1967). Each aspect of the game design, from the menus, soundtrack, script and plot, right down to specific details such as the uniform of the guards and type of gadgets and weapons used, are made to create a 1960s 'feel', echoing the period in which spy movies and television series, such as *The Avengers*, were all the rage. Even the game narrative is a pastiche of the spy movie genre, tracing the induction of Cate Archer into spy-hood, through to her betrayal by a mole in UNITY (an MI5 equivalent), to the eventual denouement in which she unravels the secret plot of HARM; not surprisingly, a diabolical organisation bent on world-domination.

NOLF is among the rising number of games that produce cut-scenes using the same graphics engine as the actual gameplay itself. This differs from games such as *Command and Conquer* (Westwood/Virgin Interactive, 1995) that utilise live-action, filmic sequences as cut-scenes, suggesting a growing concern with the safeguarding, through visual continuity, of the sense of immersiveness established in gameplay. The cut-scenes of *NOLF* still disrupt the sense of immersion, however, as the camera assumes the conventional third-person perspective – very much a filmic convention – in these sequences. The gamer's perspective is shifted to a view in which s/he looks upon himself/herself (as protagonist Cate Archer) as a character in a movie. Once the cut-scene commences, the player loses control of the character and therefore control of the camera (and the established first-person point of view). The game's shift into a more cinematic mode thus interrupts the degree of immersion that most FPS games seek to create. Such a sequence causes the gamer to lose control of the avatar, thereby allowing the game-character seemingly to take on a life of its own.

The trademarks of conventional, mainstream film-making, such as the employment of panoramic and establishing shots, are also observed in these film-like cut-scenes: for instance, the panning shot in a particular scene depicting the movement of a freight ship as it cruises past the camera. Furthermore, the use of shot/reverse-shot patterns also abides strictly to the 'classical' Hollywood 180-degree rule (exemplified in Archer's conversations with other characters). Any attempt to maintain a sense of visual continuity between the game sequence and the cut-scenes, through the consistent use of a similar 3D graphics platform, is inevitably attenuated by the employment of certain elements of cinematic style in the cut-scenes. Between the cut-scenes and the game sequence, a different relation to space, and specifically narrative space, is established. The use of the 180-degree rule and shot/reverse-shot sequences in the cut-scenes of *NOLF* is an apt exemplification of the disruption of fictional immersiveness. This occurs most often in moments of conversation between the central characters. Conversation is visually scripted to ensure that the rhythm of exchange is registered. The gamer is not distracted by the spaces around the characters, attention being directed towards the faces of characters and their expressions as they speak to one another.

As Heath reminds us, the underlying rationale of the 180-degree rule is to safeguard the illusion of spatial unity as it is framed within the limits of the screen:

> The 180-degree line that the camera is forbidden to cross answers exactly to the 180-degree line of the screen behind which the spectator cannot and must not go, in front of which he or she is placed within the triangle of representation, the space of the image projected, that is repeated in the very terms of the fiction of the imaged space. (1981: 42)

This strict adherence to the 180-degree rule, in the cut-scenes, is in contrast to the game sequence where this forbidden space *needs to* and *can be* traversed. In the game sequence Cate Archer can, for instance, eavesdrop on the dialogues between enemy guards. Some of these conversations contain information useful to the completion of the mission, while others exist merely as humorous distractions. The gamer does not get any cinematic shot/reverse-shots of these guards in conversation. Instead, s/he can attempt to creep around the guards while they are distracted, or endeavour to angle a well-aimed shot at them, as the dialogue takes place in real-time, uninterrupted by the incorporation of crucial visual and narrative cues such as the shot/reverse-shot and the 180-degree rule.

Returning again to Heath's theories, narrative space, in film, is the reconstitution and rearrangement of spatial information presented to the viewer. In other words, a fictive space is constructed, or sutured, based upon the various shots and frames of spaces in which the action unfolds. In games such as *NOLF*, narrativisation takes place as the character traverses the game space. In-game dialogue sequences between enemy guards take place as *events* in the game environment and are not narrated *as* conversations. The conversations are not remarked on as such in terms of cinematic convention. The difference between a cinematically presented conversation and a verbal exchange that takes place as an event in the game environment is an important one for they signify dissimilar modes of visualising and alternate ways of narrativising game spaces. The immersion of a gamer in an interactive simulated 3D environment, in real-time, precludes the employment of cinematic framing and editing techniques, the stylistic *modus operandi* in the construction of filmic narrative. Although games can, and often do, consist of both immersive interactivity and cinematic cut-scenes, these are two distinct modes of visualising the game-environment that cannot be synthesized. When the gamer loses control of the camera/character, thus ceding control to pre-set camera positions that direct the field of vision autonomously, in accordance with a predetermined script, the game effectively enters into something closer to a cinematic mode.

This utilisation of the virtual camera in *NOLF* is often limited to the first-person perspective of the protagonist. The gamer can swivel the camera to look freely in any direction but is unable to relocate the camera to assume a different perspective. The gamer moves freely in the 3D environment, exploring the game map via the first-person (or Cate Archer's) point of view. The sense of immersiveness is achieved, in these sequences, because the gamer is presented with a continuous screen space that the camera (assuming the first-person position) is free to explore. Real-time interactions with the game environment, rendered in a continuous, uninterrupted view, take precedence over the narrative development that is constructed with the aid of cinematic cues and stylistics. For instance, in a film, the camera can cut from the point-of-view of the protagonist walking stealthily along a deserted corridor, to another space and from another angle, showing an enemy waiting in ambush. A sense of dramatic tension and suspense, as well as some form of narrative continuity, is thus established. In a game sequence, however, the gamer is unable to relate to the environment in such a manner, as s/he assumes only the view of the first-person. There are no cuts that excise the gamer from the perspective of the character. The gamer may see a dim corridor but has no prior knowledge of the spatial design of the corridor or the possible placement of enemies lying in ambush. The gamer thus experiences a real-time interaction with the game-environment aided by the first person perspective. A different form of suspense is generated as one tries to expect the unexpected. This suspense and anticipation may diminish, however, if the gamer has to repeat an individual sequence (maybe several times) because of his/her inability to accomplish the task or clear the game-level. In games with more enhanced programming such as *NOLF*, however, the gamer cannot assume that every saved-game can be played exactly in the same manner as the previous one because the game-programming employs a principle of variation (such as the different placement of guards). Narrative space, in FPS games, can thus be said to be continuous and uninterrupted, when compared to films, whose spatial sense is rendered holistic only in the active suturing of the fragmented spaces by the viewer. The continuous view of the environment and the real-time actions cannot be sutured, in Heathean terms, because there are no discontinuous spaces framed by the camera and by editing. It follows that attention to local detail becomes more important than the cinematic construction of narrative continuity.

Such a relatively limited view might not in itself mean that the game sequence suffers in terms of narrative depth. In games like *NOLF*, (much of) what you *see* is what you *can* get. As Paul Virilio notes, in a rather different context: 'Everything I see is in principle within my reach, at least within reach of my sight, marked out on the map of the "I can"' (1994: 7). This 'map of the "I can"' is the 3D environment of the computer game. All this not only makes for a more involved gameplay, it also requires the player to construct a coherent sense of space in which the game takes place. Such involvement with the game environment invites the gamer to 'contextualise actions and goals and make [one] feel invested in what [one] is experiencing,' to cite game designer Randy Smith (quoted in Gillen 2001: 35). Thus, while it is entirely possible for a game such as *NOLF* to be scripted to emulate the sequence of a James Bond film (where for instance, Cate Archer is required to infiltrate a hidden enemy base and stop the evil villain from destroying the world), the experience of such a sequence is unique to the game, even if, hypothetically, the settings of film and game can be made to look close to identical. Games involve a process of visualisation that differs significantly from film and, as a result, a distinct sense of narrative space and narrativity is created.

The virtual camera and the visual inscription of gameplay

Another PC game that demonstrates how the process of visualisation affects the construction of game narratives and alters the definitions of gameplay is *Ground Control* (Massive/Sierra, 2000). A development from earlier real-time strategy (RTS) games such as *Starcraft* (Blizzard, 1998) and *Command & Conquer, Ground Control* is distinguished by the use of visually stunning 3D graphics and a free-moving viewpoint. The control of the virtual camera is not only vital to the enjoyment of the game but also serves as an important measure for effective gameplay. Through the manipulation of the mouse, the gamer has at his/her disposal control of a free-moving camera. The gamer is permitted to assume and organise a whole spectrum of viewpoints, ranging from that of a god-like aerial perspective of the battle field, akin to a cinematic long/establishing shot where troops appear as mere specks, to a close-up executed with a quick zoom. In close-up, a high degree of detail can be observed. Every blade of grass and even the individual rust markings on tanks are clearly rendered. The camera view, like the action-sequence, is continuous and carried on in real-time. Camera movement is smooth and the view of battle is not disrupted, despite the frequent changes in camera angles and perspectives. The gamer can focus on a particular soldier via a zoom, followed by a retraction of the camera to capture an aerial view of the whole locale, while simultaneously panning the camera 360 degrees around the field of action, all in one continuous execution.

Instead of viewing the battle arena from a fixed, oblique, top-down perspective, as in older RTS games such as *Starcraft* and *Red Alert* (Westwood/Virgin Interactive, 1996), *Ground Control* allows the gamer to be in the 'thick of the action', via the control of camera movement. The gamer is not only playing to accomplish the mission but is also actively involved in framing the game visually. S/he not only has to conceive and execute the best strategies for successful gameplay, but must also keep in mind the best positions to situate the camera for a tactically advantageous – and perhaps also aesthetically pleasing – viewpoint. The fighting of a particular battle becomes not merely the delivery of a series of instructions and actions, but also involves an active process of *visual inscription*. The gamer becomes, literally, a director of a theatre of war and a director of something like a movie on-the-go. The player can refocus on the action s/he deems most interesting and assume the position of a war reporter, reporting on his/her own battle as it is being staged. This novel use of the virtual camera redefines the visual construction of the game. *Ground Control* introduces alternative ways in which narrative space can be constructed and developed, in PC games, through the integration of a new visual textuality made possible by 3D graphics.

Ground Control establishes a scene or field of action for the gamer. The world of the game is rendered simultaneously with actions taking place in a real-time, 3D environment. In order to enjoy the gameplay, the gamer needs to develop a strong sense of awareness of, and acquaintance with, the game environment. The gamer can, for instance, land dropships in different areas of the game map simultaneously and launch flanking attacks or pincer movements in real-time. Likewise, allied troops might come under attack and require reinforcement while the gamer is engaged in another battle at the same time. The establishment of such a scene of action requires the gamer's fictive involvement and active construction of a sense of spatial coherence. The gamer's actions, in these scenes of action, might not be the sole determining factors of the game sequence. Other events that are taking place simultaneously might effect the eventual outcome of the game as well.

Similarly, in *Black and White* (Lionhead/EA Games, 2001), another real-time strategy-management game, there is simultaneity of action that occurs in various spaces. The gamer does not merely accomplish tasks in a particular village and venture forth as though each village existed in a static landscape or fixed *tableaux* that the gamer proceeds to and from. Each village continues to 'exist', with its daily routine, without the active interference of the gamer. Simultaneously co-existing spaces and characters that take place beyond the immediate encounter of the gamer appear to construct a peculiar sense of narrative totality unique to the gaming experience. Unlike the novel, in which the fictional space is an imaginary one, and unlike film, where space is constructed via the suturing of discontinuous frames and shots, the space of the game is a site of real-time interactivity. Nevertheless, the level of interactivity available in current games is limited in terms of the possible actions a character can perform and the (predictable) ramifications of such actions. In addition, game spaces are still often defined in terms of distinct 'levels' or 'maps' from which the total game-space is composed. Even so, the gamer is confronted with a different sense of fictional involvement within these distinct sites of play. Gameplay becomes more context-specific, with the gamer being required to pay more attention to local details, and to explore and relate more to the 'site' of the game, instead of merely progressing through the levels.

Closely related to this focus on a highly interactive and visually impressive game-environment, which is becoming the hallmark of 3D games, is the attending need to lend expression to or to remark on the gamer's sense of involvement. Because the virtual gaming environment is invested with fictional significance, game actions become contextualised and are endowed with specific meaning. It follows that the gamer can see, and seeks to visualise, the consequences of these actions on the virtual world. The reception and production of meaning in the narrative space of the game is thus transformed. Game-space is not merely a virtual construction rendered to the player to explore, but is presented as an active engagement and an expression of the game's fictional significance. Such expressions are realised by the highly mobile virtual camera in games such as *Ground Control* and also in *Black and White*. In *Ground Control*, the gamer is not simply mimicking memorable shots of epic war movies when attempting to execute ambitious pans and challenging zooms. These quick-styled, smooth executions permit the gamer to relate directly to a virtual 3D environment that is 'realistically' rendered. Seeking an angle by which to view one's troops as they move through a narrow ravine becomes an aesthetic possibility as well as a functional requirement of gameplay. While such moves might not in themselves affect the pre-established storyline, they permit the gamer to construct a localized sense of narrative. A low-angle shot from the ground, aimed at the skyline, not only catches a beautiful lens flare but also reveals silhouettes of enemy bunkers on the ridge. The fact that the gamer can choose to make the detection of enemy bunkers appear visually stunning, as an alternative to performing a more logical yet uninteresting aerial scan of the location, suggests that there is some form of visual narrative construction taking place in these 3D RTS games, in spite of the fact that a gamer may have chosen to perform such a gesture purely for an aesthetic purpose. This narrative is, however, based more on the ability to visualise a process or a series of actions by employing the necessary techniques of framing and selection in a real-time, continuous context than on the editing of a sequence of disjointed shots, as is the case in films.

Visualisation, narrativisation and gameplay

The gamer's relation to the 3D game environment, while at present far from completely immersive, engages him/her in a protracted sense of projected embodiedness in the virtual world. While gamers may not feel that the free-floating camera (of *Ground Control*), or the character of Cate Archer, are simple extensions of their own bodies, they are likely nevertheless to develop a sense of involvement in the spatial construction of the game-world. This sense of involvement cannot be accounted for only at the level of sense-perceptions. To achieve a sense of prosthetic embodiedness, the gamer also needs, besides the utilisation of the senses of sight and sound, a conscious appreciation of distance, height and other contextual details specific to the site of play. These elements are constitutive in the composition of narrative and important in constructing a keener sense of involvement in (and with) the fictive game-world.

Computer-based games, and 3D PC gaming in particular, therefore pose an interesting challenge to Heath's theory of the viewing subject as the one who binds the film into a narrative whole. This viewing subject is the point of convergence for all the various filmic techniques. As an example, the 180-degree rule is centred around the viewer, visually organising the onscreen conversation for his/her ease of view. Likewise, the disjunction between close-ups and establishing shots calls upon the viewer to establish a relation between two or more different spaces. In 3D games, with the exception of cinematic cut-scenes and letterboxing, there are no cinematic cues to suggest how an image should be viewed and related to other images or to the narrative as a whole. Although 3D objects, in this virtual world, are placed at strategic locations, this does not in itself constitute an act of visual framing. It is in the specific relation of the object to its surroundings (such as distance, height or lighting), and not the means by which its significance is constituted by the cinematic frame, that meaning is derived. The gamer is cued to take note of significant objects in the game environment through their spatial composition and not via camera stylistics such as close-ups, pans or shot/reverse-shots.

As this essay has demonstrated, through the examination of *NOLF* and *Ground Control*, 3D games can and do construct a distinctive sense of narrative coherence and fictive involvement through the generation of realistic 3D images animated in real-time and the employment of a free-ranging camera that breaks the rules of conventional cinema. It is because of the ability of these games to render highly immersive fictional environments that the gamer might desire to articulate and remark on his/her involvement in such an environment. Playing the game becomes a form of self-expression within the virtual world. Controlling the avatar thus becomes more than the issuing of movement commands; it also entails the imposition of a visual narrative as the camera-view selects frames and focuses on elements of the game world that interests the gamer. While the visualisation of such relationships with the game environment may not equate with Heath's notion of narrativisation, there is nevertheless a process of fictionalisation involved.

Although many PC games have intentionally mimicked and even attempted to out-do movies, this account has shown that the heavy reliance on 3D graphics in PC games has led to the development of a distinctive mode of visualisation, gameplay and narrativisation. These modes of presenting the game are specific to the demands of a real-time game environment. While the games examined here may not display strong narratives, as understood in the traditional sense, and are unlike movies because they lack defining cinematic cues that help construct narrative coherence, the process of visualisation that involves the gamer, beyond the mere issuing of reflex commands and functional orders, presents the case for a construction of narrative in games, if in a different manner. After all, what constitutes a minimal 'unit' of a narrative? Is it a sentence, an image, a sequence of images, or a scene? The newly endowed capability of games to visualise their own events and actions allows the gamer, while assuming the role of the game avatar, to re-present and express a moment of narrative significance visually and stylistically. Narrative in 3D PC games, then, takes place between and within the game itself, between the gamer and the game, within the context of the game environment.

citations

Darley, Andrew (2000) *Visual Digital Culture: Surface Play and Spectacle in New Media Genres.* London: Routledge.

Gillen, Kieron (2001) 'Ion Storm in Heaven: The Genesis of *Deus Ex 2* and *Thief III*,' *PC Gamer,* 99, August, 34–8.

Heath, Stephen (1976) 'Narrative Space', *Screen*, 17, 3, 68–112.

Mirzoeff, Nicholas (1999) 'What is Visual Culture', in Nicholas Mirzoeff (ed.) *Visual Culture Reader.* London: Routledge, 3–13.

PC Gamer Online (2001) 'The Future of Gaming: 2006', 13 April. Available on-line at: http://www.pcgamer.com.

Sawyer, Ben, Alex Dunne, and Tor Berg (1998) *Game Developer's Marketplace.* Arizona: The Coriolis Group.

Virilio, Paul (1994) *The Vision Machine.* Bloomington and Indianapolis: Indiana University Press and BFI.

chapter six

Watching A Game, Playing A Movie: When Media Collide

sacha a. howells

Game designers have long looked to Hollywood cinema for inspiration, and film-makers have certainly returned the compliment. As early as 1982, *Tron* took film audiences inside a videogame, while Atari's *E.T.: The Extra Terrestrial* (1982) took gamers inside a movie — and *Tron: Deadly Discs* (M-Network, 1982) took gamers inside a movie, inside a game. Of course, the trend continues, from *Star Wars: Episode One — The Phantom Menace*, the game (Big Ape/LucasArts, 1999), to *Lara Croft: Tomb Raider*, the movie (2001). But besides sharing themes, genres and even characters, film also exists *within* videogames.

As games grew beyond the twitch reactions of *Pong* (Atari, 1972) and *Space Invaders* (Taito, 1978), designers wanted to add narrative and character depth, elements that were difficult to express within the actual gameplay of arcade and home games. Game designers ended up turning to a proven method of narrative structure to tell their stories: film, as typified by 'classical' Hollywood cinema. Albeit in primitive form, short films called 'cut-scenes' (or, tellingly, 'cinematics') appeared early in videogame history, then exploded with the advent of CD-ROMs, and now appear in almost every game released. Cut-scenes are interspersed with the action scenes that make up the gameplay; together, the 'text' as a whole can combine active playing with a narrative that allows themes, characters and plots to develop and become resolved over the course of the game. Although the two different types of game segment ask completely different things of their audience, they end up integrated into the entire experience.

Pac-Man goes Hollywood

An example of the development of cut-scenes can be seen as early as the transition from *Pac-Man* to *Ms. Pac-Man*. In Namco's 1980 classic *Pac-Man*, after clearing certain milestones the player sees 'Intermission' screens that feature our yellow hero chasing ghosts; in one scene Blinky chases him off-screen, only to have a huge Pac-Man chase him back the other way. These intermissions were made up of visual one-liners, but had no cohesive, developing plot or story. A year later, *Ms. Pac-Man*'s cut-scenes constructed a simple narrative, even using movie-style scene markers to divide it into acts. 'Act 1: They Meet' shows the two Pacs falling in love (complete with floating cartoon heart); 'Act 2: The Chase' follows Ms. Pac-Man hunting down her man; and 'Act 3: Junior' shows a stork delivering a baby Pac-Man (who later went on to his own games).

It may have been a simplistic one, but *Ms. Pac-Man* introduced a classic narrative arc and placed the characters in a family structure. The 'Pac-Family' went on to briefly dominate American culture, spawning toys, a top-10 single and a Saturday-morning cartoon show. Obviously, there was something to be gained from giving generic game constructs personalities, families – *stories*. At the same time, games were moving out of arcades and into living rooms, where people played for hours rather than minutes, and could save games in progress and continue later – circumstances that lent themselves to character development and more sophisticated narratives. But cut-scenes were still kept relatively short and to the point; arcade boards, floppy disks and cartridges for systems like the Atari 2600 and NES had severe size restrictions that limited their data capacity. Soon, a technological advance would give designers more space than they needed, and cut-scenes would become an integral part of the language of videogames.

The CD-ROM revolution

The compact disc had been introduced as a music storage unit in 1982, and in the mid-1980s was first used to store computer data (Britannica.com). In 1989 NEC became the first game company to release a CD-ROM drive for a home system, the TurboGrafx (see Kent 2000: 328). In the next decade and a half, CD-ROM drives became standard equipment in personal computers and every home system manufacturer but Nintendo abandoned expensive, constrictive cartridges in favour of discs.

The advent of CD-ROMs as a game medium gave designers access to powerful new tools. Now, games could incorporate CD-quality music and pre-recorded voiceovers. What's more, CD-ROMs are capable of vastly more storage than their cartridge predecessors; Genesis and Super NES cartridges usually ranged from 8 to 16 MB, while Nintendo 64 carts have reached 256 MB (*Legend of Zelda: Ocarina of Time* (Nintendo, 1998)), but PlayStation and PC CD-ROMs can hold 640 MB, and the short-lived Dreamcast's proprietary GD-ROMs hold more than 1 GB of data.

While computer-rendered special effects were wowing movie audiences, game systems and home computers were limited to comparatively crude graphics. But with CD-ROMs, digital video could be recorded directly onto a CD and played back; just because a game was limited to a certain number of polygons and frames per second did not mean that cut-scene movies had to be. The result was an explosion of high-budget game cinematics that used the best digital animators, and even Hollywood actors. With their newly widespread use, cut-scenes began to fill distinct new roles.

The role of film in games

The 'come-on'

When videogames were primarily found in arcades, they did not waste much time on story or character development: they were designed to be played for short periods of time. To draw in players, designers created short looping sequences that repeated while the game was out of play, interspersing flashy graphics with action-packed gameplay excerpts – a kind of 'teaser' meant to draw in foot traffic, functioning much like a carnival barker.

As computer games made their way into the mainstream, television advertising became more prominent, and more often than not it was the polished graphics of a pre-rendered CG (computer-graphic) cut-scene that ended up in a commercial. These flashy intro movies are often distributed before a game is released (on the Internet, on sampler CD-ROMs or playing in videogame stores). Regardless of what a game actually *looks* like, the gamer's first impression is of the cut-scene, and when a player begins a game, the first thing he or she sees is the intro movie. Designers have the chance to excite the player, instilling a certain anticipation and mood with flashy graphics which, until recently, the actual gameplay was incapable of reproducing. Take, for instance, the furiously paced, slick CG action sequence that begins *Duke Nukem: A Time to Kill* (n-Space/GT Interactive, 1998); in comparison, the gameplay graphics are undeniably primitive.

Even games selling something more than arcade-style action often rely on the visual flash of a cut-scene in their marketing. For instance, the massive *Final Fantasy VII* (Squaresoft/SCEA, 1997) television campaign did not use a single shot of in-game footage, relying instead on the masterfully constructed CG cut-scenes to draw in the mainstream audience. Even outside a game's text, these scenes can become an important element of audience perception. (The perceived need for this kind of flashy visual hook has led to some strange revisions of history; for example, the *Namco Museum* series, which repackages classic arcade hits like *Pac-Man* and *Pole Position* (Namco Hometek, 2000). Even though the games themselves are exactly the same 2D, eight-colour classics that appeared in arcades twenty years ago, they are now accompanied by flashy CG intro movies, showing a fully 3D Pac-Man.)

Cut-scene as narrative segment

In his examination of classical Hollywood cinema, David Bordwell (1986) asserts that opening sequences in classical film give motivation and causal connection to the rest of the film. A sequence begins with an exposition that establishes characters, time and setting, then presents a middle period in which characters act toward clearly defined goals, and concludes with certain lines of causality closed off, while some existing ones are left 'dangling' or new ones are initiated to continue in the next sequence, giving classical film its unifying linearity (Bordwell 1986: 20). While there are certainly still videogames that forgo the constraints of character and plot, as the medium came of age many games began to incorporate action into ongoing narratives. But while a game's action is well suited to Bordwell's middle period, elements of exposition, character motivation and conflict are difficult to express within the gameplay framework. Early examples like *Ikari Warriors* (SNK, 1987) use title screens to explicate events occurring between action segments and to give the player his or her motivation for the next action sequence. With the advent of cut-scenes, film took over the role.

The intro movie introduces characters and scenario (the 'game world') and establishes the game's fundamental conflict, while subsequent cut-scenes continue causal lines, introduce new plot elements, show character interaction and continually delineate explicit goals. Once the goals have been stated, the player moves to an action sequence where he or she overcomes a series of smaller obstacles en route to the larger one. After finally accomplishing this larger goal (often a 'boss' enemy or large-scale puzzle), another cut-scene shows the effects of the player's actions and introduces a new goal. If anything, narrative videogames adhere even more rigidly to the classical formula than film; more than just giving characters believable motivation for their subsequent actions, as in a film, cut-scenes often directly give the player/spectator his or her objectives: shoot X, steal Y, jump to Z. Then the action sequence allows the player to resolve the causal line introduced by the cut-scene.

Reward

Another of the cut-scene's functions within a videogame is as reward. After particularly difficult obstacles, often in the form of a boss character, the player is given a visual reward. For example, in *Tomb Raider* (Core/Eidos, 1996), the player sees an elaborate CG intro movie showing Lara Croft's arrival on a Peruvian mountaintop. After battling through five levels, Lara retrieves the first piece of the Scion, the artifact whose recovery is the game's overall goal. After defeating a final boss (a rival treasure hunter), the player is rewarded with another slickly produced CG cut-scene of Lara's action-hero break-in to Natla headquarters, where she uncovers the next piece of the puzzle.

In narrative-driven games, cut-scenes have often come to *replace* the classic videogame reward system: points. Although there are certainly still games that keep track of points (or other markers like stars, rings or gold pieces), many of the most popular games, from *Tomb Raider* to Capcom's *Resident Evil* series, do not keep score at all. The point of the game is merely to overcome the next obstacle, get to the next level and eventually finish the game.

The 'end movie' (or 'victory movie') is a specialised reward. Successful end movies both resolve the game's narrative, wrapping up the game's goals and missions and giving closure to the characters – a kind of emotional reward – and a visual reward. Along with the intro movie, the end movie is typically the most lavish and exciting of the game's visual sequences. Intermittent cut-scenes reward the player's skill and persistence in overcoming a specific obstacle; the end movie rewards his or her skill and persistence in overcoming the dozens or hundreds of obstacles that make up the entire game. As such, players come to expect something for their trouble, and failing to serve up a worthy reward can cause a game to be remembered as a failure (for examples, see *GameSpot*'s 'Ten Most Disappointing Endings' (2001)).

End movies show their 'worth' as reward in games that offer more than one resolution to the narrative, depending on the player's choices and conduct. Games like *Deus Ex* (Ion Storm/Eidos, 2000), with three different end movies, and *Star Ocean: The Second Story* (Tri-Ace/Enix, 1999), with its eighty possible endings, inspire fans to play a game again and again, making different choices to see different outcomes. (For an example of film as a *literal* reward, see Neversoft's *Tony Hawk Pro Skater* series; while skateboarding through different arenas, players can collect rotating video tapes in hard-to-reach places, then 'cash in' to view live-action clips of professional skaters.)

'The medium is the message'

Designers use three methods of incorporating film into videogames: full-motion video (FMV), pre-rendered computer-graphic (CG) animation and in-game (or 'engine') cut-scenes. Each has distinct limitations and advantages, and each portrays something different to its audience.

Full-motion video

FMV or 'live action' cut-scenes became popular in the early and mid-1990s as games broke into mainstream culture. In particular, as movie studios experimented with videogames, they brought along their established practices and preconceptions about the definition of 'entertainment'.

Full-motion video cut-scenes portray live actors playing the roles of game characters, often in combination with computer-rendered exteriors and effects. One advantage of live-action cut-scenes is that human actors are more capable of expressing emotion than digital constructs, making it easier for players to identify with their in-game personas (although technology is rapidly closing the gap). Another obvious benefit to game designers is that FMV allows them to use recognizable actors, tapping into the celebrity power that fuels the film and television industries. But early games were unable to secure big-name talent, and had to settle for B-list actors like Corey Haim (*Double Switch* (Digital Pictures, 1993)) and Tia Carerre (*The Daedalus Encounter* (PalmSoft, 1993)); as a result, full-motion video became associated with substandard quality.

Sometimes designers use existing live-action footage to associate a game with a familiar film or character. For example, *The World Is Not Enough* (Electronic Arts/Black Ops, 2000), based on the James Bond film of the same name, intersperses its action segments with footage from the actual film, perhaps the most *complete* example of 'film-in-game'. Here, the live-action footage both reinforces the film-viewing experience that the audience is presumed to have had, and gives the player the feeling that he or she is 'in' the movie – an oft-stated goal of videogames.

Full-motion video has not proved very effective. Because videogames tend to have fewer resources than movie productions, everything suffers: lesser actors, poor direction, lower production values. Another problem is the jarring transition between the games' action scenes and the movies. As the game strives to make gamers *believe* the imaginary, computer-generated – and often blocky and pixelated – game world, the transition to full-motion video reminds gamers that this is, in fact, *not* real, breaking the suspension of disbelief. Paradoxically, FMV's realism makes the game itself seem less real. As improved game-engine graphics allow for more detailed, realistic depictions, FMV cut-scenes have largely fallen out of favour.

Pre-rendered computer graphics

Computer-graphic cut-scenes are made by artists and animators using much more advanced hardware than the game console or PC on which the game will eventually be played. They are then recorded directly onto the CD-ROM and played back when triggered by gameplay conditions. The major benefit of CG cut-scenes is an obvious one: without the limitations of system hardware, they can be as elaborate and flashy as the animator can envision. This adds to their value as reward, and often features heavily in a game's advertising and marketing. CG cut-scenes can even become iconic of a game, standing in for it in the public mind; the Lara Croft that burned into the cultural consciousness in 1996 certainly was not the blocky polygonal mess who appeared in *Tomb Raider*'s actual gameplay, it was the high-res heroine of the cut-scenes who featured in so many television and print ads.

But like FMV cinematics, CG movies invariably knock the player out of the game world, disrupting the experience. And although CG has been an important part of some of the most significant games of recent years, as system advances make in-game graphics all the more impressive, more and more designers have moved toward using the actual game engine to portray cut-scenes.

Game engine

Elaborate CG and live-action cut-scenes can succeed in giving player/spectators high production values or recognizable faces, but they inevitably impose a major rift in the game's structure. The suspension of disbelief that allows the player to 'exist' within the game world is unavoidably broken when cut-scenes look completely different from in-game action.

Rather than pre-recorded, immutable movies, game engine cut-scenes are generated 'on the fly', using the graphics and physics engine that powers the game itself. As such, characters, props and environments that the player interacts with during gameplay are consistent with those he or she sees in cut-scenes, unifying the experience and linking the elements of active playing and passive watching. Another benefit of engine cut-scenes is that they allow for better continuity. Pre-recorded CG or live-action cut-scenes are *fixed* – every time they play out in exactly the same way. In-game cut-scenes, generated by the game engine as they are triggered, allow for variation. If the in-game character is carrying a certain object, wearing a certain costume or standing next to a certain character during gameplay, the cut-scene can reflect the same 'reality'. Again, this enhances the player's uninterrupted involvement in the game world.

The major flaw with in-game cut-scenes is that they are limited by the engine's capabilities. But in 1997, Activision's *Interstate '76* showed that those limitations could be overcome. Cut-scenes that involved vehicles and backgrounds were generated by the same engine that powered the game, and while pre-rendered CG cut-scenes were in fact used to portray the game's characters, they used a polygonal art style that reflected the in-game graphics, giving players a consistent experience. *I-76*'s cinematics won much critical acclaim, sparking new interest in engine cut-scenes. Subsequently, as PC and console hardware have become more advanced, the limitations are fading; with the PlayStation2, GameCube, X-Box and PC graphics cards like nVidia's GeForce 3, the visual difference between in-game performance and prerendered CG cut-scenes will all but disappear.

Another problem with in-game cut-scenes is that because they are rendered on the fly, they are prone to bugs, which can be just as disruptive to the player as changes in visual style. For example, in *Blair Witch Vol. 1: Rustin Parr* (Terminal Reality/GodGames, 2000), the mysterious 'Stranger' approaches the game's heroine, Elspeth Holliday, in a cut-scene after a bloody encounter with zombie townspeople. But depending on how the action unfolds, the bodies around Holliday may mean that the Stranger cannot reach the spot where he has been programmed to stand; throughout the cut-scene, he often ends up wandering around in circles. These kind of bugs can be programmed around, but tracking down every possible glitch is time-consuming and expensive.

Identification and disruption

Even game-engine cut-scenes cannot overcome the biggest hurdle in combining the active, involved entertainment of *playing* a videogame with the relatively passive entertainment of *watching* a cut-scene. (As many have argued, film audiences actively participate in constructing a film out of discrete images, and a narrative out of discrete scenes; here, I use passive to mean that they do not physically interact with a film as game audiences do with a game). The player learns the rules of interacting with the game's universe – how to move, what objects can be manipulated, how the game should be approached – and then when a cut-scene starts he or she is abruptly wrenched out of this established world and thrust into a new one, where the role of active participant is abandoned.

In discussing the pleasures of watching film, Laura Mulvey describes the process of identification. Rather than the reflected self of the mirror, the spectator of a film sees an idealised version of him- or herself onscreen and becomes entangled in the 'fascination with and recognition of his like' (1986: 202). Through this identification with the onscreen characters, the viewer becomes personally involved in a film.

Players of a game are even more actively involved with the game's characters; besides just observing, they actually control the onscreen characters – their movements, what they look at, what they pick up, what they *do*. Insofar as the player is invested in the game, he or she is 'hurt' when the character is – the character's injury or death punishes the player, who has to expend collected resources, spend time finding new resources or replay a difficult segment. While movie viewers certainly identify with on-screen characters, game players are more strongly involved with their on-screen personae.

Christian Metz (1986) argues (with others) that audience identification with a film's characters is secondary to the primary identification with the camera itself; the same can be argued for videogames. While players control on-screen characters, they also control the camera, sometimes overtly, sometimes less so. Third-person games such as *Tomb Raider* have one set of controls for the character, and another for the camera, while those such as *Rune* (Human Head, 2000) centre the camera immediately behind the character, making camera and character control the same. Similarly, first-person shooters such as *Quake III Arena* (id Software/Activision, 1999) and *No One Lives Forever* (Monolith/Fox, 2000) offer a first-person view that means controlling the character *is* controlling the camera. Even third-person games such as *Resident Evil* (Capcom, 1996) and *Nocturne* (Terminal Reality/GodGames, 1999), which use a single, fixed camera angle for each area, or node, still give the player indirect control over the camera; he or she steers the character from one node to the next, so the angles are still contingent on the player's actions.

Aside from those games that allow players to identify with a single character (or at least one at a time), there are also the aptly named 'god games' (*Populous* (Take 2/EA Games, 1998), *Black & White* (Lionhead/EA Games, 2001)) and real-time and turn-based strategy games (*Command & Conquer* (Westwood/Virgin, 1995), *Shadow Watch* (Red Storm, 2000)), which put the player in an omniscient, all-seeing role. Here, while players do control on-screen characters, their primary connection with the game is with the camera – moving the camera is how the player observes and interacts with the world, an even more literal extrapolation of Metz's primary identification.

As such, player identification with a game character (or with the camera itself) is arguably even stronger, and certainly more overt (playing *Tomb Raider*, the player 'is' Lara Croft) than a mainstream film audience's identification with onscreen characters. And even game-engine cut-scenes that maintain the gameplay's graphics and physics force a significant break: the player suddenly relinquishes control of character and camera, and sees the character who presumably 'is' him or her doing things he or she never instructed. Frankenstein's monster does not just come to life; it takes over the Doctor's body. But while this should be terribly disruptive, even traumatic, to the gaming experience, the audience accepts it unthinkingly as just another piece of the overall spectacle. The player is seamlessly transformed into spectator, and back again.

Turning players into spectators

As David Bordwell has said, 'The spectator comes to a classical film very well prepared' (1986: 28), armed with what Christian Metz called 'the mental machinery ... which spectators "accustomed to the cinema" have internalized' (quoted in Creed 2000: 77). The film audience is conditioned to expect the 'canonic' story of characters working toward causally motivated goals, to recognise conventions of particular genres and to anticipate linear narratives that move from one sequence to the next following distinct paths of cause and effect (see Bordwell 1986: 28–30).

Game designers rely on this same 'mental machinery' to separate gameplay from cut-scenes. As players, gamers expect certain things from a game: control of the onscreen images, outside stimuli that require physical reactions, interaction with surroundings. When gameplay ends and the audience is confronted with a cut-scene, it expects the same things it expects from film: exposition, resolution of some causal lines, introduction of others. By using cues to prepare us, reinforced by familiar filmic techniques – making cut-scenes 'look' like film – designers transform their audience from players to spectators without disruption.

Cut-scene signifiers: how we know to stop playing

Of course, in the case of FMV or CG cut-scenes, the change in visual style instantly alerts the player to the change in his or her role. But even live-action and pre-rendered cut-scenes use filmic conventions to prepare the audience for a new format. A common method of separating gameplay from cut-scene is by 'letterboxing' game movies. During gameplay, the player usually sees the entirety of the (square) PC or television screen; when a cut-scene starts, black bands across the top and bottom of the screen emulate the aspect ratios we see in cinema. The cut-scene is separated from the gameplay by visually defining it as 'film', triggering a different set of responses. We find letterboxing across the spectrum, in FMV (*Wing Commander IV* (Origin, 1995), *Heavy Gear* (Activision, 1997)), CG (*Resident Evil: Code Veronica* (Capcom, 2000), *Driver 2* (Reflections/Infogrames, 2000)) and engine cut-scenes (*Metal Gear Solid* (Konami, 1998), *Deus Ex*) – in fact, this particular device is all but universal. The technique was initially useful in keeping the viewing area small to allow for smoother playback, but while current technology does not suffer from the same limitation, designers have recognised the usefulness of letterboxing as a signifier.

While a game interface refers to how we act upon a game – the keyboard, joystick, or gamepad – it also describes how we get information from it. Most videogames provide some kind of visual interface that overlays the game's action. Often known as a HUD ('heads-up-display'), it may include a targeting reticle, a directional arrow or status bars that track resource levels. When a cut-scene begins, these gauges are almost always omitted. This, too, is all but universal; when players see that the interface has disappeared, they understand that they no longer need to be prepared to interact with the game. The spectating has begun.

Of course, the fundamental difference between gameplay and cut-scene is the change of camera angle; although they may include shots that recreate the in-game experience (for instance, the cockpit view which appears in *Heavy Gear*'s intro movie), cut-scenes use different perspectives from gameplay sequences. When the camera suddenly moves to a location that the player could *not* have chosen within the gameplay, he or she knows that the cut-scene has begun, that control has been surrendered. How designers manipulate those angles and shots plays even further into replicating the audience's expectations for filmic entertainment.

Classical film style in videogame cut-scenes

After using these devices to tell the audience to stop playing, game designers use classical film techniques to present the cut-scenes themselves, reinforcing that the player is now expected to use the mental machinery of a film spectator, not of a game player. Just as a film audience is prepared to make narrative leaps, so do specific shots hold codified meanings. A long shot of a building that cuts to a scene of two characters in a room is immediately interpreted by the audience: *these people are in the building* (see Bordwell *et al.* 1985: 63). Crosscutting between two locales tells the audience that the events are happening simultaneously, and given a shot/reverse-shot succession, the audience infers that the two characters are looking at one another (see Dayan 1992: 188–9). Sound bridges lead from one shot to the next, unifying them; these things the audience understands.

The entire library of codified shots is reproduced in videogame cut-scenes, presenting a game's plot and story content in filmic terms. By making cut-scenes 'like' the movies they know the audience is accustomed to, designers seamlessly transform us into (relatively) passive observers rather than active participants. For example, in Monolith's *No One Lives Forever*, an early cut-scene introduces us to Cate Archer, female spy, and her superior, Bruno. The scene opens with a game-engine, letterboxed shot of a telephone sitting on a nightstand, accompanied by the sound of a running shower. The shot then switches to Cate in the shower, with the camera slowly tracking toward her; a phone rings, and the shot returns to the nightstand. As we hear Cate pick up the phone and talk to Bruno, we see a tracking shot of her bathroom counter, holding a barrette, a perfume atomizer, a gun and a machine gun, all objects she will use in the game. The phone conversation ends with an agreement to meet at a restaurant, and the scene immediately cuts to a long shot of Cate and Bruno sitting at a restaurant table. Then follows a succession of shot/reverse-shots between Cate and Bruno's heads, with middle-ground shots to present the two and one long shot when a waiter interrupts. Cate tells Bruno her fundamental problem – she can't get real field assignments – and a cell-phone call summons them both to agency headquarters. Bruno closes, saying, 'I'll meet you there'. Using film's library of shots and devices, we are introduced to the two main characters, discover the overall 'problem' of the game and are given a causal line that leads us into the gameplay: 'I'll meet you there.'

Because cut-scenes *look* like movies, from screen aspect ratio to shot sequences, the audience knows what to expect from them. The player/spectator does not try to run, shoot, or move a box; he or she watches and takes in information, allowing the game's movies to work with its action to form a satisfying, unified whole.

Half-Life and the future

Of course, as any medium matures, its creators begin to manipulate the very mental machinery they rely on. Valve Software's highly acclaimed first-person shooter *Half-Life* (Valve/Sierra, 1998) approaches cut-scenes with its trademark originality. While standard cut-scenes slip into classical Hollywood cinema's existing systems of linear causality and shot sequences, *Half-Life*'s introductory 'movie' (one of only two in the game) is revolutionary precisely because it does not bow to that existing framework – it remains a game, the player stays in control. As Gordon Freeman, the player boards a monorail car that takes a trip through the Black Mesa Research facility; there is no letterboxing or other signifier because it is *part* of the game. Although nothing significant happens, it introduces locations that the player will encounter later. Most important, he or she is free to move about the car at will. As such, the game never causes the disruption discovered in other narrative games that use cut-scenes. The player never sees a camera angle that is different from the gameplay angle and never loses control of the character.

Does the future of cut-scenes lie in this kind of removal of disruption? Is the classic cut-scene obsolete? Until our mental machinery is reprogrammed to expect plot, characters and causality within the gameplay format, the odds are against it. As box office results show, audiences *like* watching movies, and are satisfied with how they present their stories. And while *Half-Life* was able to get across certain plot points with in-game devices, it was not capable of the depth of *Deus Ex* or *Final Fantasy VIII*.

Once again, it is a technological advance that promises to make the next significant development. Already, game engines are pushing into the realm of CG cut-scene quality, and new hardware will remove the differences altogether. In May 2001, *Next Generation* reported: 'It wasn't long ago when we first sat in front of games like *Tekken* and *Panzer Dragoon*, and, watching their beautiful pre-rendered intros, pondered the question, "When are we going to play games that look like *that*?" That question was answered when nVidia revealed the GeForce 3 chipset' (Russo 2001: 5). The time is here.

The next generation of consoles and PC drives has also embraced DVD-ROM capability. Now audiences are able to watch movies on the same machines they use to play games, making further crossover inevitable. Before long we may see something of a reversal: just as designers use cinematic conventions to enhance their games, so directors may soon borrow game conventions to add new layers to their films. Videogames have grown up since *Ms. Pac-Man*, and cut-scenes have come a long way from 'Act 1: They Meet'. Poised on the verge of yet another quantum leap in technology, games and cut-scenes are about to undergo yet another transformation, one that will doubtless impact film, television and the very idea of 'entertainment'.

citations

Bordwell, David (1986) 'Classical Hollywood Cinema: Narrational Principles and Procedures', in Philip Rosen (ed.) *Narrative, Apparatus, Ideology*. New York: Columbia University Press, 17–34.

Bordwell, David, Janet Staiger & Kristin Thompson (1985) *The Classical Hollywood Cinema: Film Style and Mode of Production to 1960*. New York: Columbia University Press.

Britannica.com (2001) *Encyclopedia Britannica*. 27 May. Available on-line at: http:/www. britannica.com/eb/article?eu=1432

Creed, Barbara (2000) 'Film and Psychoanalysis', in John Hill & Pamela Church Gibson (eds) *Film Studies: Critical Approaches*. Oxford: Oxford University Press, 75–88.

Dayan, Daniel (1992) 'The Tutor-Code of Classical Cinema', in Gerald Mast, Marshall Cohen & Leo Braudy (eds) *Film Theory and Criticism: Introductory Readings*. Oxford: Oxford University Press, 179–91.

GameSpot (2001) 'The Ten Most Disappointing Endings'. 20 May. Available on-line at: http://www.gamespot.com/features/tenspot_badendings/index.html.

Kent, Steven (2000) *The First Quarter: A 25-Year History of Video Games*. Bothell, WA: BWD Press.

Metz, Christian (1986) 'The Imaginary Signifier [Excerpts]', in Philip Rosen (ed.) *Narrative, Apparatus, Ideology: A Film Theory Reader*. New York: Columbia University Press, 244–78.

Mulvey, Laura (1986) 'Visual Pleasure and Narrative Cinema', in Philip Rosen (ed.) *Narrative, Apparatus, Ideology: A Film Theory Reader*. New York: Columbia University Press, 198–209.

Russo, Tom (2001) 'Realtime Graphics Go Big Time', *Next Generation*, May, 5–7.

chapter seven

Videogames as Remediated Animation

paul ward

Many contributors to this volume usefully explore the relationships between games and other media forms, whether at the level of spectator/player positioning or the specific aesthetic strategies used. This essay attempts to locate videogames in relation to some theories of animation, arguing that we can only fully understand how videogames work if we acknowledge the role that animation plays. Certainly one can achieve much by carrying out close readings of games in terms of their links with other forms of representation. However, it is only through recognising that we are talking about a mode of animation that we can fully make sense of these 'localised' readings. In many respects, this should therefore be seen as a call for a more detailed consideration of how 'animation' might encompass a range of media — including videogames, special effects and other computer-generated imagery.

There are three main areas of consideration. First, I outline the ways in which theories of animation might be useful in discussing videogames in general. The second area borrows Jay David Bolter and Richard Grusin's (1999) concept of 'remediation' to further refine the discussion of the relationship between film and game. Finally, I consider the ways in which animated films have figured as source material for games, suggesting that what is involved is more complex than the usual notion of one being 'based upon' the other. Via analysis of *Toy Story 2* (1999) and the associated game, *Buzz Lightyear to the Rescue* (Activision/Disney Interactive, 1999),[1] I discuss the ontological dimensions of both film and game, to suggest that the ways that 'reality' is figured in these worlds takes us to the root of the interface between films and games.

Animation/representation/'realism'

It seems obvious that there is considerable overlap between animated films made using computers and videogames that consist of animated characters and actions. They are two manifestations (or applications) of the same technology. It is important to note, however, that animation as a distinct category (which is to say, *all* animation, even the most 'traditional' types such as cel, puppets, claymation) has some useful theoretical common ground with digital imagery (whether that imagery is used in a film or a game). In the case of a videogame (or any computer-generated, digital imagery) objects and actions are mathematically modelled and manipulated, and the text is stored as binary code. There is therefore no action that has been 'captured': all that we eventually see is a complete creation, or simulation (the obvious exceptions to this are animated films and games that use motion-capture techniques). In traditional forms of animation a corresponding thing happens in the sense that any movement or action is not 'captured' but is rather *created* (or simulated) frame by frame. As Giannalberto Bendazzi points out:

> In live action cinema, actions are filmed exactly as they take place, at twenty-four frames per second, whereas in animation the action is constantly reinvented. ... In an animation film, [the depicted] events [take] place for the first time on the screen. (1994: xvi)

This raises some important issues in relation to conceptions and relative degrees of what is understood as 'realism', more of which presently. The central point here is that both modes of representation have in common a distancing from their referent. For example, a film such as *Toy Story 2*, or the game *Buzz Lightyear to the Rescue*, *totally* creates the diegetic space and characters.[2] A more traditional animated film such as *Chicken Run* (2000) is different in the sense that it films 'real' models and sets, but the *movements* of characters are totally 'created'. Therefore, both of these examples show us something that has a mediated relationship with the 'real world'. Although we need to be wary of suggesting that live-action film is a simple transcription of a pro-filmic reality, while the various forms of animation are constructions, it is the case that conventional live-action cinema tends to have a higher level of correspondence to an external reality. Indeed, one of the things that interests us here is the way certain animated films and games deploy such a 'correspondence' in their representation of their totally created worlds. Certainly there are differences between the analogue-based animated film and that produced using digital techniques. What they have in common though is the fact that what they 'show' us — totally created world or totally created movement — only exists and has only ever existed in the simulated representation itself. This process is taken a stage further in the real-time generation of the animated sequences experienced during active gameplay. When responding to the player's actions, the game engine draws upon a library of short, pre-rendered animated sequences. These are combined and recombined in the real-time of the gameplay, with the result that the complete animated sequence as experienced by a particular player on a particular occasion (during a fight scene, for instance) comes into existence *only* at the point of playing the game.

Andrew Darley (1997) writes usefully about aspects of computer animation and the uncanny relationship such animation can have with conceptions of realism. This is particularly important when we discuss videogames, as notions of verisimilitude and plausibility are often central to our understanding of gameplay and the player's interaction with the represented world. Darley suggests the term 'second order realism' as a category helpful in understanding the mediation seen in computer animation. As he explains it, the term alludes to 'an attempt to produce old ways of seeing or representing by *other means*' (1997: 16, emphasis in original). Darley links his example — *Red's Dream* (1987) — to a tradition of cartoonal realism, but recognises that there are 'levels' to the realism. The aesthetic of the film is one that draws attention to its own ability to represent with an eerie accuracy. As Darley suggests:

> In terms of plasticity, texture, look (particularly the illusion of three-dimensional space) and movement, [*Red's Dream*] certainly involves a much higher degree of surface accuracy than has hitherto been the case in the animated cartoon ... [there is] a displacement away from concentration on the story ... towards the allure of the image itself. (1997: 18)

A major part of such 'allure' is the 'ambiguity' inherent in the imagery, and Darley argues that this stems from an uncertainty on the part of the viewer. We are 'uncertain of [the imagery's] status in terms of means of origination: is it animation, live action, a combination of these ... or what?' (1997: 18). This is a characteristic of some recent digitally animated films made for the cinema, such as *Shrek* (2001) and *Final Fantasy: The Spirits Within* (2001). What we have is a highly specific mediation of certain forms of cinematic realism, used as a special effect. When Darley talks about *Red's Dream* producing 'old ways of seeing ... by other means' he is pointing out two things. Firstly, that the film buys into the dominant way of representing perspectival space, or the 'old ways of seeing'. This is important because it underlines the fact that what we have in these animations (and his point applies just as much to *Shrek* and *Final Fantasy* as it does *Red's Dream*) is not an out-and-out rejection of (or refusal to represent) a pre-existing reality, but rather a *continuation* of a particular tradition of representation, and one that, moreover, seems to privilege 'naturalistic' depiction as an end in itself.[3] His second point appears to contradict the first somewhat in that it suggests that the film(s) use new technology to simulate — but refashion — pre-existing ways of seeing, and do so in such a way as to draw an uncanny/eerie attention to how detailed it can be. The 'ambiguity' or contradiction to which Darley alludes is of central importance to Bolter and Grusin's concept of remediation (1999), something I return to below.

Before moving on, we need to clarify some terms, especially the notion of 'realism'. It is a notoriously difficult concept to pin down with any certainty, mainly because it is a quality so often established in relative rather than absolute terms. It is frequently used in a 'commonsense' way to suggest forms deemed to capture a close approximation of the surfaces, details, textures and events of the 'real' world — the world exterior to the representation. What is deemed to be 'realistic' in particular circumstances, however, is often judged against other, more established forms of textual production. That which has already gained the status of the 'realistic' (a particular form of cinematography, for example) is as likely to be the measure of the degree of 'realism' associated with other textual forms (such as videogames) as any reference to the exterior world. Maureen Furniss offers a useful model here for defining animated forms, allowing for the essentially comparative dimension of degrees of 'realism'. She proposes a continuum in which the *relative* positions of all 'motion picture production' (1998: 5) can be mapped. Thus:

> Although the terms 'mimesis' and 'abstraction' are not ideal, they are useful in suggesting opposing tendencies under which live-action and animated imagery can be juxtaposed. The term 'mimesis' represents the desire to reproduce natural reality (more like live-action work) while the term 'abstraction' describes the use of pure form — a suggestion of a concept rather than an attempt to explicate it in real life terms (more like animation). There is no one film that represents the ideal example of 'mimesis' or 'abstraction'. ... The point is that the relationship between animation and live action, represented by mimesis and abstraction, is a relative one. They are both tendencies within motion picture production, rather than completely separate practices (1998: 5—6).

Games such as *Silent Hill* (Konami, 1999), *Metal Gear Solid* (Konami, 1998), or *Max Payne* (Remedy/GodGames, 2001), and more 'cartoonish' games such as the *Crash Bandicoot* series (Naughty Dog, 2001), or *A Bug's Life* (Traveller's Tales/SCEA, 1998), can all therefore be described as more or less 'realistic'. The degree of realism (or otherwise) associated with each, however, is defined in relation to other games and other representations such as animated and live-action cinema. Their imagery combines, in a manner that varies from one example to another, the kind of precise rendering of surface details associated with mimesis and more outlandish 'abstractions' of character and action. The tension between these two tendencies is a significant factor in the quality of many games.

In none of these games, however, does the sense of 'realism' come anywhere near that established by films such as *Toy Story 2*, *Shrek*, or *Final Fantasy* (or even the 'less advanced' *Toy Story* (1995)). The issue here is not just that of the reality of the image, but also that of the movement; or, to coin a phrase, we are considering the realism of the *animation*. As noted earlier, the real-time movements of characters during active gameplay (as opposed to cut-scenes) are determined by the combination of pre-rendered animated fragments. Limitations to the range and quality of animated movement can be explained by the fact that such 'combos' draw on a finite library of fragments, the extent of which varies from one case to another. A trade-off exists here between the quality of the resolution of these images and the number that can be stored, and thus the number of available movement options; a trade-off, in other words, between one variety of animated realism (that of surface detail) and another (that of movement).

This limitation might be overcome, however, as a result of recent developments in real-time simulation. New physics engines being used by some game developers are, in the words of Mark Frauenfelder, 'pumping games full of dynamic realism to match their visual verisimilitude' (2001: 118). The gap between realising a highly detailed setting (visual verisimilitude) and achieving equally accurate movements (dynamic realism) is closing fast. At the moment, it is the size of this gap that is responsible for some of the jarring contradictions in the perceived realism of gameplay. This can certainly be seen in many games, where the movements of characters are what can detract from the degree of plausibility constructed within gameplay. This is not to say that games should attempt simply to copy 'real' movement, but that the animation can offer more compelling gameplay if certain rules (such as those of gravity and the solidity of objects) are obeyed up to a point even when characters are performing actions that seem unbelievable by real-world standards. A certain degree of 'plausibility' at one level helps to emphasize the pleasure of engaging in vicarious activites that go beyond the bounds of normal physical capability. I return below to the notion of animated movement and how it impacts on the characters in *Buzz Lightyear to the Rescue*. For the moment, it is worth noting Steven Poole's observation that 'it is lack of coherence rather than unrealism which ruins a gameplaying experience' (2000: 64). The suggestion is that we can accept any level of 'unrealism' or departure from the world as we know it (as games such as *Pac-Man* and *Space Invaders* prove), as long as the rules of the game — including those of movement or animation — remain consistent. That is, the aim is not to achieve a zenith of naturalism, but a game in which movements and actions are plausible in their own terms. As Poole makes clear, the concern with verisimilitude is particularly complicated in the case of movement in videogames. The more realistic a game attempts to be in terms of *mise-en-scène*, action, thrills and the like, the more likely players are to become frustrated by inconsistencies in the abilities of the animation to fully represent a whole range of movements. Poole's main example here is Lara Croft:

> In the [relatively] naturalistic milieu of the *Tomb Raider* series (Core Design, 1996—), the bolted-on possibilities of movement that are added in each sequel only serve to remind the player how odd it is that Lara can run, swim, crawl and jump, but cannot punch or kick an assailant. (2000: 67)

A similar point is made by Hugh Reynolds, of the software company and physics-engine specialist, Havok: 'Game physics is about consistency, not realism' (quoted in Frauenfelder 2001: 121). As Frauenfelder adds:

> Although game developers like to boast about the realism of the experiences they create, they're actually talking about making sure that

the world within a game, which may be entirely unlike the one we live in, is consistent and accessible. (2001: 121)

A game such as *A Bug's Life* or *Crash Bandicoot 3* (Naughty Dog/SCEA, 1998) – or, indeed, *Buzz Lightyear to the Rescue* – offers us a simple, coherent world in which the movements are carried out by an insect, a bizarre marsupial and a toy. Limitations of animated movement are therefore not complicated by references to anything but the most general sense of reality and the world of the game seems largely self-contained.

Remediation/animation/games

As pointed out above, both videogames and recent cinema computer animation have a complex – and potentially contradictory – relationship with theories of realism. The seemingly relentless progression towards 'more realistic' modes of representation can be taken as 'common sense': as computers have become more powerful, and audiences more discerning, it appears to go without saying that the films and games have become more convincing in their illusionism. As Poole puts it, relating the increasing realism of videogames to changes in art in general:

Videogames, as with the strain of Western art from the Renaissance up until the shock of photography, were hell-bent on refining their powers of illusionistic deception. (2000: 137–8)

The problem with this formulation is that it falls into the same idealist trap that characterises, say, André Bazin's writings on cinema. The increasing realism of the representations is seen as an inevitable form of progress rather than an historically/ideologically/technologically contingent development. The idea that specific strategies which appear to increase the illusionism of a representation have come about *because* of their ability to do this is a fallacy. More convincing is the argument that suggests a dynamic, dialectical relationship between the function of realism in any particular text and its immediate context. As has been argued persuasively in relation to cinema, for example (see Winston 1996: 10–38), the gradual 'invention' and diffusion of what are, for idealists such as Bazin, 'more realistic' techniques and technologies – sound, colour, widescreen – did not lead to these technologies being used for 'realistic' effects, but for 'special' effects. The new technologies and aesthetic strategies were used in such a way as to foreground their position *as* effect. In other words, they were not there to play a role in a seamless, believably realistic world, a closer approximation to how 'we' actually perceive the world. Rather, they were used to emphasise the spectacular: sound used for musical extravaganzas, colour for swashbuckling historical epics, for example. The relationship between 'realism' and 'spectacle' is a complex one, here and in the case of animated videogames. We need to negotiate the contradiction inherent in situations in which we, as viewers/players, are asked to marvel at and revel in *how* illusionistic and transparent a particular representation is. How do we conceptualise a scenario where the transparent and naturalistic is *looked at,* and marvelled at, rather than simply, unproblematically *there*?

Bolter and Grusin's concept of remediation is useful here, suggesting that relationships within and between different media are complex and dialectical. They argue that remediation is the foundation upon which all new media developments are based, and that rather than 'new' media simply replacing 'old' media they will, at any historical point, necessarily *remediate* previous media forms. By remediation they mean the ways one medium appropriates the representational strategies of another, ostensibly in order to further its transparency/immediacy but with the apparently contradictory consequence of foregrounding the process of mediation itself. An example they offer is the way contemporary news coverage strives for an up-to-the-minute, on-the-spot and immediate approach to events, but does so in a manner that uses hypermediated strategies (for example, the marking out of the screen into areas that resembles a web-page using a variety of simultaneous inputs). As Bolter and Grusin argue, remediation works as a form of double logic involving both immediacy and hypermediacy. On the one hand, representations appear to offer a direct experience of something (immediacy); a process that, by definition, tends to mean that the process of mediation itself must be effaced. On the other hand, remediation relies, paradoxically, on an amplification of the process of mediation (hypermediacy).

We can argue that the kind of computer animation seen in films such as *Toy Story 2* is actually remediating animation as a whole, because of its simultaneous drive towards increased illusionism/transparency *and* provoking a 'look at that!' kind of reaction from the viewer. The former clearly involves the creation of a sense of immediacy, in its use of an increasingly 'naturalistic' technical repertoire (as noted by Darley (1997) in relation to *Red's Dream*); the latter equally clearly is based on spotting *how real* it all looks and is therefore based on opacity and actually seeing the mediation that is occurring. As Lee Unkrich, one of the assistant directors on *Toy Story 2* suggests, this paradox was at the centre of the film-makers' working practices:

> He [Al, of Al's Toy Barn] is such a realistic person, but at the same time it's good to point out that we never set up for ourselves that we would try to recreate reality. We're not trying to make a human on the screen that people will think is a real human interacting with the toys. ... [W]e stylize the humans somewhat and give them a caricatured look. At the same time we've made the skin very realistic with hair on it. Al has hair on his arms, beard stubble and little hairs in his nose. All those things add up to a viewing experience that makes people think to themselves, 'I know that what I'm seeing is not real, but it really does look real'. (quoted in Cohen 1999)

Bolter and Grusin argue that 'animated films remediate computer graphics by suggesting that the traditional film can survive and prosper through the incorporation of digital visual technology' (1999: 147). In other words, film has co-opted CGI for its own purposes. This is something Hollywood has always done — absorbing new technological developments into its dominant paradigm.[4] Importantly though, this is another indicator of quite how commonplace remediation is as a process. They also point out that:

> Toy Story ... borrows the graphic power of digital media but removes the promise (or threat) of interactivity. Toy Story shows that the 'new' digital film can maintain a conventional relationship with its audience — that linear media such as film and television can exploit the computer's power to create visually convincing worlds without the troubling notion that the user must be in control of these new worlds. (1999: 149)

What I am arguing is an extension of their point. They suggest that some animated films remediate computer graphics. I am suggesting that computer games now remediate specific animated films. There is plenty of rhetoric about the graphics in the games being on a par with those in the film. A typical positive review of the PlayStation version of the game gushes:

> I loved the first movie, I loved the second movie, and I loved how this game looked. It looked just like the movies. ... When someone else is playing and you are watching, the bright colorful smooth graphics make you think you are watching the movie. It's incredible. (GameGenie 2001)

However, it is obvious to anyone directly comparing the two that the game's interactivity or 'control' comes at the price of resolution of graphics and complexity of movements. This is not a problem in itself: as already pointed out, plausibility and consistency of movement and graphics in the context of the game are more important than out-and-out 'accuracy' in relation to the film or the 'real world'. (Especially, it is worth adding, when so many games contain caricatures, toys, monsters, and so forth). Neither should we forget that how realistic a game feels is inextricably bound up with the logic of the gameplay. That is, a game is never just judged on its visual verisimilitude or the accuracy of how characters move, but on the ways in which the player can and does achieve particular objectives in the course of actually playing the game. Nevertheless, we still need to consider in more detail precisely how degrees of 'reality' are figured in both game and film. It is also worth asking whether one can have *too much* realism. These are questions to which we now turn in relation to *Buzz Lightyear to the Rescue*'s 'adaptation' of *Toy Story 2*.

Animated films as a source for games: *Toy Story 2*

The film version of *Toy Story 2* begins with Buzz Lightyear flying through space in Gamma Quadrant 4, landing on a planet and exploring hostile-looking terrain. This is soon revealed to be inhabited by innumerable robots out to destroy

Buzz. He prevails and the planet surface opens, taking him to a confrontation with the evil Emperor Zurg during which Buzz is destroyed. It is then that the film cuts to reveal that what we have just viewed is a game-within-the-film, played by Rex the dinosaur with Buzz as onlooker. A variety of film and game joke-references are set in motion during this sequence. The overdetermined technology of the robot soldiers who Buzz single-handedly defeats — complete with gun turrets within gun turrets — is a parody of that seen in films such as *Robocop* (1987) and the *Star Wars* films. When Buzz discovers the source of Zurg's power, it comes in the game-like form of a levitating battery. To reach it, he has to negotiate a vertiginous abyss via a walkway of disks that play Strauss's *Thus Spake Zarathustra*, a theme strongly associated with *2001: A Space Odyssey* (1968).

One of the pleasures of the game is the access it gives the player to a measure of control over a recognisable film character, as well as the approximation offered to the film's diegesis. However, it must be reiterated that the game, for all its 'realism', never approaches that seen in the film on which it is based. A useful distinction can be made here between the qualities associated with the terms 'simulation' and 'emulation'. Both mean 'to copy', but they have differing connotations. To simulate something is defined as: 'To assume the likeness or mere appearance of; to counterfeit, to feign, to put on, to mimic' (Oxford Concise English Dictionary). The connotations here are negative, suggesting a fake that falls short of its target. To emulate, on the other hand, is defined as: 'To try to equal or excel; to rival; to imitate with intent to equal or excel'. Here, copying is given more positive connotations. Simulation, is seen as a sham, a 'mere' attempt to copy, while emulation is viewed as a nobler attempt to equal if not to better the original.

I would suggest that what we see happening with many contemporary computer animated films, and also videogames based on computer-animated films, is a complex negotiation between simulation and emulation. It is as if the viewer is invited to marvel at quite how real a computer can make a scenario seem (such a trajectory is emphasised by people noting how much 'better' — that is, 'more realistic' — the animation in *Toy Story 2* was than that of its predecessor), but always with an implicit recognition of the role of the computer (that is, a recognition that it is, precisely, 'only' a simulation). Simulation and emulation have particular meanings in the world of computing and cybernetics. As one web-based definition puts it: 'An emulation is based on duplicating the specific structure and content of a real brain whereas a simulation can be more abstract and take certain shortcuts' ('Whole Brain' 2001). This is interesting because it suggests that emulation is an attempt to be much more precise and actually capture a 'specific structure'. If we apply this to the various nuances associated with concepts of realism, it is tempting to conclude that the sometimes uncanny surface details seen in some recent computer animation films are a result of emulation. Whereas, in the world of computer games, with their considerably more limited powers of representation (or rather, their need to devote considerable space/memory to elements that need not bother the linear world of a narrative film, such as interactivity) we see simulation. That is, the game is 'more abstract and take[s] certain shortcuts', in that the graphics are less detailed and movement is limited by preset programming.

Such a formulation is an oversimplification, however. It is more helpful to suggest a complex *negotiation* or interaction between qualities such as simulation and emulation. Conceptualising the relationship in this way is more in keeping with Bolter and Grusin's dialectical notion of remediation. For, despite the fact that certain computer animated films and computer games do offer a form of 'realistic' experience, it is hardly likely that one can be mistaken for the other, or that either can be mistaken for representations of reality such as cinematography or television. It is of course possible that there may come a time when technology progresses to such a point that it will become virtually impossible to tell computer-generated imagery from that produced by more 'conventional' means, but that time has not yet arrived.

We are usually *aware* of the status of what we are watching or interacting with. Players are unlikely to mistake a computer animated videogame game for a computer animated film not only because the animation is 'not as good', but because a game will have someone *playing* it. As Noel Carroll suggests:

> Standardly, when one attends a film, one does not have to guess — on the basis of how it looks or sounds — whether it is fiction or nonfiction. Nor does one typically guess whether a written narrative is a novel or a memoir. The film and the writing come labeled, or, as I say, *indexed*, one way or another, ahead of time. (1996: 287)

Although recent technological advances are increasingly blurring the differences between specific types of representation, it is important to remember that our consumption of and interaction with these representations is not usually blind, but is subject to such 'indexing', usually via phenomena such as advertising, our own prior knowledge of particular genres and so forth. No matter how 'real' the world of a film like *Toy Story 2* or *Shrek* appears to be, therefore, we *know* it is animated, partly because it is *coded* as such. Indeed, its coding as hyperreal animation (rather than, say, attempting to be passed off as live-action), is its main selling point and again underlines the centrality of the experience of remediation. For, if audiences watched the films *as if* they were live action, not knowing (if this were possible) their indexed status as animation, much of their current entertainment value would disappear. The pleasure of these films and games lies in the way they *knowingly flaunt* their ability to imitate certain other representations (including each other).

The temptation to efface the differences between computer animated films and games must therefore be resisted. To do so would be to fall into the trap, cited earlier, of the game reviewer who suggests that watching someone playing the game *Buzz Lightyear to the Rescue* is just like watching the film *Toy Story 2*. This suggests that the game is truly emulative, in the sense that we are 'tricked' into thinking it is something else (the film). This is mere hyperbole, but more importantly, such an approach masks the central importance of the dialectical relationship that Bolter and Grusin identify. To reiterate: the 'uncanniness' of the computer animations in question is predicated on their being perceived as *simultaneously* highly naturalistic/transparent *and* hypermediated/opaque; this combination appears to be central to their allure.

Thus, computer animations such as the *Toy Story* films, and the videogames based on such animations, are attempting to mimic and copy a sense of external reality — or the 'realistically'-coded textures of other forms of representation — but in a manner that draws attention to the process of representation. A route through this conceptual paradox is provided by Bob Hodge and David Tripp's use of the term 'modality'. Modality refers to 'the reality attributed to a message', or the level of certainty or belief that one might have in an image (1988: 104). It is helpful because it gives us another framework in which to discuss the various 'levels' of realism that obtain in relation to computer animation films and games.

We can only understand and conceptualise how 'realistic' these forms are by reference to our actual lived reality — including, however, our experience of other media representations such as 'realistic' live-action films. Modality provides a framework in which to place the various degrees of realism we experience, and is particularly useful in relation to computer-generated imagery such as that found in the *Toy Story* films. The films (and to a lesser extent, games) offer a technological 'appropriation' of the real, where what is flaunted is the ability of the representations to reproduce an approximation of an action, location, etc., in sometimes uncanny surface detail. Hodge and Tripp suggest that 'underlying every modalized statement is an unmodalized positive' (1988: 105). In other words, if something is stated in the negative (they use the example of the statement: 'There isn't a monster in that room'), in order to understand it, we first of all need to 'imagine the possibility ... and then negate that thought' (1988: 105). The 'realism' of computer animation seen in the *Toy Story* films and many recent games works on a similar basis: we recognise that what we are looking at is *not* real, but can only do so by invoking an idea of the 'reality' — or the other forms of representation — the film or game is trying to emulate.

But is 'realism' the most important issue anyway? In his discussion of educational multimedia simulations, Peter Standen argues with the assumption that 'more realism is better' by pointing to the complexities of a real world scenario that

> may not optimally represent consistent elements of tasks; doesn't optimally sequence events for training; may overload attentional resources; and can cause frustration and poor performance. (2001)

Although Standen is discussing training simulations such as flight simulators rather than games, the relevance of his point to debates about realism and computer-game imagery should be obvious. 'Reality', and attempts to represent it with increasing accuracy, is not perhaps what should most worry game designers, as 'reality' is a messy place that is not conducive to the levels of control that make gameplay so enjoyable. Thus, when Standen states that a common suggestion is that 'training devices should incorporate as little fidelity as will achieve required training outcomes', it is easy to replace 'training devices' with 'games' and 'training' with 'gaming'. In this sense, the 'appropriation of the real' in computer animated games can be seen as a means to an end rather than an end in itself. Impressions of realism are only one of the pleasures offered by computer animated films and games, and not necessarily the most important ones.

Conclusion

One of the most interesting aspects of the relationship between computer animated films and the videogames based upon them is that which distinguishes one from the other — what we might call the 'ontological gap' — is much smaller than is the case with other games. Despite my scepticism towards claims that playing *Buzz Lightyear to the Rescue* is 'just like' watching *Toy Story 2*, it is undeniable that these two representations are, relatively speaking, *very* similar. No one playing *GoldenEye 007* (Rare/Nintendo, 1997), for all its manifest qualities, is likely to argue the game is remotely 'as realistic' as the film on which it is based, in the sense of reproducing something like the textures of the external world. Bond films and games share mediation through the conventions established in the 007 franchise, but they differ greatly at the level of the ontology of the image. They exist in very different ontological registers — those of cinematographic live-action and of digitally-generated, animated gaming. While both can be described as more or less 'realistic', in their own terms, they occupy widely separated positions in the broader continuum explored in this essay. As Poole puts it: 'Even watching the most 'cinematic' of videogames is still like watching a really bad, low-resolution film. A video game is there to be played' (2000: 99).

In the case of the *Toy Story* film and game, there is a blurring between the two, because both are located in the spectrum of computer-generated animation. The discourse found in some of the reviews is a manifestation/ symptom of this blurring. Three distinct levels of imagery can be identified, however, if comparison is made between the film, the cut-scenes included in the game and the rest of the game. The cut-scenes in *Buzz Lightyear to the Rescue* are lifted directly from the film *Toy Story 2* and appear to have the same lustrous quality as the video or DVD. This similarity serves to highlight the *difference* between the animation in the film and the animation in the rest of the game, however; a point underlined by the fact that, as is conventional in such games, the full-quality animated cut-scenes take on the form of a 'reward' for the completion of levels. The extracts from the film are part of the game, yet marked-off from the activity of gameplay. The player, having been immersed in the interactive, 'realistically' animated world of the game, is compelled to contemplate the *'more* realistically' animated, *non-interactive* world of the film via the cut-scene. It appears, therefore, that such computer animated films and games offer a particularly instructive example of the process of remediation. While both clearly oscillate between immediacy and hypermediacy, they also both exist *as animation*.

notes

1 To avoid confusion, I am using the title *Buzz Lightyear to the Rescue* to refer to the PlayStation game. Some sources call this game *Toy Story 2: Buzz Lightyear to the Rescue* or, more confusingly, just *Toy Story 2*.

2 Although many computer animations are based on some form of motion capture software — where 'real' movements are captured and then translated into computerised movements — *Toy Story 2* does not use such software. As Karl Cohen states: 'Pixar never uses motion capture according to [Ash] Brannon [co-director of *Toy Story 2*]. "It isn't right for our film since it is a very caricatured world."' According to Kit Laybourne, such computer animations use a technique known as 'inverse kinematics', where 'realistic' movement is simulated via computer algorithms (1998: 241). In such programs, figures' movements are simulated by mapping where specific joints should be in relation to one another. Instead of realistic motion being captured therefore, it is *created*.

3 Brian Winston is instructive on this issue, though he is by no means alone in pointing out that cinema, television, and even more recent modes of representation (such as digital imaging) have in a sense 'inherited' aspects of earlier ways of representing perspectival space. Winston borrows A.D. Coleman's term 'lens culture' (1996: 22) to describe this hegemonic way of representing space, a mode that seems to be alive and well, and operating in a computer animated film or game near you.

4 Indeed, a number of the most important players in recent Hollywood production have been companies like LucasArts and Industrial Light and Magic, innovators in the area of digital imagery. This suggests, of course, that they have played as much of a role in shaping the 'dominant paradigm' as they have been 'absorbed' by it.

citations

Bendazzi, Giannalberto (1994) *Cartoons: One hundred years of cinema animation.* London: John Libbey.

Bolter, Jay David & Richard Grusin (1999) *Remediation: Understanding New Media.* Cambridge, Mass: The MIT Press.

Carroll, Noel (1996) 'Nonfiction film and postmodern skepticism', in David Bordwell & Noel Carroll (eds) *Post-Theory: Reconstructing Film Studies.* Madison: University of Wisconsin Press, 283—306.

Cohen, Karl (1999) '*Toy Story 2* is not your typical Hollywood sequel.' *Animation World Magazine*, 4, 9. Available on-line at: http://www.awn.com/mag/issue4.09/4.09pages/cohentoystory2.php3

Concise English Dictionary. Poole: New Orchard Editions, 1988.

Darley, Andrew (1997) 'Second-order realism and post-modern aesthetics in computer animation', in Jayne Pilling (ed.) *A Reader in Animation Studies.* London: John Libbey, 16—24.

Frauenfelder, Mark (2001) 'Smash Hits', *Wired*, 9, 8 (August), 116—21.

Furniss, Maureen (1998) *Art in Motion: Animation Aesthetics.* London: John Libbey.

GameGenie (2001) 'Toy Story 2: Buzz Lightyear to the Rescue'. 3 July. Available on-line at: http://www.gamegenie.com/reviews/psx/toystory2.shtml.

Hodge, Bob & David Tripp (1988) *Children and Television.* Cambridge: Polity Press.

Laybourne, Kit (1998) *The Animation Book.* New York: Three Rivers Press.

Poole, Steven (2000) *Trigger Happy: The Inner Life of Videogames.* London: Fourth Estate.

Standen, P. (2001) 'Realism and imagination in educational multimedia simulations', in C. McBeath & R. Atkinson (eds) *The Learning Superhighway: New world? New worries? Proceedings of the Third International Interactive Multimedia Symposium.* Perth, Western Australia, 21–25 January. Available on-line at:http://cleo.murdoch.edu.au/gen/aset/confs/iims/96/ry/standen.html.

'Whole Brain Simulation & Emulation' (2001) Last updated 1 January 2001. Available on-line at: http://www.cybernetics.demon.co.uk/WBS.html.

Winston, Brian (1996) *Technologies of Seeing: Photography, Cinematography and Television.* London: BFI.

chapter eight

What's That Funny Noise?
An Examination of the Role of Music in *Cool Boarders 2*, *Alien Trilogy* and *Medievil 2*

david bessell

What's that funny noise I can hear in the background when I'm not blowing up aliens? Who is playing the organ in the old west wing of the castle and which cool 'choon' shall I choose to accompany my latest freestyle stunt? These and other questions which might not have occurred to you while hacking the heads off demons are considered here. The three games in question are: *Medievil 2* (Sony/SCEA, 2000), a comedy horror hybrid involving completion of set tasks, slaying of adversaries and acquisition of weapons and tools in various ghoulish settings against the backdrop of a quite elaborate narrative involving resurrected dead knights; *Alien Trilogy* (Acclaim/Probe, 1996), which revolves around shooting aliens in a variety of science fiction environments, the loose narrative and scenarios of which rely heavily on the movie *Alien* (1979); and *Cool Boarders 2* (UEP/Sony, 1997), a snowboarding simulation where points are accumulated by performing elaborate stunts on a variety of downhill courses.

Measured against the yardstick of conventional film music usage, questions addressed here include: does the music in these three PlayStation games share a common identity or function; how might this relate to the function and style of film music; does the technical format of computer games have an impact on the way music is used in these games; does the nature of music as a linearly-ordered medium conflict with the concept of interactivity and its inherent uncertainty; and do certain styles of music accommodate this element of choice better than others? These questions will be addressed after a description of the musical material and techniques found in each game.

At first sight it might seem that a great deal of common ground exists between the typical use of music in Hollywood films and that of games. This initial impression is further reinforced by games such as *Alien Trilogy* (actually just a single game), a direct spin-off from the *Alien* films. Such overt reference to film on the part of this and many other games would seem a fairly blatant attempt to hijack some of the marketing hype surrounding major studio releases and to tap into what is perceived as a ready-made audience. A closer examination of the exact nature and usage of music in the three games considered here, chosen for their differing approaches to the role of music, reveals, however, some interesting divergence from typical film music practice.

Of the three games it is not *Alien Trilogy* but *Medievil 2* that strives to mimic most closely the sound of traditional Hollywood film music. In particular, the opening pre-rendered animation sequence, a feature common to many games, takes a straightforward filmic approach. A large Romantic orchestra is used, playing material loosely in the late nineteenth-century style that has become associated with film soundtracks. Specific events and scene changes are often accompanied by synchronised musical events such as sudden changes in dynamics or percussion 'hits' and the music evolves in a continuous linear progression without significant repetition. For example, the summoning of a demonic force in the opening sequence is accompanied by both a simulation of special effects lighting and a sudden orchestral crescendo led by prominent cymbal swell. The musical effect climaxes as the demonic force bursts through the window and escapes out into the street.

There is also a suggestion of the use of a common film music device in the association of a childish musical theme in a light mood with the appearance of a child and scenes of everyday life at the start of the opening sequence. This theme is then contrasted with music of a more dramatic character as the scene changes to the interior of a room where a sinister figure is conjuring dark forces. In addition it might be suggested that the music references the style of Danny Elfman's soundtracks to films such as *The Nightmare Before Christmas* (1993) or *Batman* (1989). Such stylistic allusions are difficult to quantify but the inclusion of some late 1950s or early 1960s Broadway musical influence in the rhythms and accompaniment, combined with a light-hearted approach to ostensibly dark material, would be the decisive indicator in this case. Elfman was of course at the height of his popularity as a mainstream Hollywood film composer at the time of the game's creation.

When the gameplay proper begins, it seems at first that the music recommences in the same filmic manner as in the introductory sequence, or at least that the game programmers have striven to create this illusion. However, in this transition between opening sequence and the game itself, both visuals and music are interrupted simultaneously, which only serves to emphasise the discontinuity between the two sections. Someone more versed in film technique and less intent on just imitating the sound associated with film soundtracks might perhaps have tried to minimise this rather awkward transition with a continuity of music sometimes referred to as a sound bridge.

137

On closer examination, it can be observed that the music, though superficially similar to the opening, now consists entirely of what in the film world would be called an underscore. An underscore comprises a section of music that sets the general mood for a scene and provides added emotional support for the visual element but contains none of the synchronised musical events or themes that were a feature of the opening sequence. In addition, as the game progresses, the continuous music reveals itself to be a loop lasting approximately one minute that repeats continuously regardless of the gameplay until the end of the first scene/level is reached. Recognisable musical events that do occur, such as the fairly prominent crescendos in the first level or the sudden change of mood halfway through the loop that accompanies the second level, can seem incongruous due to their non-synchronised relationship to the action of the game.

In the initial phase of the game a narrator/ghost figure appears from time to time to give instruction to the novice player. These spoken interjections interrupt the music in an arbitrary manner; afterwards, resumption of the music is from an equally arbitrary point in the underscore loop. From time to time throughout this level, specific actions initiated by the player are used to cue spot sound effects that are overlaid on the music track but none of these have any musical content. Subsequent game levels, which follow the completion of the initial scene by the player, are musically similar, although the actual music contained in the underscore loop changes with each new part of the game. This renewal of the underscore loop provides a sense of reward for the player on the attainment of the new level while the maintenance of similar musical means and mood is intended to provide continuity in the game as a whole. The rather generic nature of the soundtrack, and the inability of game programmers to synchronise music and game play in any meaningful manner, have some consequences for the use of common film score techniques in this case. Little continuity of musical themes is in evidence between these different underscore loops, in contrast to the use of Wagnerian leitmotifs (recurrent short musical themes or motifs that recur in different guises and are consistently associated with particular characters or events) common in films that utilise this musical style.

There are short pre-rendered links between level changes in *Medievil 2*, each of which uses new music in a similar synchronised non-repetitious manner to the opening sequence. These also function as a reward for completion of the previous level but the game's programmers have not chosen to utilise the opportunity for a musical transition to contrasting material, of the type that is common from one scene to another in film. Although the actual notes change, the style, mood and technical musical means remain substantially unchanged giving a rather one-dimensional impression in comparison to most film scores.

In *Alien Trilogy* the game programmers have perhaps surprisingly taken a less overtly film-score approach to the use of music. Gerry Goldsmith, one of the leading contemporary exponents of the 'classic' Hollywood film music style, composed the original *Alien* (1979) film soundtrack. As mentioned above, this style involves the use of large orchestral forces and a type of harmony and orchestration associated with nineteenth-century composers such as Wagner. In common with many films in the science fiction and horror genres, moments of particular drama are occasionally highlighted by the use of more dissonant twentieth-century orchestral harmony. The subsequent films in the *Alien* series, although composed by others, take their general style from this original Goldsmith score.

In contrast, the opening sequence of the *Alien Trilogy* game – prerendered, and therefore non interactive – is scored with electronic music loosely in the style of Vangelis' score for *Blade Runner* (1982). Somewhat incongruously, a short 'fight' scene, which comes towards the end of this sequence, is highlighted by the sudden appearance of 'Heavy Metal' distorted guitars in a manner that would not be out of place in a Japanese Manga animation. In a sense the game still references film as a model for the musical approach taken; there is a fairly well established precedent for the use of electronic soundtracks in science fiction films and the particular Vangelis style hinted at has been referred to by the composer himself as electronic orchestration, utilising as it does elements of more traditionally filmic nineteenth-century harmony. It is a matter of speculation why the programmers of the game decided to diverge from the musical style of the original films. Perhaps this orchestral approach was deemed a little too conservative for the newly emerging field of videogames.

In common with *Medievil 2*, the opening music for *Alien Trilogy* contains synchronised musical events such as the heavy metal guitars/fight sequence already mentioned and does not employ repeating looped segments. The music that accompanies the start of the gameplay also changes, as in the previous game, although here the boundaries between music and sound effects start to become more blurred. At the very onset of the first level, the soundtrack comprises electronic effects of the sort associated with the older analogue type of synthesizer, typically consisting of whooshes and bleeps that fall between the conventional fixed pitch of traditional music and the unpitched noise of most sound effects. These effects run in a loop similar to the music of the first game, but here each repetition of the loop is interspersed with a period of silence. After a short period of this effects loop alone, a second loop comprising primarily electronic music emerges. This manages to reference both traditional film music, with the use of a prominent orchestral string-like sound, and popular music, with the inclusion of a synthesized drum pattern reminiscent of the German electronic pop group Kraftwerk. These two loops run independently of each other and give rise to a continually evolving texture of underscore from the combination of these two individually repetitious segments. This continuous evolution allied with the lack of any really distinctive musical landmarks means that the underscore in *Alien Trilogy* manages to function in a more successfully filmic manner than the more overt orchestrations of *Medievil 2*. Perhaps the varied nature of the musical styles incorporated here can also be traced back to a more recent trend in film soundtracks to incorporate an eclectic mix of popular styles and traditional orchestration in what can only be described as a rather scatter-gun approach to audience maximization, as in *Strange Days* (1998), for example. As in the previous game new levels are associated with new musical loops but the technique remains the same throughout.

Cool Boarders 2 presents an interesting contrast to the other two games in its approach to music. In this case it is hard to see any direct connection with the traditional role of music in film. The opening sequence, which in this case utilises both pre-rendered animation and 'real' video footage, is accompanied by music in a popular subcultural style known as 'indie' or alternative rock, featuring medium-distorted guitars, real drums, bass guitar and vocals. This has little in common with the games mentioned above, except that it too is presented in linear non-repeating form. No synchronised musical events are evident so the general high energy level of the music can be viewed as functioning as a rather frenetic underscore, although the analogy becomes a little strained by the prominent nature of the music.

Again the musical approach changes when the gameplay begins, although *Cool Boarders 2* allows an element of choice/interactivity at this point. Among the options given to the player at the start of each level is the choice of an accompanying tune, selected from a menu on a virtual 'ghetto blaster'. The music on offer is all variations on the popular dance styles of Jungle, Techno and Trance, which rely significantly on heavily repetitive short looped material (loosely similar in style to that of the group The Prodigy). This reliance on looping, of course, allows the continuous music to repeat until the end of the gameplay for that level is reached, no matter what the duration. A significant feature of all the music on offer is the fast pace, typically 150 beats-per-minute (bpm) and higher, and the busy percussion parts, which induce a sense of urgency and high energy intended to enhance the game play-experience. This type of generic popular musical accompaniment has more in common with the television presentation of extreme sports programmes aimed at a youth audience such as those found on 'Extreme' channel's Adrenalize for example (Sky Digital).

Although some recent films have opted for musical content comprising mainly or exclusively popular material (such as *The Matrix* (1999)) these are almost always either pre-existing well-known tunes or by well-established artists likely to have a high recognition factor with a potential audience, which is not the case here. Only the style is familiar to the target audience. In common with the other games, the music can be changed with each new level. *Cool Boarders 2* additionally allows the music to be changed for each subsequent replaying of the same level. This interchangeability of the available musical material further underlines its generic underscore function. Overlaid on the music is a commentator's voice-over, synchronised to give encouragement (or not) depending on the successful completion of various snowboard stunts.

Having established what musical material we are dealing with in these games, we are now in a position to ascertain what they have in common and what they do not. All three exhibit a difference in musical practice between the introductory scene setting or title sequences and the main body of the gameplay. The possible reasons for this will be examined later. For *Alien Trilogy* and *Medievil 2*, the film model offers a good fit in these opening sections, although the specific style differs from one to the other. Both exhibit all the hallmarks of film practice: enhancement of mood combined with specific synchronised aural and visual events. To call the generic 'indie' music of the opening sequence of *Cool Boarders 2* 'filmic', however, seems to be stretching the point somewhat. The model here is closer to that of pop video or youth television. It is interesting to note, however, that even in the case of *Medievil 2*, where the traditional film score is obviously the main model for the role of the music, when play commences and the game becomes truly interactive the programmers struggle to follow this model as closely as they might like. Here the underscore method begins to look a little shaky and there is almost a sense that the functional role of the music during interactive gameplay is somewhat at odds with the model it is ostensibly trying to follow. To some extent this discrepancy is addressed by the rather ingenious programming of the two independent loops in *Alien Trilogy*, while in *Cool Boarders 2* the problem has been largely side-stepped by adopting a different paradigm from youth 'extreme' sports television. The lack of even a pretence at narrative in this game is significant here; more on this later.

There are, I believe, two main factors causing this partial mismatch between the Hollywood model of music usage and the realities of the game environment. The first of these is the actual technical format of the games themselves. At the present moment games are marketed primarily on CD which has a finite data storage capacity (this data capacity will inevitably expand in this fast-moving area but will continue to be a factor for some considerable time yet). The sound and video files that are important components for computer games are notoriously large and, as video often seems to take priority for the programmers, sound is often subject to fairly strict capacity restrictions. The repeated looping of sections of music is undoubtedly a response to limited storage capacity and necessarily involves a trade off with the continuous flow of music desirable for a true movie soundtrack experience. Money may also be a constraint here. Games do not normally have access to the type of budget for music normally afforded to a mainstream Hollywood production. The typical roles the underscore would fulfil in a Hollywood film, such as smoothing continuity between scenes and adding to the emotional impact of the visual element, are often undermined by these constraints. Awkward transitions, abrupt interruptions and uninvolving repetitive musical loops are often the result.

The second and perhaps more fundamental factor, in its implications for the use of the film music paradigm, is the concept of interactivity. Once past the opening sequence, it can readily be seen that all these games present a variety of possible routes determined by choices made by the players. The main consequences for the role of music are the uncertain amount of time that any section or event may take and the unpredictable ordering of events within the game. Music, of whatever style, has traditionally been regarded as a series of finite proportional events that proceed in a fixed order; indeed it might be argued that the emotional power of the favoured nineteenth-century orchestral style stems partly from these very properties. The typical Hollywood film, involving a strong narrative thread, fits well with this linearly ordered model of music. But the inherent uncertainty engendered by interactivity presents some difficult problems in relation to music in general. How can the music be structured if the order of events are uncertain? How can music be constructed to occupy a time of uncertain duration without tedious direct repetition? The consequences of these problems can be seen at work in the variable approaches taken to the music outlined in the three games examined in this essay.

Each of these games attempts to deal with these problems with differing degrees of success. *Medievil 2* suffers the most because of its attempt to adhere to the sound of film music while losing sight of its *raison d'être*: the heightened emotional impact provided by the close synchronisation of musical and visual events, the use of leitmotif to facilitate character identification and the smoothing of visual transitions and breaks in continuity. *Alien Trilogy* fares a little better by keeping its focus on the intended function of film techniques such as underscore rather than blindly imitating the sound itself. The ability to generate an apparently less directly repetitious sequence through the use of two independent non-synchronised loops is crucial here. *Cool Boarders 2* goes even further, adopting a style of music primarily comprised of short looped sections and abandons the classic Hollywood orchestral style altogether in a fortuitous marriage of popular stylistic relevance and practicality. As *Alien Trilogy* suggests, there are possible programming solutions to some of these problems involving layering of musical elements, but too literal an attempt to adhere to film music practice seems at the moment to be restricting innovation in this area which could, I would suggest, be taken much further. Perhaps as the computer games industry matures this will change, but at the moment games manufacturers seem heavily dependent on pre-existent models from sources such as film and television for their sound strategies. This seems to be the case despite the ill-fitting nature of some of these models to the task in hand, which is essentially different in some crucial respects from that of the traditional film. This can be seen particularly in relation to the non-linear form of games that arises as a result of their interactive structure.

Lessons might be learned from other musical fields that have dealt with the problem of non-linearity that film has not been required to address. Composers associated with the twentieth-century avant garde, such as Boulez and Lutoslawski, have become interested in the problem of indeterminate form for quite different reasons and have proposed in their works possible solutions to the dilemmas that I suggest games programmers currently face. While it is true to say that much of the music of these composers is associated with a level of dissonance currently unacceptable in the commercially-driven games world, the principles embodied in the music could be transferable.

Examples can be given from each. The music of Lutoslawski involves short repetitious sections for individual instruments. These many overlapping non-synchronised sections are of differing lengths for each instrument involved, resulting in a continually evolving musical texture composed of short loops that can be stopped at any point in time by a cue from the conductor (*Symphony No.3*, 1994). This has obvious parallels with the approach taken by the *Alien Trilogy* programmers.

Similarly, Boulez has experimented with new types of musical form that allow multiple readings of a score in which the individual components of a piece can be played in a variety of orderings while maintaining the fundamental character of the piece (*Pli Selon Pli*, 1983). This technique is sometimes combined with the freedom to overlap different sections and vary the speeds of the different components at the players discretion (*Rituel*, 1975). In game terms, Boulez has introduced interactivity into musical form while managing to maintain a common identity between different readings of the piece. This new Boulezian model of musical structure has not generally been taken up by Hollywood film composers precisely because of its incompatibility with linear narrative, but its usefulness to game programmers struggling with non-linear forms seems self-evident. Film composer David Hirschfelder has noted, however, that the increasing use of non-linear editing techniques in modern film production, which often results in last-minute recutting of sections after completion of the music, has prompted him to search for a more flexible approach to musical form (see Buskin 1999: 123–4). It may be that films, and therefore the film score, will in future become more interactive in response to technological development. The attempt to provide the DVD format with an interactive element could perhaps be seen as the first stirrings of this tendency.

It is perhaps not that surprising that games programmers are not up to speed on developments in the musical avant garde, but more puzzling is the infrequency with which another relevant model is utilised. In the presentation of television news, music is often required to fill a link of uncertain length but also to cue a specific event or new segment with a musical event at the end of the link. This is precisely the problem facing game programmers. The solution as used by BBC News 24, to take just one example, is to have a rhythmically repetitive short musical loop over which a percussive or dynamically distinctive, but pitched, musical 'sting' or 'hit' is superimposed at the required moment (in a similar manner to the treatment of the sound effects in *Medieval 2*). This type of solution is referred to as a theoretical possibility by Steven Poole in *Trigger Happy: The Inner Life of Video Games* (2000: 83), but examples of its actual musical implementation are curiously difficult to find in the games arena. This is doubly surprising since television news is the kind of source with which one would expect game programmers to be familiar.

One notable response to the difficulties identified in this essay has been to make rather minimal use of music. The influential *Tomb Raider* series (Core/Eidos, 1996–2000), for example, adopts a musical strategy in which short continuous musical sections in conventional orchestral style are cued by specific events and certain locations in a manner similar to the use of sound effects in the other games considered here. No underscore substitute is attempted and consequently large sections of the games have no music at all. This does circumvent the repetition problem, with its associated danger of boredom on repeated playings, but leaves the game rather bare musically speaking and bereft of the potential for heightened emotional impact that Hollywood has long exploited.

In this fast-moving area, predictions of future developments are hazardous at best. Perhaps as the games industry becomes more established it will begin to forge new working practices based on musical notions similar to those of the musical avant garde or television news presentation. The perceived cultural gap between *Cool Boarders 2* and Boulez may be at least partially responsible for the lack of cross fertilisation between these two areas at present. Perhaps in the not too distant future the next gaming sensation will be sparked off by a musical programmer with a secret taste for Boulez? Strange Days indeed!

chapter nine

From Hardware To Fleshware: Plugging into David Cronenberg's *eXistenZ*

steve keane

As Allegra Geller (Jennifer Jason Leigh), the heroine of David Cronenberg's *eXistenZ* (1999), informs us: 'eXistenZ is not just a new game — it's an entirely new game system'. Characteristically, Cronenberg provides us with little explanation of the principal differences between 'game' and 'system'. Project manager Wittold Levi (Christopher Eccleston), however, does go some way to providing an initial distinction. On one level the members of the focus group who gather for the test launch at the beginning of *eXistenZ* are there to try out Antenna Research's new hardware, the MetaFlesh Game-Pod. Where the game pod (complete with brand new UmbyCord) can be referred to as the ostensible games console in this respect, *eXistenZ* is the software, the actual game which Allegra, the designer, and marketing trainee Ted Pikul (Jude Law) go on to play during the film. A provisional distinction can be made between the two. Principally, however, while *eXistenZ* lends itself well to exploration of the immersive and interactive nature of videogames, I would like to focus on the point of entry: the consoles that players use and the hardware Cronenberg effectively turns into fleshware in the film. The framework for this essay is provided by a number of qualifications of the distinction between 'real' and 'imaginary'. Beginning with a consideration of current videogame hardware, I will then suggest some points of comparison and contrast with Cronenberg's game pods. Much of the distinctiveness of the film lies in its deliberate resistance to similarities with prior videogame and virtual reality films. Part of that distinctiveness is exactly the fact that Cronenberg concentrates so much on the physical interface between player and game. The focus of this essay, then, is provided by hardware and the activity of playing games. My aim is not necessarily to explain how *eXistenZ* works as a videogame film. Rather, I would like to ask: what are some of the material processes at work in playing games, and how does Cronenberg exaggerate those elements of physical connection and control?

Designs for life

To date, there have actually been very few videogame-themed films. If we can look back on *Tron* (1982), *War Games* (1983) and *The Last Starfighter* (1984) as constituting a slight trend in the early 1980s, science fiction films of the 1990s have tended to pass over videogames in favour of the wider vicarious thrills afforded by imaginary versions of virtual reality.[1] Virtual reality is both a technology and a mode of representation, and, as such, remains symptomatic of the current development towards what R. L. Rutsky (1999) has termed 'effacement', 'transparency', and 'invisibility'. Principally, where prior, modernist machines were identifiable as machines, postmodern technologies have shifted the focus from forms of hardware to modes of simulation (1999: 110–12). It could be argued that the main problem in looking at hardware, therefore, is that it ignores the very process of becoming immersed in virtual reality and videogame environments. Hardware, in this sense, is a means to an end, and VR films follow that 'transparency' in terms of both reflecting the current drive towards increasing miniaturisation in technology and favouring the representational aspects of VR. Hardware comes in all shapes and sizes in VR films: the cumbersome chair-cum-life-support system used in *Total Recall* (1990), the gyroscopes and teledildonic bodysuits of *The Lawnmower Man* (1992) and the headpieces worn in *Strange Days* (1995), for example. Pointing towards an increasingly intimate interface between humans and hardware, all of these films remain relatively consistent in terms of immersion. Once the characters are equipped or strapped in, the main aim of VR films is to transfer one of the central precepts of virtual reality onto the screen — disembodiment. The principal appeal of virtual reality is to our senses, and for cinema this naturally translates to essentially visual representations of the virtual.

Virtual reality technologies lend themselves well to imaginary representation because VR is itself so much a forthcoming technology. Without a similar gap, the principal danger in making specific comparisons and contrasts between Cronenberg's imaginary game pods and current videogame hardware would be that 'invention' is pulled down to more literal observations regarding 'awareness' and 'intention'. The other extreme, however, would be to read the film in complete isolation from the current context of videogames.[2] Before even attempting to approach such comparisons and contrasts, therefore, it would be useful to establish how important videogame hardware actually is. Successively, the release of new games consoles has raised the stakes in what have been termed the 'console wars'. On one level, the progressive battles can be traced through the advances in graphics, sound and subsequent gameplay promised by successive 8-bit advances.[3] The current 128-bit revolution is, however, notable for a number of factors beyond technical specifications and the ways new-and-improved capabilities translate to 'better' games. Partly because the years 1998 to 2002 have seen the release of four new 'superconsoles', what distinguishes the current state of play, most of all, is that interest in hardware has almost superseded interest in the actual games. With the qualification that this represents, a particularly concentrated flurry of activity in reporting on specifications and capabilities has been joined by equal consideration of design and function.

Specifications and capabilities point towards what happens 'inside' games consoles and how that translates to what appears on the screen. Design and function bring attention back to the fact that consoles are pieces of hardware — objects of desire and control. The design aspect is relayed in terms of style. Primarily, if consoles are, indeed, becoming part of the 'cultural furniture' (Poole 1999: 16), they should not look out of place. In contrast to current superconsoles, the earliest consoles simply stood out as machines. For all its subsequent 'new flesh' imagery, for example, Cronenberg's *Videodrome* (1982) provides a number of telling glimpses into the hardware available in the early 1980s. In the first major transformation scene, in particular, we see Max Renn (James Woods) placing the throbbing Videodrome tape into his video recorder. The television set is itself identifiably of its time (literally big enough for Renn to be consumed by it) and we might also point out that the video recorder is a bulky Betamax machine; but more pertinent with regard to the current inquiry is the fact that there is a games console on top of the television. Surrounded by game cartridges, the buttons, wooden sides and principal 'radiator' fronting identify the machine as an Atari VCS 2600. The look of this Video Computer System, released in 1978, is in stark contrast to the progressively streamlined consoles released by Nintendo, Sega and Sony throughout the 1980s and 1990s.

Where design might well point to a certain gloss on the matter — or, alternatively, the way consoles are becoming an increasingly inconspicuous part of the home — function refers to the various internal and external mechanisms that allow for more interactive control over what is happening on screen. It can well be argued, in the first instance, that while a number of aesthetic, textual comparisons can be drawn between games and films, the most important, situational, difference is that games players do not just sit back and watch events unfold before them. While there is a visual, psychological link between the film viewer and what is occurring on screen, there is a very literal physical connection between player and game. As Steven Poole argues, control systems represent the most 'unreal' aspect of videogames, in which simply pushing buttons, for example, is radically removed, structurally, from the often-athletic feats enacted by the game characters on the screen. This cybernetic connection and control is, however, fundamental to both the omniscient control over, and further involvement in, videogames: 'the videogame is not simply a cerebral or visual experience; just as importantly it is a physical involvement — the tactile success or otherwise of the human-machine interface' (Poole 1999: 73).

To refer to this as a 'cybernetic' connection is not merely a casual association. Consoles can be located between computers and arcade machines in terms of physical connection and involvement, the greater distance between player and screen traversed by a number of wires and at least two pieces of hardware (console and controller). Referring principally to game controllers but also extending to genre-specific steering wheels and light-guns, for example, peripherals represent both add-on extension and more involved connection with the console and games. First of all, peripherals follow on from the points raised earlier regarding design. Again, looking back at the brief glimpse we are afforded of the Atari console in *Videodrome*, one might also notice the very basic joystick — little more than a stick in a box, allowing the player to move their ship, pong paddle or pixel character left, right, up or down. This is in further contrast to the PlayStation joypad or the Nintendo 64 controller, moulded for use by both hands and containing a combination of analog and digital buttons, miniature joystick and under-hand trigger. Design in this respect points to ease of control and the relative invisibility of the controllers once control has been mastered. All of these elements translate to freedom of movement within the games themselves. Or at least this is the promise. Exactly how do the various devices outlined above contribute to the ways in which we interact with videogames?

'Interactivity' has become a loose term in analyses of videogames. Although useful in initially trying to distinguish games from literature and films, for example, it is now simply taken as read that videogames are interactive or at least more interactive than reading a book or watching a film. The main distinction that needs to be made, however, is between the physical activity of playing a game (what happens on this side of the screen, as it were) and the subsequent results. As Andrew Darley defines the term, interactivity refers to 'a distinctive mode of *relating* to audiovisual representations or fictions. The player is provided with a way of directly taking a leading role in what occurs, given the means to control — at least in part — what will unfold within the scene on the screen' (2000: 156). This is a useful definition that carries with it an equally important qualification. It makes the common-sense point that has, therefore, rarely been made: that gaming begins with the player. Foregrounding the fact that playing games is always, initially, a physical activity, Darley's definition acts as a reminder that interactivity begins with the interface between player and hardware. I refer to this in 'initial' terms because the physical aspect is most apparent when first playing games or mastering the controls of a new game. All games and game genres rely on different combinations of button-pushing moves and the initial task is to gain competency in navigation and basic fighting moves, for example. Hence, whilst gaming might well become a battle of wits between programmer and player, the first steps are very much dependent on the player getting used to the control system.

From 'hands-on control' to achieving a sense of 'agency' within a game (to use two phrases already parenthesised by Darley), there is no doubt that, once mastery has been achieved, the physical aspect of gaming merges into the background. Interactivity becomes habitual, involvement automatic and even instinctual. It is not so much that the physical aspect becomes unimportant as the fact that it has become part of the very flow of the game. This ongoing synthesis between player, system and game is, in fact, an essential part of the much valued 'difficulty curve' of videogames. Primarily embedded in the design of a game, the success or otherwise of the curve is also dependent on retaining the player's sense of involvement throughout. Practice levels or training modes are entirely predicated around the player getting used to control systems. Difficulty curves work through the gradual introduction of other activities and added combinations.

Part of the limitation and success of current videogames is, of course, the fact that interactivity is itself something of an illusion. This not only applies to players finding out that they are taking part in pre-determined narratives unfolding in circumscribed spaces but also the fact that actual physical control is both incongruous and restricted. Buttons are not limbs and the same buttons are often used, in the same way, for wildly different moves such as opening a door and shooting a gun. Such standardisation also applies to the various vibrating mechanisms — Sony's 'Dual Shock' controller, Nintendo's 'Rumble Pack' and Sega's 'Jump Pack' — which still, nevertheless, do little to distinguish between gunshots and explosions. The myth of total control can also be undermined by a number of simple observations: players are only given moves relevant to the game and certain actions can only be performed in certain places. Darley sees these physical restrictions as being most apparent in narrative-based adventure games. Stripped of such 'textual' considerations, it is principally action games — so-called 'twitch' games — that provide for the ideal balance of skill, sensation and the illusion of taking part in acts of spectacular risk. This 'vicarious kinaesthesia' (Darley 2000: 157) is a fundamental part of the willing suspension of disbelief in our senses that in effect compensates for the technical limitations of current videogames and videogame systems. What such restrictions reveal is that there is still a developmental gap that can be exploited by science fiction cinema. Similar to the promises heralded by VR throughout the 1990s, in fact, those restrictions can be ignored, corrected, overcome or overcompensated as appropriate. Technology provides for ideas as much as raw material.

The pleasures of the interface

As David Cronenberg has stated in a number of interviews, his approach to *eXistenZ* involved 'subtraction'. Referring primarily to its low-tech setting and the drained look of the film, numerous references to *The Lawnmower Man* and *Strange Days* make it clear that he wanted to escape comparisons with previous VR films. 'I didn't want to make a VR movie ... I wanted to make something else' (quoted in Floyd 1999: 60). That 'something else' could quite simply be a videogame film but even here Cronenberg originally envisaged not showing the actual game: 'I'd allude to the game and you'd see people playing it, but the audience would never get into it. It would be like an elegant frustration. But that didn't last long! Once I'd started, I thought, "I wanna see what this game's all about!"' (quoted in Rodley 1999: 9). If what we are seeing on the screen remains a film — naturalistic in terms of setting and absent of the usual, computer-generated trappings of virtual reality and VR films — one of the main consistencies is provided by the game pods. Consistent in terms of both Cronenberg's original intention of not wanting to enter into the game and *eXistenZ*'s final development towards switching between the 'real' world and the 'game' world, the game pods remain evident throughout most of the film.

Insofar as one can arrange *eXistenZ* into a successive chronology of game systems — providing the advances with a discernible structure, as it were, and while we must be aware that all of the events in the film might well be controlled via an even more advanced and unspecified system — there are three main companies that use three different systems: Pilgrlmage's VR system used for playing transCendenZ; Antenna Research's central MetaFlesh Game-Pod used for playing eXistenZ; and the 'game' version of Antenna's system, Cortical Systematics' Micro-Pod, used to play the games on sale in D'Arcy Nader's Game Emporium. When rearranged in this way, the advances principally point to the decreasing size and increasing invisibility of the respective systems. Hence, the principal move from the players who wear Pilgrlmage's VR equipment on their bodies; through the MetaFlesh Game-Pods that plug into the players' spines; and onto the Micro-Pod, which is small enough to literally disappear into a player's body. External in effect becomes wholly internal, the intermediate level afforded by the MetaFlesh Game-Pod being that of the spine connecting to the brain.

One of Cronenberg's most specific observations of videogame hardware and the experience of playing games is very telling in beginning to chart the successive developments represented in *eXistenZ*:

> It seemed to me that what people are really doing in computer and video games is trying to get closer and closer to fusing themselves with the game. The idea that a game would plug right into your nervous system made perfect sense to me, because putting on glasses and gloves is a crude attempt to fuse your nervous system with the game. So I went that little bit further — if I want to be the game, the game will also want to be me. (existenz.com)

A number of observations can be brought to bear on Cronenberg's 'game made flesh' philosophy. Again, notice the way Cronenberg refers to the game rather than what might be termed the whole system. Plugging and fusing, however, are essentially physical terms, the sort of engineering carried out by the garage mechanic Gas (Willem Defoe) in the film. Secondly, notice Cronenberg's most specific reference to hardware: glasses and gloves. The headpieces and wristbands worn by the players of transCendenZ at the end of *eXistenZ* represent the main concession towards previous VR films and the current intersection between videogame and virtual reality hardware. While the game architecture is obviously much more advanced than present superconsoles, the equipment looks not so far removed from a combination of Sony's Glasstron monitors and their recent motion-sensitive wrist controller, Evolution, or alternatively the current arcade system, Virtuality. As John Luther Novak further explains in his novelisation of the film, these VR sets are, in fact, necessarily retrograde, mockups used on this particular audience in order to test the equipment and gather feedback on the players' responses to the game, system and overall experience:

'The sensation this little gizmo can give you! I've never felt anything like it! And I love the thumb-hole. What a thrill!' (1999: 228).

Where PilgrImage's VR system concludes and brackets the film as a whole, Antenna's MetaFlesh Game-Pod remains central in that it acts as both the physical point of entry into eXistenZ and a self-projected 'object' and 'theme' within the game. In terms of its size and shape, there is little doubt that the MetaFlesh Game-Pod is comparable to a games console rather than a computer. Portable enough to be carried around in Allegra's ski-shoes, its appearance is all surface, with two 'nipples' substituting for on/off buttons and the main body moulded for use by two hands. The new system allows up to thirteen players to play eXistenZ. Allegra's is the 'master' pod and, once the game architecture has been downloaded into the other, 'slave' pods, all the players stroke their modules in order to take part in the game. Hence, while playing the game remains a cerebral experience for the most part, there are still elements of dextrous control wherein stroking and squeezing the pods indicate different moods and levels of exertion. The main point of comparison in these terms would be a central console with twelve controllers for taking part in a multi-player game. These are, however, only surface comparisons. In contrast to the sleek designs of current consoles and the overall circuit of connections between player, controller, console and screen, the MetaFlesh Game-Pod bubbles and breathes. The interface between human and machine is in part negotiated, therefore, by the fact that the pod is already half organic. It plugs into the players, rather than vice-versa, and as part of the removal of identifiable hi-tech extensions the pods are relatively self-contained. The UmbyCord is well conceived in this respect, as internal connects with internal. The pod works through a combination of technology and biology, the most specific details of which are provided by games doctor, Kiri Vinokur (Ian Holm). Grown from amphibian eggs, spliced with synthetic DNA and laced with neural webbing, the pod is both primordial creature and state-of-the-art nanotechnology. Once ported, the pod both stimulates and feeds off the player's emotions, the reciprocal relationship being such that the added stimulation leads to extra bio-chemical energy providing power to the pod itself: '*You're* the power source. Your body, your nervous system, your metabolism, your energy. You get tired, run down, it won't work properly.'

This preoccupation with the body is a defining characteristic of Cronenberg's films. Understood as an organic system, the body is made up of parts contributing to the whole. Understood as a solid, material entity, there are still boundary disputes at work in the connection between self and world. Often categorised under the term, 'body horror', what such a definition only partly touches upon is the fact that the body and mind are inextricably linked in Cronenberg's films (see, for example, Rodley 1997; Grant 2000). Whenever the body is infected, penetrated or undergoes complete mutation, changes in psychology and behaviour inevitably follow. Similarly, it becomes difficult to distinguish whether the events, and in particular the various bodily transformations depicted in *Videodrome* and *eXistenZ*, are really happening at all; they represent the psychosomatic nightmare of losing control of the body. As Scott Bukatman states, a third element is also introduced into many of Cronenberg's films. Referring specifically to *Scanners* (1980), *Videodrome* and *The Fly* (1986), what we are also faced with in *Crash* (1996) and *eXistenZ* are scenarios 'in which the apparent mind/body dichotomy is superseded by the trichotomy of mind/body/machine' (Bukatman 1997: 79). From the hyperreality of *Videodrome* to the virtual reality of *eXistenZ*, Cronenberg's films also remind us of the importance of the corporeal. Modified in its connection with other objects or entities, the Cronenberg body is always caught in an interface and becomes part of a unique process.

The body works on three levels in *eXistenZ*. First of all the MetaFlesh Game-Pod plugs into the body and the game is effectively transferred through to the brain; secondly, the players' bodies are residually transferred into the game itself; thirdly, while playing the game there are numerous references to the bodies left behind in the ostensible real world. Where the experienced Allegra sees all this as perfectly natural and finds the initial interface and subsequent disembodiment pleasurable, games 'virgin' Pikul acts as a translator, voicing his concerns about being penetrated and worrying about what is happening to his real body while the game is taking place. Once fitted and ported, Pikul's role as translator, therefore, becomes important in terms of *our* understanding of *their* involvement in the game. The viewer having been provided with a dissection of the MetaFlesh Game-Pod, Pikul's commentary on the actual experience of taking part in eXistenZ explains both the physical and then psychological effects of playing the game. On first entering into the game, for example, Pikul looks down at his feet and checks his body: 'That was beautiful. I feel just like me. Is that kind of transition normal, that kind of smooth interlacing from place to place?' 'It depends on the style of the game,' Allegra replies. 'You can get jagged, brutal cuts, slow fades, shimmering little morphs.' As Novak develops this point, Allegra's preferred method, the 'dissolve', is in stark contrast to the more immediate entries designed to 'shock' players into responsive action in martial arts and explore-and-conquer games (Novak 1999: 103–4).

eXistenZ is not a primarily physical game. Travelling between the respective locations (the game emporium, trout farm, Chinese Restaurant and breeding pool) is carried out through next-level scene changes. And in what is for the most part a dialogue-driven game, eXistenZ principally progresses through Allegra and Pikul walking around and talking to the main characters. As Steven Poole reiterates, different games require different modes of thought and control. It is in this respect that Poole begins to question whether the increased cybernetic control promised by peripherals and potential developments in virtual reality hardware will actually 'narrow the field of possibilities'. Suitable for straightforward exploration games, what will happen to 'the pleasurable unreality of human-body physics' that allows a player to somersault like Lara Croft or deliver crippling moves in martial arts games? As Poole concludes:

> Counter-intuitively, it seems for the moment that the perfect videogame 'feel' requires the ever-increasing imaginative and physical involvement of the player to stop somewhere short of full bodily immersion. After all, a sense of pleasurable control implies some modicum of *separation*: you are apart from what you are controlling. You don't actually want to

be there, performing the dynamically exaggerated and physical perilous moves yourself. ... You don't *want* it to be too real. (1999: 76—7)

This is the obvious next step taken by all videogame and VR films — taking part in the simulated environments *does* become too real. As I have already argued, while playing any given game the cybernetic (human/machine) gives way to the virtual (player/game). From actively porting in to the rather restricted movement allowed within the game, playing eXistenZ appears to follow the same development. This is primarily signalled by Pikul's increasing expressions of concern over losing touch with his body. 'I'm very worried about my body,' he states during his 'sex' scene with Allegra. 'Where are our real bodies? Are they all right? What if they're hungry? What if there's danger?' In a trance-like mumble Allegra replies: 'Where we left them. We're sitting quietly, eyes closed. Just like a magic dream.' 'I'm feeling a little disconnected from my real life,' he further complains, 'Kind of losing touch with the texture of it ... I mean, I actually think there's an element of psychosis involved here.' Allegra sees this as a 'great sign ... it means your nervous system is fully engaging with the game architecture'. It is at this point that Pikul decides to pause the game in order to get back in touch with himself. We too are taken back to the chalet, where we are given the first opportunity to see what involvement in the game actually entails. Or, exactly how are they playing the game? Express physical activity has given way to unconscious mental activities, as we see the two players lying on a bed, passive, stirring, strung out. Existence is itself temporarily on pause. 'Let's go back,' states Allegra, 'There's nothing happening here. You're safe. It's boring.' Walking around with the UmbyCord hanging out of the back of his shirt, Pikul replies, 'It's worse than that. I'm not sure that here, where we are, is real at all.' This is the first sign that something has slipped over the edge. Control has been lost. The game is clearly taking over.

Outside in

Cinema has always offered its own vicarious pleasures. Videogame and VR films can be distinguished by the fact that they base their appeal, at one remove, on what videogame and VR technologies already appear to offer. Having looked at some of the ways players interact with games and how the players participate in eXistenZ, all that remains to be asked is: what is *our* involvement with the game in the film? How are we, as viewers of the film, invited to engage with the game element? For science fiction cinema, the principal task is to imagine what videogame and VR technologies might *possibly* go on to offer. For recent postmodern and cyberpunk science fictions, this is less to do with insightful 'prophecy' and meticulous 'extrapolation' than all-round 'observation' and often striking 'exaggeration'. From *Videodrome* and *Neuromancer* (1984) through to the similar bracket afforded by *eXistenZ* and *The Matrix* (1999), the collapsing distinction between present and future is further accompanied by the blurring of boundaries between technology and the organic (see Csicsery-Ronay Jr. 1992). Hardware is disappearing. Reduced to neural jacks and connective wiring in cyberpunk fiction and film, *eXistenZ* slows that process down to a certain extent by bringing us back to the body and lingering so much on the interface between players and pods.

Beginning with the game systems in the film, there is little doubt that they have an 'uncanny' feel to them; an appropriate term, I would suggest, not only because they are strangely familiar but also because they are as much part of the playful 'horror' elements of the film as the 'science fiction' aspect. On being asked whether he foresees the otherwise science fiction game pods becoming 'science fact', Cronenberg replied: 'That's a classic sci-fi thing, like Arthur C. Clarke saying, "I invented satellites ten years before they happened." I'm not interested in being that kind of techno-prophet. However, I'm very aware of what's happening with computers and I find it exciting' (quoted in Rodley 1999: 9). This 'not ... however' is symptomatic of the way Cronenberg squares 'interest' with 'invention'. The differences between real and imaginary devices, then, are part of the *interest* of the film. But the hows and whys, I suspect, are less to do with what we have come to expect from science fiction than the fact that the pods are the sort of hard-wearing, soft-to-the-touch organic systems that only Cronenberg could conceive and that rabid games players would welcome.

One of the defining characteristics of VR films is that they offer something of a 'contradiction' between narrative and spectacle, 'between what we are told at one level and invited to enjoy on the other' (King 2000: 191). What we are actually being told is that too much virtual reality is bad for you. 'What if' becomes 'hopefully not', and one can only suggest that this is a case of an established technology (cinema) attacking new technologies (VR and videogames) for the commercial threats they pose. But all this is still a matter of competing modes of simulation: film versus software. A comparable conclusion with regard to cinema versus hardware would entail equal consideration of the cinematic apparatus. This in itself would be a large undertaking, mindful of both a retrospective history of cinema-as-technology and the recent convergence between cinema and digital technologies (see, for example, Darley 2000; King 2000). Can we really say that *eXistenZ* is primarily a cinematic experience? Where VR films benefit from widescreen sights and stereo sounds, *eXistenZ* remains dark, contained, enclosed, and arguably works better on the small screen — the natural home of videogames.

The game pods in *eXistenZ* are in part a way of making sense of the film. That is, when we see the two test enclaves or Allegra and Pikul porting in and taking time out, we, the viewers, are offered an external perspective on 'breaks' in the game. When the game appears to take over and the central MetaFlesh Game-Pod is decimated, there is a sense in which we too are not altogether sure whether the central characters are locked 'inside' or 'outside' the game, as Allegra expresses it. To some extent the pod is revealed as little more than protective casing. Vulnerable throughout, shocked and infected, Allegra's pod is finally machine-gunned, but only after Vinokur has managed to replicate its 'entire nervous system ... complete with contents' for Cortical Systematics. 'I murdered your pod,' he states, but then qualifies, 'Your game is healthy and happy.' Or, boiling this down to the essence of the system, the hardware's ruined but the software is safe.

Looking at hardware is only half the inquiry. While acting as a way in, *eXistenZ* itself remains a very external affair. Where mainstream VR films work towards involving the audience in both the visual and physical experiences of virtual reality — crosscutting between first- and third-person perspectives, for example — the physical experiences of porting in and playing eXistenZ are represented in third-person and the subsequent involvement of the audience in the film/game is, if anything, much more cerebral than kinaesthetic. Lost in the spectacle and warning against the effects of becoming lost in spectacle, the main dislocation of VR films is nevertheless important in what they have to offer in terms of the push-and-pull of viewing and involvement. Detached in terms of both its clinical approach to physical sensations and the interesting but unexciting game, *eXistenZ* is food for thought rather than feeling. But there is a sense in which videogame and VR films do simply short-circuit the viewer. Flashing between the human characters, snippets of hardware and moments of visual splendour, the appeal is initially conceptual and ultimately frenetic. *eXistenZ* is conceptual and deliberating. It strips away the spectacle and offers a narrative without resolution. But the process of losing ourselves in the screen still remains and is in part born out of the fact that physical points of reference do dissolve as the film progresses. Beginning with the interface and following the players into the game, *eXistenZ* finally leaves the body behind and leads us into uncertainty.

notes

1 I use the term, 'videogame-themed', to distinguish films in which characters actually play games from straightforward adaptations and any number of films that could be said to make use of videogame aesthetics. This obviously narrows the field even more and it is in this respect that *Tron* and *War Games* become even less free-wheeling videogame-inspired films than *Hackers* (1995) or *The Matrix* (1999), for example. This distinction between the 1980s and 1990s also carries a few exceptions, most notably the 'virtual reality' film, *Brainstorm* (1983), and the very specific videogame-themed film, *Brainscan* (1994). For a useful summary of VR and videogame films in this respect, see Newman (1999).

2 Specific details relating to Cronenberg's knowledge of videogames include early discussions with Salman Rushdie regarding videogames as a potential new art-form; visiting internet gaming sites and chat rooms; and the fact that, while he has played *Myst* (Cyan/Broderbund, 1993) and *Gadget*, Cronenberg's experience of games principally relates to looking over his son's shoulder (see Rodley 1999; Richards 1999; Wise 1999). What we must also bear in mind is that specific elements of aesthetics and design were agreed in collaboration with the film's production team. Red Orb Entertainment and Electronic Arts, for example, provided *eXistenZ*'s designers with a number of games, some of which — principally *Gene Wars*, *Moto Racer* and *Road Rash* — appear in 'alternate' form in D'Arcy Nader's Game Emporium. One of the most interesting contextual factors is that the film was part-funded by Sega. While having no bearing on the actual production, the British video release of *eXistenZ* carries the clearest signs of this advertising deal; the reciprocal relationship being such that the box is marked with the Dreamcast logo and the video begins with a commercial for *Tomb Raider: The Last*

155

Revelation (Core/Eidos, 1999). Designed to advertise the recent release of Dreamcast and show off its new-and-improved graphics capabilities ('Dreamcast's 128-bit processor makes Lara more beautiful than ever before'), the contrasts between this glossy commercial and Cronenberg's film are tremendous.

3   Bits primarily refer to the processing power of games consoles. The dominant console of the 1980s was the 8-bit Nintendo Entertainment System (NES), which was released in 1983. Having effectively brought an end to Atari's aspirations in the domestic market, the NES held a virtual monopoly until Sega introduced its 8-bit Master System in 1986 and quickly proceeded onto its 16-bit Mega Drive in 1988. Nintendo did, however, go on to win back lost ground with the release of its 16-bit Super NES (SNES) in 1990. The first acknowledged 'console wars' came about in the mid-1990s with the release of the 32-bit Sony PlayStation in 1994 and Sega Saturn in 1995: the principal development from this point being the fact that Sony has established a seemingly unstoppable lead. Where Nintendo found itself alone with the release of the Nintendo 64 in 1996, the current 128-bit revolution has been referred to as 'console wars II', initiated by the Japanese release of the Sega Dreamcast in November 1998. Sony has merely gone on to extend its lead with the PlayStation 2. Nintendo will go on to complete the expected range with its GameCube and Microsoft's X-Box looks likely to disrupt the plans of the established games companies in 2002.

citations

Bukatman, Scott (1997) 'Who programs you? The science fiction of the spectacle', in Peter Brooker & Will Brooker (eds) *Postmodern After-Images: A Reader in Film, Television and Video*. London and New York: Arnold, 74—88.

Csicsery-Ronay Jr., Istvan (1992) 'Futuristic Flu, or, The Revenge of the Future', in George Slusser & Tom Shippey (eds) *Fiction 2000: Cyberpunk and the Future of Narrative*. Athens and London: The University of Georgia Press, 26—45.

Darley, Andrew (2000) *Visual Digital Culture: Surface Play and Spectacle in New Media Genres*. London and New York: Routledge.

Floyd, Nigel (1999) 'The Meaning of eXistenZ', *SFX*, 52, June, 60—4.

Grant, Michael (ed.) (2000) *The Modern Fantastic: The Films of David Cronenberg*. Trowbridge: Flicks Books.

King, Geoff (2000) *Spectacular Narratives: Hollywood in the Age of the Blockbuster*. London and New York: I.B. Tauris.

Newman, Kim (1999) 'Time machines', *Sight and Sound*, 9, 4, 11.

Novak, John Luther (1999) *David Cronenberg's eXistenZ*. London: Pocket Books.

Poole, Steven (1999) *Trigger Happy: The Inner Life of Videogames*. London: Fourth Estate.

Richards, Sam (1999) 'Profile: David Cronenberg', Arcade, 9, August, 37.

Rodley, Chris (ed.) (1997) *Cronenberg on Cronenberg*. London and Boston: Faber.

___ (1999) 'Game boy', *Sight and Sound*, 9, 4, April, 8—10.

Rutsky, R. L. (1999) *High Techne: Art and Technology from the Machine Aesthetic to the Posthuman*. Minneapolis and London: University of Minnesota Press.

Sheff, David and Andrew Eddy (1999) *Game Over: Press Start to Continue*. London Cyberactive Media Group.

Wise, Damon (1999) 'One on One: David Cronenberg', Empire, 120, June, 104-8.

chapter ten

Run Lara Run

margit grieb

Style eclipses content: reinventing popular appeal

When Tom Tykwer's film *Run Lola Run* premiered in Germany, where many domestic films cannot compete with the heavy line-up of Hollywood blockbusters,[1] it became one of the twenty most successful films of 1998 and the second most watched of all the German films that year (Joseph Vilsmaier's *Comedian Harmonist* ranked first) (see Schroeder 1998). It also faired well in the United States, winning the Sundance Audience Award and collecting praise from critics as diverse as Janet Maslin of *The New York Times* and Peter Travers of *Rolling Stone*. What is particularly remarkable about *Run Lola Run* is that, although wide-ranging in its appeal, its filmic structure does not conform to conventional strategies in popular film traditions.

The film's narrative incorporates digressions, repetitions and disjunctures while also limiting the opportunity for viewers to identify with the film's main characters. In fact, their personality traits are not admirable at all; they are social misfits with a leaning toward unlawfulness. Reinforcing the spectator's distance from the protagonists, the film never tries to hide its artificial construction. On the contrary, it revels in its hypermediacy.[2] *Run Lola Run* confronts its audience with multiple visual media: video, 35mm film stock, cel-animation and still photography, and bombards it with fast cuts and 'unnatural' camera angles. Of course, the three segments that tell the same tale with slight changes and different endings are far removed from normative diegetic exposition and might frustrate the viewer's desire for closure. Yet, Tykwer's film was very successful, even with audiences accustomed to dominant cinematic fare, precisely because it was *not* referencing classical film conventions. Rather, I contend, it appealed to viewers through another, less obvious, though also immensely popular medium: the videogame, a form Tykwer uses as a stylistic template to structure *Run Lola Run*.

Videogames have surpassed all other game media in both popular appeal and economic success. Not surprisingly, then, *Run Lola Run* makes abundant allusions to this digital medium in addition to conventional games. However, I intend to show that *Run Lola Run*'s primary goal is not to capitalize on the popular appeal of videogames through imitation. Rather, the film reflects critically upon its own medium and attempts to relax the narrative and visual conventions of dominant cinema practices. By adopting conventions used in videogames *Run Lola Run* acknowledges, even highlights, the limits of its cinematic apparatus, but also demonstrates that its restrictive and static nature can be subverted. Tykwer uses an ostensibly simple concept to accomplish this task. The film is fashioned around the theme of games; however, the viewer is a spectator in the unfolding of the play, rather than an active participant.

Apart from *Run Lola Run*'s latent manifestation of videogame aesthetics, the film includes plenty of overt references to games in general. The opening quote 'After the game is before the game', attributed to Sepp Herberger, one of the most famous German soccer coaches, is immediately followed by the announcement that: 'The ball is round. The game lasts 90 minutes. Everything else is theory', spoken by one of the film's secondary characters, the bank security guard. Since *Run Lola Run*'s approximate running length is also close to 90 minutes (81 minutes, to be exact), this declaration can be extended to apply to the film as a game as well as to a soccer match. These scenes are presented within the first few minutes of the film and establish a leitmotif for everything that ensues.

To expand the game allusion beyond the sports references and to arrive at a more general definition, *Run Lola Run*'s diegesis also includes the game of dominoes and an animated roulette croupier announcing, *'Rien ne vas plus'*, signaling that the 'game' (film) has begun for the main character. In response, Lola runs to save the day and win her game. She eventually succeeds, of course, when this trope comes full circle and she triumphs against incredible odds in a game of roulette at a casino. Finally, embedded in the overall narrative structure of the film, lie the rules to which all players/characters must adhere. When Lola breaks the law, Manni dies; when Manni breaks the law, Lola dies. When both pursue the DM100,000 more or less legitimately, they live happily ever after. 'Law and order' functions as a metaphor for rules, and, since rules are essential elements of games, they cannot be broken to win.

Because of technical limitations, *Run Lola Run* must do without traditional game features such as competition (player vs. player and/or game), interactivity (input leading to response) and winning/losing in the traditional sense; yet it still retains a playful overall ambience. Therefore, it seems fitting that the film uses the references to soccer — a spectator game par excellence, and especially popular in Europe — to frame the action and prepare the audience for an uncon-

Figure 12 Kick-off for Lola (*Run Lola Run*, 1998)

ventional visual experience. Viewers are 'passive', as the traditional film medium demands, but at the same time engaged in the experiencing of a kinetic extravaganza styled like an interactive videogame. Tom Tykwer explains the film's effect fittingly when he remarks: '*Run Lola Run* is supposed to exert thrill, it should have the effect of a roller coaster on the viewers who will be made to quake and quiver' (Tykwer 2001).

Prior to *Run Lola Run*'s domestic release in 1998, the computer/videogame *Tomb Raider* (Core/Eidos, 1996) hit the world's gaming market, becoming an instant market success, so much so that it spawned several equally or even more popular sequels, each one improving upon its predecessor. Lara Croft, the game's star, is now as famous as any film star, with innumerable fan clubs and internet sites as well as a monthly German magazine (there is also an English one, probably others too) devoted to all aspects of her *non*-being. She can be seen worldwide in computer-generated television and magazine advertisements peddling products such as Nike, Pepsi and the Lucozade energy drink, which has been renamed in her honour as 'Larazade'. Finally, her flesh-and-blood counterpart, Angelina Jolie, portrays her in the film *Lara Croft: Tomb Raider* (2001). In Germany, Lara enjoys tremendous success not only as a game character, but also as a poster child for commercial products. She has appeared on magazine covers and newspapers such as *Die Welt*, *Stern*, *Focus* and in television commercials for the magazine *Brigitte*. The popular German rock band 'Die Ärzte' profited from her audience appeal when they cast her in the music video for their song 'Männer sind Schweine' (men are pigs).

159

Figure 13 Lara Croft in *Tomb Raider* and Lola in *Run Lola Run*

Films and games: a winning combination?

> The hybrid of the meeting of two media is a moment of truth and revelation from which new form is born. For the parallel between two media holds us on the frontiers between forms that snap us out of the Narcissus-narcosis. The moment of the meeting of media is a moment of freedom and release from the ordinary trance and numbness imposed by them on our senses. (McLuhan 1994: 55)

It is no secret that videogames are becoming a force in mass entertainment with which few other media are able to compete. Even films, once considered *the* premier choice of entertainment and bringing billions of dollars each year to the United States, recently gave way to the lucrative gaming industry. In 2000, videogame software and hardware sales reached $8.9 billion versus $7.3 billion for movie box-office receipts (Poole citing the *Wall Street Journal*, 2000: 7). However, for the most part, films and videogames do not appear to take part in any competitive scrambles resulting from or spawning such comparisons. In fact, they often exist symbiotically, promoting and remediating each other and each other's stars and themes through cross-media and trans-media campaigns, financing each other's endeavors (for example Sega and Cronenberg's *eXistenZ* (1999)) and adapting each other's stories and characters to film and game screen.

Many videogames openly emulate the older medium of film. According to Bolter and Grusin these games do the only thing 'any new technology can do: define itself in relationship to earlier technologies of representation' (2000: 28; emphasis in original). This imitative style is immediately apparent in the FMV-scenes (full-motion-video or cut-scenes),[3] but also includes use of camera angles,

160

point-of-view shots, visual effects, sound effects and inclusion of non-diegetic music. On the first level of *Tomb Raider*, for example, when Lara enters the caves, she looks up at an opening to the left, ostensibly indicating the direction in which the player is to go. The player her/himself never initiates this look.[4] It is pro-grammed to occur as Lara reaches a certain point in the cave corridor. While this 'directed' and 'manipulated' point-of-view is clearly a nod to film, it is also an ironic device, because strategically the player would do better to ignore this left passage and continue straight ahead to a dead-end room with tasks to accomplish first. However, not only do films affect games, but the opposite is also true. Films remediate computer technology relying on CGI (computer-generated imaging) and action sequences that extend the boundaries set by conventional techniques which employ staging, lighting and non-digital special effects.[5]

Most of the time, when critics discuss how videogames have influenced film techniques and aesthetics, the discussion remains confined to the impact that computer-generated special effects have made, and arguments centre predominantly on post-production concerns. This is not surprising since it is rare to encounter a film that consciously fashions itself according to computer game aesthetics: that is, using narrative practices, spatial and temporal devices, atmosphere and rhythm, unique or at least ostensibly tailored to a computer game world. Upon closer inspection, however, some slight changes that can be traced to computer technology as well as to games are slowly transforming the structure of popular films. This is precisely where Tom Tykwer takes his cue and, with *Run Lola Run*, offers a film that tries to accomplish a double task: openly emulating videogame aesthetics while retaining an overall filmic structure, both strategies translating into an entertaining and popular film. However, *Run Lola Run* attempts to engage the viewer in the production of meaning rather than simply playing to the 'passive' audience generally associated with this popular entertainment form. Let's walk through *Run Lola Run*, in the double sense of a game walk-through and a slowing down of the film's motifs.[6]

Conquering space through speed

> The true problem with virtual reality is that orientation is no longer possible. We have lost our points of reference to orient ourselves. The de-realized man is a disoriented man. (Virilio 1996b: 326)

Run Lola Run's similarities to *Tomb Raider* are not just confined to superficial characteristics of the protagonists, Lola and Lara. Apart from the obvious, but maybe coincidental, name resemblance, the action attire and the quest for for-tune that both women share, they are also similar in other, less noticeable, ways. Lola's fantastic control over her environment, things and people, while travers-ing a space full of obstacles — as well as her seemingly superhuman powers to change the fate of others as well as her own — are key elements of *Run Lola Run*'s narrative flow. These characteristics directly correspond to Lara's capabilities in *Tomb Raider*. Most importantly, it is both women's incessant drive to reach their destination that brings them together. The viewer's identification with both characters is not so much embedded in an emotional response as it is kinetic. After watching *Run Lola Run* one can almost physically feel the exhaustion of the main character. In *Tomb Raider,* running is Lara's default propelling action, as is Lola's in the film. In order to make Lara *walk* instead of run the player must use a special keyboard command or game pad combination.

The navigation and mastery of 'virtual' environments — for example the artificial, dense, and heavily accessorised space created for *Tomb Raider* and in *Run Lola Run,* the use of images from Berlin, German urban space par excellence — can be linked loosely to the experience of entering and interacting with 'real' urban spaces. Exploring the simulated places staged in a videogame is initially likely to take the shape of an aimless 'stroll', apprehensive of what one might find and disoriented by the unfamiliar space (one that does not always adhere to realistic conventions) or navigational controls (not an intuitive physical walking, after all). Such wandering is therefore not unlike the Dadaist excursions through the urban landscape of Paris in the 1920s. Indeed, several new media critics — Florian Rötzer, Lev Manovich and others — have linked the navigation of virtual spaces to *flânerie.*[7] However, rather than trying to come to terms with the alienating speed of modern life, the 'landscapes' of many games are mastered/achieved by *utilising* this fast pace in order to explore the game world, perform the various required tasks and advance to the next experience. Speed is no longer something with which we have to come to terms, but rather something that has become an instrumental part of everyday life. Constituents of communication, manufacturing, travel and technology are moving at an incredible speed. Virilio's 'disoriented man' (see opening quote) is adjusting quickly to this new situation; her or his points of reference have changed.

Rather than the passive, goalless discoveries of Dadaist *flânerie,* the experience of the videogame is an excursion that invites interaction rather than observation. It is therefore more closely aligned with the Situationists' *dérive,* a playful interaction with space that calls for contact and intervention, albeit the ultimately teleological (progressionist) drive has been voided of any of the Situationists' political dimension. The *dérive,* what the Situationists call 'a technique of transient passage through varied ambiances' (Andreotti & Costa 1996: 69), makes it possible to 'apprehend the experience of ... space not as spectator but as actor' (Hollevoet 1992: 45). Similarly, a game makes it possible to grasp that which we commonly call 'virtual space,' physically (through the joy stick, game pad or other input device) and cognitively through manipulating its constructed environment. That, as Guy Debord notes, 'written descriptions can be no more than passwords to this great game' (1996: 26) is as much true of the videogame as it is for the *dérive*; it must be experienced and navigated first-hand not second-hand.

In *Tomb Raider,* as well as some other games in its genre, there exists no topographical representation of the game space one is supposed to traverse. On the contrary, a representational aid such as this would greatly reduce the pleasure of exploring and diminish the degree of difficulty associated with certain areas. Like a *dérive,* where 'one or more persons ... let themselves be drawn by the attractions of the terrain and the encounters they find there' (Debord 1996: 22), the sites that exist in adventure/exploration games such as *Tomb Raider* are not necessarily thought of as a mapable area for the player; they are conceptualised as, for example, 'the room with the vicious bear', or 'the cave with the movable wall'. In other words, they are tied closely to the interactive experience that awaits the player,[8] to the extent that often the game retains sinister signs, such as carcasses, of a player's earlier interaction with a particular site.

Although the commonly encountered architectural terminology tempts us to connect the virtual with the physical, it is really only movement that defines most videogame 'spaces'. If the player chooses not to encounter a certain 'room', it simply does not exist for her/his game (except maybe in its absence, legible as a reduced score or a failed objective). This is a characteristic that these types of videogames have in common with popular films. In the latter, as well, only space that is filmed exists on screen for the observer. Space outside the frame, especially the physical realm of the viewer, is seldom acknowledged, since it would compromise the illusion of the film's autonomous reality as well as interrupting the act of 'losing oneself' to some extent in the film's staged world. *Run Lola Run* does not use common narrative strategies, such as character-development devices, to guide and engage its audience; rather the story develops and is driven by the navigation of space, a common diegetic tool in videogames.

In *Run Lola Run*, the urban setting of Berlin, a place commonly loaded with ideological meaning for other German films,[9] has become a virtual setting; a city that never had a Reichstag, a Wall, or a Cold War 'evil twin'.[10] Although an aerial view of the supposed film location is presented to the viewer early on in the film, most of the space revealed in the film frame reflects only those paths and locations that Lola uses to get the DM100,000 and to meet up with Manni, her boyfriend. There are some flashbacks that violate this principle, but they are presented in stark contrast to the general flow of the film, in black-and-white film stock. Similarly, the episodic flash-forwards, that preview the fate of the secondary characters after interacting with Lola, are also marked-off distinctly from the fast-flowing diegesis, as photographic still images. Finally, all scenes that do not involve either Lola or Manni are filmed in video rather than 35mm in order to achieve 'a kind of synthetic, artificial world' (Tykwer 2001). Tykwer is not interested in complicating his tale through weighing down a specific urban landscape with meaning. Instead, his approach allows meaning only where Lola interacts. Tykwer's aesthetic use of landscape corresponds to the techniques used by videogames to deal with their virtual environments. Steven Poole observes that the space/character relationship is precisely what informs the basis for game architecture (2000: 212). The environment of *Tomb Raider*, for instance, is built to accommodate Lara: the height of ledges is designed according to Lara's ability to climb and jump; the length of underwater passages are adjusted to her ability to hold her breath; and so on. The topography of a videogame adheres to set rules in a way that a film set does as well; virtual and filmic space are both prescribed and distinctively meaningful. All items and locations in a computer game have a function, even if this function is limited to being a device to deceive or create atmosphere. Everything important looks staged, so as to attract attention and to prompt the player to interact.

Correspondingly, in *Run Lola Run*, the *mise-en-scène* gives the impression that it is arranged in this videogame-like fashion in order to provide Lola and Manni with an interactive environment. The film even goes so far as to disregard the laws of physics when the situation demands it, as in the scene in which Lola and Manni converse through a store window as if it were not really there. Additionally, the secondary characters featured in the film interact with Lola and Manni in two ways; they either hinder or advance them in their quest, as in the case of the nun. However, like the store window, when something or someone would detract or be utterly useless, such as traffic, it simply vanishes. This is especially evident in the final scene in which Lola looks for Manni, who is getting out of a car in the background. She stands superimposed on a motionless background with neither the moving cars nor bustling pedestrians that would render this city space 'real'. The space through which Lola navigates seems to be responding to her every move; it creates the illusion of existing solely for her passage. If she interacts with this space in slightly different ways, the story takes a different course. In a Votivkino interview, Tykwer himself alludes to this when he mentions that Lola's interaction with Berlin is based on the Pippi Longstocking motto 'I shape the world to be the way I want it to be'.

Lara and Lola traverse their constructed diegetic spaces at a frantic pace,[11] running to convey a certain rhythm; a significant mood and stylistic device employed in both game and film. This incessant attempt to keep player and viewer in a dynamic relationship with their respective representational medium can be seen as part of a larger trend in recent entertainment and commercial venues, such as advertising and pop videos.[12] Popular cinema has had to adopt a

Figure 14: Virtual Berlin — *Run Lola Run*

modified style to satisfy this expanding media sensibility of viewers. David Bordwell characterises this adjustment as a gradual development over the last thirty years, evident in an increase of shots per film or reduction of shot length and hyperactive camera employment (the camera continually moves as it records).[13] *Run Lola Run* exaggerates these techniques so that most cuts separate shots lasting barely a second (often less), an editing mode that contributes significantly to the film's dynamic style. When shots do last longer, they are tracking shots where the camera is moving at the same speed as the *mise-en-scène*. These 'traveling shots' appear most notably when the camera follows Lola as she runs to complete her task in only twenty minutes. The sequences shot in video also tend to include longer takes, but keep the viewer actively involved in decoding the images because of the unstable hand-held recording technique. When Lola and Manni slow down their lives and engage in their inter-segment 'pillow talk', recorded in relatively long takes, the audience feels encouraged to take a break as well. Overall, however, these breaks intensify the film's fast pace because they provide a standard for gauging the speed employed in the rest of the film. Although these kinetic techniques can be linked to general developments in advertising, pop videos and film, *Run Lola Run* also uses the fast pace to lend it the feel of a game, a race against time.

The quest for narrative

> Caring nothing for the division between good and bad literature, narrative is international, transhistorical, transcultural: it is simply there, like life itself. (Barthes 1982: 252)

Tykwer abstains from conveying interrelationships of events and continuity by negating notions of sequence, logic and causality, elements that make up the basic principles of common diegetic progression. Although each segment in *Run Lola Run* follows basic laws of cause and effect, the film interrupts its own diegetic flow with alternating divergent media, going from 35mm to video to animation to still photography, as well as using various filmic techniques such as split-screens, black-and-white versus colour images and slow motion shots.[14] These techniques highlight the constructedness of the story and therefore interfere with the viewer's immersion into the story. Also, the flash-forward fragments, associated with some of the secondary characters, are extra-diegetic elements that interfere with the continuity of the main plot. But most of all, the restarting of the narrative and replaying of many of the scenes with only minor changes sets Tykwer's story apart from conventional narratives. As Lev Manovich points out, 'narrative cinema has avoided repetitions; like Western fictional forms in general, it put forward a notion of human existence as a linear progression through numerous unique events' (1999: 187).[15] In *Run Lola Run*, repetition is used as part of the film's logic; since the protagonists are not ordinary humans, the film's structure cannot be ordinary or conventional either. Repetition and non-linear narratives are, of course, also at the heart of digital entertainment. Websites, hypertext stories, interactive CD-ROMs and videogames are all excellent examples of

165

this. The technical limitations and benefits of the digital medium encourage an approach to narrative different from that found in older media.[16]

Both film and videogames construct their narrative through a trajectory that connects actor/player with their interactive space. Although Lola ostensibly relives the basic story three times, each segment is very different from the preceding one. Otherwise, it would be impossible to keep the viewer's interest. Instead of altering the plot significantly, however, Tykwer changes the setting; each episode of the film explores a new space, but the narrative still tells the same basic story of Lola attempting to get DM100,000 for Manni. In the first segment the action takes place in the bank, the second uses a retail store and the third episode plays in the casino. This change of location prevents the film from inducing boredom in the viewer. It is predominantly the change of scenery rather than the development of narrative or character that keeps the audience anxious to see more; the seduction is visual. In videogames, where elaborate narratives are difficult to sustain, the variation of environmental conditions is also the primary device for keeping the player interested in the avatar's fate. Every level in *Tomb Raider*, for example, features new surroundings, environmental conditions, and appropriate adversaries (for example, bears and bats are encountered in caves).

Movement for players in videogames is almost always synonymous with interactivity. Interactivity, in turn, cannot necessarily be equated with freedom in narrative production as various critics have pointed out.[17] Thomas Elsaesser argues that interactive environments are static in the sense that they have a terminal, unchanging overall construction. A player may create unique trajectories, but s/he may not create completely new paths; 'rather than begin to explore a game environment, [s/he] explore[s] its narrative architecture: its paths and its detours, its branching and its multiple choices' (1998: 217). Additionally, interactivity in videogames is a hyper-structured endeavour because, if the player does not end up with a certain number of discovered secrets and items, her/his game enjoyment may suffer or even come to a halt. A game is an environment that must be navigated to some extent in the way that the creators imagined it. Only paths that are given can be explored, only items that are programmed to be there can be found, and all entities with which one interacts have previously been added to specific places and situations. The fun lies not in *creating* a narrative in a literary sense, but in *uncovering* a story through actions. This interactive element sets games apart from films, because in the cinema viewers more 'passively' consume the narrative; yet not as far as one might think, because of the restrictive nature of a programmed, pre-created narrative that both cinema and literature share sometimes with games.

Nevertheless, interaction of the players with the game can change the flow of narrative immensely. Essentially, no game ever unfolds in the same way twice. The player gains more experience each time s/he interacts with the game. Experience enables the player to react differently, adjust to dangers and obstacles and move in more advantageous directions. *Run Lola Run* alludes to this integral element of game play within the three segments that have slight changes according to how Lola and Manni interact with their environment. Although on the surface level Tykwer appears to fashion these alternating segments as a fictional treatment of 'chaos theory', on the level of style these episodes represent an exposition of how player experience (Lola) can alter the outcome of the game (film). A single moment in Tykwer's film makes this intention obvious. In the first episode Lola draws a gun on a security guard at the retail store which Manni is robbing. Because Lola does not know how to unsecure the gun's safety mechanism, she is instructed by Manni to move a lever near the weapon's trigger. However, in the second episode, Lola does not waver when she is in an almost identical situation.

Conclusion: popular cinema, ideology, and reflections on originality

Run Lola Run reaches out to a transnational, heterogeneous audience by employing internationally recognisable style and content.[18] This is achieved through the game-like structure of the film, its nondescript locations, and its overly simplified narrative and character development. Whereas the directors of the New German Cinema of the 1970s and 1980s acknowledged their cultural and political baggage and embedded these themes into their films and characters,[19] *Run Lola Run* avoids any references that would limit its appeal to a particular target audience.[20] The non-diegetic techno soundtrack, further enhances the film's 'cool' and therefore attractive atmosphere.[21] Tykwer's approach is surely motivated, at least in part, by economic interests, using a 'lowest common denominator' market strategy. However, beyond these economic considerations, the film is also an experiment in style.

As I have argued, *Run Lola Run*, an undeniably postmodern product, wallows in the remediation of other representational media, frequently quotes secondary cultural materials and even refuses to lay claim to an ultimate conclusion in the narrative. Tykwer never privileges originality as a mandate for his style; the film is unconventional, yet strikingly familiar. This 'unoriginal' and 'open' attitude of Tykwer's film again connects it to the videogame scene, where borrowing of stories, themes, techniques, and to some extent even code, is an accepted and standard practice. Through remediation of practices and aesthetics of another medium, Tykwer's attempt at subverting convention and undermining cinematic constraints, while still retaining popular appeal, has been a successful one, and consequently *Run Lola Run* has attracted large audiences in Germany and abroad.

notes

1   In 1998, the percentage of the market share for German films in the domestic market was only 8 per cent (of DM 692 Million). American imports, in contrast, made up for 85 per cent of the total market (statistics from *Wolken am deutschen Kinohimmel*).

2   The term 'hypermediacy' here refers to Bolter and Grusin's use of the term in their book *Remediation: Understanding New Media*. They define it as a 'style of visual representation whose goal is to remind the viewer of the medium' (2000: 272).

3   FMV scenes are generally used to advance the story of the game, similar to the function

of recitative in opera. They are also presented as a reward and respite to players finishing a particular task or level in a game and can serve as establishing scenes to introduce the player to the game's plot and general objective. In *Run Lola Run*, the initial sequence, in which Manni narrates the events leading up to his predicament, acts and feels very much like a game cut-scene.

4   In the game, Lara's point-of-view can be deliberately controlled with a keyboard or game pad and the player can have 'a look around' the 3D environment.

5   There are also plenty of films using gaming as a topic for their narrative, for example *Tron* (1982), *WarGames* (1983), *The Last Starfighter* (1984), and *eXistenZ* (1999), or adapting a game to the screen, for example *Mortal Kombat* (1995) and *Lara Croft: Tomb Raider* (2001).

6   A computer game 'walk-through' is a detailed description of a game's topography and interactive setting and the trajectory of the player through both.

7   Manovich expands on the link of navigable virtual space and its *flânerie* counterpart to some extent in his essay 'Navigable Space' (1998). Florian Rötzer also uses the Baudelaire/Benjamin reference in *Digitale Weltentwürfe* (1998).

8   Although it must be mentioned that most games use official designations for different 'worlds' or 'levels' of the game. But this is usually tied to marketing purposes, atmosphere enhancement, or the designation of a location that the player has reached in a particular game.

9   Some notable examples are *Berlin, Symphony of a Great City* (1927), *The Marriage of Maria Braun* (1979), *Wings of Desire* (1987), *November Days* (1992), *Life Is All You Get* (1997) and *Heroes Like Us* (1999).

10 Although Lola mentions a 'Grunewaldstrasse in the East', she only recounts this potentially geo-political detail as an explanation for her late arrival.

11 This is not to say that *Tomb Raider* never contains slow-paced sections. In fact, other action games, such as *Quake* (id Software, 1996) for example, are much faster in comparison.One must even deliberately reduce Lara's speed to complete a task in some cases. Also, the overall speed is controlled by the player, and therefore the game's pace can be decelerated or halted completely at any time. This is not unlike the pace set for *Run Lola Run* where Tykwer also slows down or stops the action at times. However, Lara and Lola both run when moving from one location to another, setting a certain base rhythm for game and film.

12 Underlying this stylistic employment of 'speed', through fast cutting, camera-movement and choice in subject matter, is the need to make visual material, once thought of as fulfilling an audience's desire for passive pleasure, more 'interactive'. In *Die Eroberung des Körpers: Vom Übermenschen zum überreitzten Menschen*, Paul Virilio (1996a) argues similarly that the passive and immobile lifestyle of the postmodern subject demands increased stimuli from the media as compensation.

13 Most films today use 2,000 to 3,000 shots, with an average shot length of no more than 2—3 seconds (Bordwell 2001).

14 According to Tykwer, juxtaposing these heterogeneous elements represents an experiment with and a comment on the limits of the film medium *per se*.

15 In the mainstream Hollywood film *Groundhog Day* (1993), the disdain for repetition becomes the topic of the film's story. The protagonist's main objective is to escape from the redundancy of reliving the same day over and over. Repetition is cast as a punishment

for the hero who will only avoid it through improving his disposition.

16 In *Hypertext 2.0*, for example, George Landow has shown how this alternative approach manifests itself in hyperlinked texts. Instead of following a linear expository trajectory, hypertext has the ability to let the writer go off on tangents; it enables writers to consider facts that 'resist linearization' (1997: 59). It does not rely on normative argumentation but favours a dynamic presentation of views (following links transversely).

17 Both Elsaesser's 'Digital Cinema' (1998) and Poole's *Trigger Happy* (2000) discuss this phenomenon to some extent.

18 However, eliminating national particularities from a film is not necessarily a mandate for subtitled European films to succeed internationally, as films such as *Il Postino* (1994), *Buena Vista Social Club* (1999) and *La Vita è Bella* (1999) have shown. Popularity cannot simply be conflated with universal appeal.

19 The 'Oskar scream', appropriated from *The Tin Drum* (1979), serves an exemplifying function. Whereas Grass's and Schlöndorff's Oskar screams to defy authority figures in Nazi Germany, Lola screams to defy the universal force of fate.

20 Nevertheless, the film's theme, character, soundtrack and atmosphere tend to privilege a younger audience.

21 Caryl Flinn points out that *Run Lola Run*'s soundtrack is globally recognisable because variants of this style can be found in many countries, and techno crosses national boundaries so easily because it uses 'sampling, modulating, remixing, and looping' techniques that 'deflect any claim to authorial, romantic expressivity, authenticity, or originality, not to mention copyright'. Furthermore, music and games both transcend linguistic national barriers because of their focus on nonverbal language.

citations

Andreotti, Libero & Xavier Costa (eds) (1996) *Theory of the Dérive and other Situationist Writings*. Barcelona: Musée D'Art Contemporani.

Barthes, Roland (1982) 'Introduction to the Structural Analysis of Narratives,' in Susan Sontag (ed.) *A Barthes Reader*. New York: Hill and Wang, 251—95.

Bolter, Jay David & Richard Grusin (2000) *Remediation: Understanding New Media*. Cambridge, Massachusetts: The MIT Press.

Bordwell, David (2001) 'Intensified Continuity: Aspects of Visual Style in Contemporary Hollywood Film.' Midwestern Conference on Film, Language, and Literature. Northern Illinois University, DeKalb. 23 March.

Debord, G. (1996) 'Theory of the *Dérive*,' in Libero Andreotti & Xavier Costa (eds) *Theory of the Dérive :And Other Situationist Writings on the City*. Barcelona: Museu D'Art Contemporani, 22—7.

Elsaesser, Thomas (1998) 'Digital Cinema: Delivery, Event, Time', in Thomas Elsaesser & Kay Hoffmann (eds) *Cinema Futures: Cain, Abel or Cable? The Screen Arts in the Digital Age*. Amsterdam: Amsterdam University Press, 201—22.

Flinn, Caryl 'That Music that Lola Ran To', in Nora M. Alter & Lutz P. Koepnick (eds) *Sound Matters. Essays on the Acoustics of German Culture*, forthcoming.

Hollevoet, Christel (1992) 'Wandering in the City *Flânerie* to *Dérive* and After: The Cognitive Mapping of Urban Space', in *The Power of the City: The City of Power*. New York: Whitney Museum of Art, 25—55.

Landow, George (1997) *Hypertext 2.0. The Convergence of Contemporary Critical Theory and Technology*. Baltimore and London: Johns Hopkins University Press.

Manovich, Lev (1998) 'Navigable Space.' Available on-line at: http://www.manovich.net/texts_00.htm.

___ (1999) 'What is Digital Cinema?' in Peter Lunenfeld (ed.) *The Digital Dialectic. New Essays on New Media*. Cambridge, Mass. and London: MIT Press, 1999: 173—92.

McLuhan, Marshall (1994) *Understanding Media: The Extensions of Man*. Cambridge, Mass.: MIT Press.

Poole, Steven (2000) *Trigger Happy: Videogames and the Entertainment Revolution*. New York: Arcade Publishing.

Rötzer, Florian (1998) *Digitale Weltentwürfe*. München: Carl Hanser Verlag.

Schroeder, Joerg (1998) *Die erfolgreichsten Filme 1998 Deutschland*. Available on-line at: http://online.prevezanos.com/skf/statistik/rueckblick/1998-3.shtml.

Tykwer, Tom (2001) *Anything Runs. Interview mit Tom Tykwer*. Votivkino. Available on-line at: http://www.votivkino.at/328intv.htm.

Virilio, Paul (1996a) *Die Eroberung des Körpers. Vom Übermenschen zum überreizten Menschen*. Frankfurt am Main: Fischer-TB.-Vlg.

___ (1996b) Interview with Louise K. Wilson. 'Cyberwar, God and Television: Interview with Paul Virilio', in Timothy Druckrey (ed.) *Electronic Culture: Technology and Visual Representation*. New York: Aperture Foundation, 320—9.

Wolken am deutschen Kinohimmel (1999) Informationsdienst des Instituts der deutschen Wirtschaft Köln. Ausgabe 49, 9 December. Available on-line at: http://www.iwkoeln.de/IWD/I-Archiv/iwd49-99/iwd49-99-8druck.htm.

Laura Mulvey in the pivotal 'Visual Pleasure and Narrative Cinema' (1990)) yet the passivity and castigation integral to such models has to be reconciled, in some way, with Lara's explicitly sadistic and penetrative appetites. In certain respects Lara resembles Ripley from the *Alien* films, in that she has battled monsters in strange places and survived unaided. While Ripley has been exhaustively analysed, her meaning as gendered being has never been fully resolved. Her identity, authority and her function within the narrative have disrupted reductive or essentialist readings of her gender. Binarist models problematised by Ripley's identity are completely scuttled by Lara's. Lara is a peculiar mutant; her motion relies on her occupation: she requires a driver.

In recalling Ripley, my point is not to reopen the debate of who Ripley is or what she may mean, but rather to site the accumulation of theoretical attention she has received as a point of reference from which to proceed to an examination of *Tomb Raider* (Core/Eidos, 1996), a point from which to begin a consideration of the ways in which cinematic accounts of pleasure, identification and gender may translate, or fail to translate, to an interactive medium. It is not their sameness that is being considered, but rather their difference. Ripley must elude death (at least until the end of *Alien*[3]) and the whole point of our fear, and our fears for her, is loaded by our investment in her survival. She runs on fear, and our emotive succumbing to her endangerment propels the narrative to its climax. Lara, on the other hand, can die repeatedly and temporarily. Her infinite and mechanical resurrections change the dynamics of our investment in her safety. Each of the women is available to us, as viewers, via a screen, but the bodies they risk originate differently, as do the spaces they must cross. Differences inherent to the media, and their particularities of access and pleasure, have to be considered. Given the unique, specific role of an avatar, as image and as vehicle, watched and played, it is possible that Lara manages to function as objectified on-screen woman, even as she simultaneously functions as sadistic agent relative to those she so effectively and relentlessly annihilates.

Ripley, and the theoretical attention she has received, is a resource, a base from which to proceed into the less charted territory of *Tomb Raider.* Throughout the *Alien* cycle dialectically informed attributes and values emerge as mythic operatives. The complex, livid universe Ripley occupies lends itself to emotive and sensual existence in the eyes of the recipient. Her embodiment as endangered and gendered being in a compellingly imagined universe has generated multiple readings.[2] Her role places her at the epicentre of meaning, within complex worlds, and against sets of hierarchical relationships. As Barbara Creed has argued in her work on the *Alien* cycle, its geography and its abject monsters are gendered in pre-Oedipal fantasies of maternal draw and abhorrence.[3] The films lock Ripley and the alien queen in a relationship that traces the terms of their difference as it negotiates their semblance. Processes theorised as integral to our sense of self remain susceptible to anxiety concerning our origins: our remaining receptive or sensitive to notions of reunification with the maternal body informs both the terrors and the pleasures of *Aliens* (1986) in particular. The *Alien* films are, at least in part, horror movies; they intend us to take pleasure in our fear of the carnivorous womb at their centre. As Carol Clover (1992) has pointed out, horror films and their squirming audiences problematise viewing models that insist on positioning the female on screen as inevitably the object of a sadistic or controlling gaze. The pleasures of horror involve surrender, passivity and discomfort, rather than, or alongside, pleasures of sadistic control. The environment of *Aliens* and the characters that fill it are loaded with information, from the implicit gendering of a craft or a creature, to the hyperbole of close up wide-eyed terror. Ripley is positioned in a mobile frame of enacted values, her meaning extricated from a web of jostling elements. While Ripley can be read as ideological or psychoanalytic figment, as 'Final Girl' (Clover 1992: 35) in a loaded space, Lara is the only girl in an empty space. The proliferating detail of filmed space presents the reader/viewer with a range of sensual information and emotive investment notably absent from the echoing sterility of Lara's world.

The places Lara infiltrates are redolent of painstaking assemblage and technological accomplishment. In consequence, and despite all the game's shadowy vast chambers, game-space cannot attain the kind of creepy enigmatic or suggestive depths that Ripley encounters. While the areas that Lara explores can be complex, visually pleasing or intriguing, they remain sterile and profoundly organised. They are not vicariously tactile. There is a feeling that the places could not smell, that even the water is not damp. Traps and predators arrive on schedule to be dodged or despatched. Monsters attack suddenly and fatally, but the fright they evoke is contained, utilitarian rather than uncanny.[4] Cinematic space is haunted by what remains just off-screen, especially in a scary movie, but digital game space seems less able to evoke such resonance. The creepiest monsters in *Tomb Raider* are those that manage, in their murmurings and groans, to attain a kind of uncanny, auditory ambiguity despite their digital construction.

The terms of our visually consuming on-screen film space are pre-arranged, then naturalised, via continuity editing, shot and reaction shot, while the camera orchestrates our motion through the screen space. Notions of film immersion as a subtle and encompassing process do not translate comfortably to a necessarily interactive medium. Lara is a vehicle, and she will only move if, as and when the player compels her to. While gazing at a film screen, our looking is choreographed and the limits of the frame become naturalised, denied or surpassed. Our motion though the onscreen space is pleasurably fuelled by a dreamlike disembodiment or surrender, while distance is cut, soared through. By contrast, in *Tomb Raider* players cross a space that is rarely abbreviated, running behind Lara, who is mostly on foot. Participants trail her in a third-person perspective. Players are able to partially manipulate the screen frame using Lara's location as a fulcrum: to look up or down for example. Whereas cinematic immersion involves denying our containment by a frame, the options offered by *Tomb Raider* centralise the issue of choice, and as a reductive side effect make explicit the limits of those choices. Interactivity makes a point of access, and thus the terms of access are never neutralised. We aim Lara, but her mechanised progression has the effect of emphasising the insistent limits of our options.

Much of *Tomb Raider* involves steering Lara from behind through various trials and onwards through a sequence of zones or levels. The barriers between subsequent zones are overcome once the relevant levers or keys have been activated. To cross a barrier is to enter the next sector. Penetration, novelty and accumulation are the rewards of performance. Death can be sudden (by yeti or archaeological death trap) or gradual (venom, drowning), accidental or strategic. If a poorly handled conflict has resulted in the squandering of various resources, such as health or ammunition, Lara is sacrificed, the confrontation played over and the text perfected. This kind of replay does not represent real options in terms of interactive intervention in narrative outcome: as a player, I can do, undo and redo until Lara has effectively performed the challenge presented to her by the game, but I can only proceed through the game, through the space itself, if I perform the task as the game demands. Scaling a series of monoliths or chasms, for example, calls for a precise and predetermined series of jumps, holds and steps. For each puzzle or obstacle, there is generally a single solution. To discern that solution and then perform as necessary is your aim. The solutions clearly pre-exist your participation. Players have options about the speed with which space is crossed, the ferocity with which enemies are despatched and the meticulousness which each nook, cranny, or cave is explored, but we do not author our trajectory. Solutions are not freestyle. A player will systematically experiment, and after trial, error and accidental death, correctly perform the intended and necessary response. The conditional terms of our motion through space are thus rendered explicit. We do not write our own narrative, we uncover a pre-existing text and conform to its injunctions.[5]

Tomb Raider is nostalgic in a boys' own adventure, Indiana Jones, style. The game supposes that there are still empty spaces to be revealed, entered and pillaged, invaded places that have lost their names and occupants, where a lone, wilful adventurer can defy death and gravity.[6] In his analysis of film noir Slavoj Zizek describes nostalgia as involving an intensification of gazing pleasure: contemporary viewer gratification is buoyed and buffered by the gazing of some past, imagined audience. Zizek explains the relishing of film noir as being informed by this ghostly doubling:

> What fascinates us is precisely a certain gaze, the gaze of the 'other', of the hypothetical, mythic spectator from the 1940s who was supposedly still able to identify immediately with the universe of film noir. What we really see when we watch a film noir is this gaze of the other. (2000: 527)

When I play Lara, I play in the company of her creators, and in the shadow of the desiring gaze that her breasts and short shorts were formed to address. Extragamically Lara Croft is repeatedly posited as technological innovation, as dreamed up, cutting-edge cheesecake, while each new *Tomb Raider* episode, and each subsequent Lara, is heralded as the offspring of creative and technological innovation. Game magazines mix glowing reviews of *Tomb Raider* with detailed accounts of Lara's construction, as if leering over Dr Frankenstein's shoulder. Driving Lara means occupying a place shaped and then vacated by her designers. Each impressive interior or frustrating puzzle is resonant of their will. Lara's is an imagined world, and the fact of its invention is never denied or superseded. Her body and its capabilities have shaped the spaces through which she is steered, obstacles have been designed and placed with specific and achievable solutions in mind. Lara runs in the company of these ghosts, the eyes she seems built to please, and the creative intention, the will, of her makers. Somewhere near the crux of her desirability resides a digitally immaculate primal scene. As players we occupy a zone strung between this loaded moment and some imagined reception, a mirage target of desire. Lara herself is intertextually narrativised as rising directly from technological innovation and implicitly paternal 'authors'. She has come into being parthonogenically, shaped by a fictional beckoning appetite that is gendered male, as relentlessly as she herself is gendered female.[7]

Gendered bodies, big guns

Cycles of representation initiated by the image of woman on screen, of 'lack' and subsequent castration anxiety (as elaborated in psychoanalytically informed film theory), cannot be held to translate directly from an image of flesh to an image of digital conception. Given Lara's digital history, can it be assumed that the viewer, of whatever gender, accepts on some necessary and unconscious level that the figure on screen is persuasively sexed? Is she 'woman enough' to instigate the castration anxiety on which Mulvey's benchmark analysis of narrative pleasure hinges? By Mulvey's account, the screened image of woman inevitably gives rise to castration anxiety in the male viewer, and such anxiety (associated with her 'lack') is manifest in either scopophilic or sadistic scenarios.[8] Superficially there are alignments between Mulvey's explication of sadistic looking and the trauma undergone by Lara on screen. It is completely possible that the urge to punish and control her are crucial to the relationship between Lara and her player. Nevertheless it would be deceptive and reductive to dismiss Lara as a figment of hypersexed objectification. Perhaps the cycles suggested by Mulvey as being an inevitable aspect of gendered looking are being evoked, mobilised and exploited, only to be rendered ironic or subsequently compromised by Lara's construction and expendability. Her emphatic proportions would seem to confirm that she operates as object for the screen viewer, and as such calls into play the models of looking described by Mulvey, but levels and degrees of flux and exchange made manifest by the console complicate attempts to cement a static subject/object allocation. Lara is watched, while she is being driven. Her physicality and gender invite objectification, yet she operates as perpetrating and penetrative subject within the narrative. This duality involves a certain delegation of agency between on- and off-screen positions.[9]

Watching a film may of course involve shifts in processes of looking and identification, but driving an avatar involves utilising a console, identification is occupation: literal and mechanised. This flux in agency is the price we pay to play. When Lara dies her temporary mortality returns the role of subject to her operator. She exerts violence with us, and then she dies for us, over and over.

Certainly Lara suffers (to the extent that a non-biologically generated and infinitely resurrectable character can be held to suffer) in a manner that recalls Mulvey's account of on-screen woman as the object of punitive ordeal. But are

Lara's travails experienced by the viewer's unconscious as credible; does digital pain count?[10] She is not impaired by her wounds. She runs on, relentless and unmarked, and only a small indicator in the top right of the screen gives any clues to the extent of damage sustained to her wellbeing. The novelty and variety of her deaths are diverting, and occasionally spectacular, but her resurrection is constant and guaranteed. Lara is punished in ways that are suggestive of objectified castigation, but the rapidity and repetition of her revivals indicate the presence of a different, perhaps simultaneous dynamic. It is not just about her pain or suffering, but about her renewability. Her primary adaptation is this facility to shed lives. This discarding and resuming sites her as subject, not object, within a sadistic formula. She is the agent of repetition, the perpetrator, while her victims are the numerous, the interchangeable and the expendable. At the same time as she carries out her penetrative exercise in slaughter and acquisition, she fulfils the role of object for the spectator. She takes lives and we take hers. Her hyperbolic breasts are decoys: her sex toy physicality is a mantle of objectification, as her deaths are a pretence of fallibility.

Lara models an objectified female casing, but she is the sadistic force in *Tomb Raider.* She is the subject (the transgressor, the survivor, the perpetrator) at least relative to the other occupants of her world. The sadist requires objects as fodder, and the sadistic scenario demands repetition. This is where the parade of victims, in their numbers and by their interchangability, come into play. Sadistically informed narrative is associated by Deleuze in *Coldness and Cruelty* (1991) with post Oedipality, with will, law, demarcation and penetration. Lara's violence and mobility are fuelled by just such appetites. Perhaps this is precisely the value of her cipherdom, and the fulcrum of the subject/object flux between player and avatar. Empty, she enables occupation. Her driver is the 'male' agent whose will to penetrate is teased and appeased by the game's terms of pleasure and reward. The function of her elaborately gendered chassis is to act as psychic mattress. Progress is a *fort-da* oscillation,[11] onward motion is gendered male, and penetrative success and acquisition are transmitted directly past the avatar to the player (of whatever gender). Failure, on the other hand, is snared by Lara's body.[12] Her unexpected deaths or sudden fallibilities recall and reinstate her limitations. The limitations reside in her body and her body is gendered female.

Gaylyn Studlar (1985) has adapted Deleuzian accounts of masochism in order to explore aspects of identification and film fantasy, and to propose that cinema evokes the seductive possibility of symbiosis in a dynamic that draws on fantasies of regression. As per *Coldness and Cruelty,* masochism is pre-Oedipal, involving a subject's vulnerability to the lures of maternal plenitude and reunification. Accordingly, the un-nameable maternal body operates as a structuring vortex around which an elaboration of dialectics, suspense and elaboration orbit, the 'eternal timeless supremacy of the mother can only be expressed in the language of myths, which is therefore essential to masochism' (Deleuze 1991: 63). Studlar traces structural similarities between the thematics of masochism and elements of film spectatorship. Further to associating masochism with the elaboration and suspense of film narrative, she links masochism's drive towards maternal reunification with the film screen itself. Studlar wonders if aspects of viewer submission enable a restoration via the screen to the 'sense of wholeness of the first symbiotic relationship' (1985: 614). The pleasure of symbiosis (viewer with viewed) is enabled by a selective collaboration on the part of the spectator. It is a process reliant on surrender (and of course it is a tendency, not a proscribed or inevitable aspect of viewer immersion). We also watch Lara via a screen, but in a game, the conditions in which a fantasy of regressive symbiosis between viewer and screen could operate are undermined or ruptured. The masochistic seductions of infantile regression and obliterating maternal reunification cannot thrive in a site where participation is performative. The pleasures of cinematic identification involve an emotive immersion or investment in the body, and the environs of the body on screen, in processes engaging the unconscious and fuelled by elements of spectatorial passivity. The games console, by mechanising elements of identification, arguably undercuts the pleasure potential of such processes. Lara remains under the viewer's control, identification is explicit: we drive, direct and occupy her. The console umbilically links the off-screen participant to the on-screen world and enables their agency within that world. The console embodies the difference between the two media, from surrender to interaction. The console involves skill and proficiency, any accumulation of which is demonstrable, on-screen. As the film screen offers the dream of symbiosis, the console offers the dream of control.

In *Coldness and Cruelty*, Deleuze counters Freudian allocations of masochism and sadism as complementary Oedipal perversions, by describing sadism and masochism as contrasting complexes, with different structuring fascinations. Sadistic fantasy is Oedipal, it 'negates the mother and inflates the father' (1991: 134), while the pre-Oedipal urges of masochistic fantasy involve self-abasement, symbiosis and the lure of the maternal body. Sadistic fantasy involves taking the role of the controlling parent in the punishment, objectification or debasement of a parade of nameless victims. *Tomb Raider* is driven by just such concerns, especially in its element of formulaic repetition. Additionally, at an extra-gamic level, the attention paid to the terms and details of Lara's construction are suggestive of a concern with origins and paternity that recall sadistic preoccupations. As masochism involves the draw of maternal symbiosis, sadism involves the idealisation of the father. Lara's digital origins are resonant of parthenogenesis, of an expulsion of biology that recalls sadism's drive to exalt the paternal.

Deleuze describes the dialectical, elaborative proliferation of sensual description in masochistic fantasy as a kind of circling, an approach to a gravitational namelessness: the lure of reunification with the maternal body (hence masochism's association with self-obliteration, absorption). On the other hand, the 'sadistic hero appears to have set himself the task of thinking out the Death Instinct (pure negation) in a demonstrative form' (1991: 31). Repetition is the sadist's tool in approaching this negation. In *Tomb Raider* pleasures and frustrations grate against each other in repetitious rituals of obedience and conformity that lead, via homicidal incident, onward (or inward) to new territories. Deleuze writes that 'in sadism, it becomes possible for the boy to play the role of a girl in relation to a projection of the father' (1991: 68), and that 'the sadistic fantasy ultimately rests on the theme of the father destroying his own family, by inciting the daughter to torture and murder the mother' (1991: 59). To bear his account in mind, is to open a space in which to imagine our weakness for Lara across gender and against more obvious tidal patterns of desire, sexual demarcation or appetite. If it is feasible to gender the hermeneutic 'secret' as the deepest female aspect in the game, the implication is that the androgynous daughter (Lara, and the player in Lara's guise) is expiating or exposing the maternal on behalf of the exalted and absent father.[13] This notion of play as an attempt to placate a paternal authority is suggestive of the obedience inherent to our conditional progression through the game, and recalls again the pathenogenic construction of Lara and her world.

Conclusion

Lara is an agile cypher, a vehicular android, a smooth-seamed femme-bot. She is hyperbolically gendered, but having digital origins and an avatar function significantly effect the ways that she is visually consumed. *Tomb Raider* is fuelled by sadistic preoccupations at the primary (apparatus) level, and at a subsequent or thematic level. Lara is the perpetrator, her victims are numerous, unnamed and disposable. On screen, in her world, she takes on the role of subject. Yet, simultaneously, Lara's exaggerated dream girl proportions are inflated by a reactionary imagination; she does function as object for the viewing/playing subject. I propose that this 'doubling' is enabled by Lara's peculiar origins, her construction and her vacuity. She is a vehicle, and she freezes should players lift their fingers from the console. This is a constant reassurance that she acts for the player, and thus that there is no will pre-existent to the player's. The player is effectively confirmed as sadistic operative, and as subject. This reassurance is then confirmed and cushioned by Lara's physicality. Her sex-doll attributes are the clear signals of a familiar, cosseting objectification that eases a delegation of agency from player to avatar. Extra-gamic sniggering about Lara's desirability further deflects potential anxiety regarding subject fluctuation. The outcome is that Lara relays her penetrative, wilful and lethal agency on to the player. This, perhaps, is why despite all her lone adventuring and valiant perseverance, she reaffirms more borders than she crosses. The fact remains that I have enjoyed Lara's company, and will continue to do so, but as the *Tomb Raider* games have moved closer to cinema in terms of characterisation (via increased use of animated inserts and dialogue for example) there is less flexibility in Lara's identity, and more a sense that a woman on the console is, at some level, a problem. While this girl-on-girl dynamic remains largely unacknowledged, it seems implicitly present in attempts to standardise the pleasures Lara offers her operators. Lara's expanding biography is, via her latest incarnations (*The Chronicles*, the *Lara Croft: Tomb Raider* film (2001)), problematising my relationship with her in new ways. The more elaborated, fixed or otherwise legitimised her 'story' is, the more it seems that a desiring and specifically male consumer is being imagined, addressed and constructed, and the more untenable any neutral participation by players outside this particular demographic seemingly becomes.

notes

1   Remembering Ripley involves grappling with psychoanalytically informed models of representation and subjectivity. My intentions are speculative rather than prescriptive, and I am not presuming that a particular, specific or static player is constructed by the text, or that the pleasures offered by the text are necessarily constant from player to player.

2   For an account of the problems Ripley has raised for feminist film theory, see Elizabeth Hills (1999: 38).

3   Barbara Creed's 'Alien and the Monstrous-Feminine' is included in *Alien Zone; Cultural Theory and Contemporary Science Fiction Cinema* (Kuhn 1990). This anthology contains a selection of work on the *Alien* cycle, and thus offers an overview of the various conclusions theorists have reached concerning the meaning of Ripley.

4   Julia Kristeva (1982) links the hybrid and the ambiguous with the abject. If the game spaces are digitally constructed and overtly assembled, its sheer intentionality would seem to make it difficult to employ ambiguity at a visual level. Using darkness works to an extent, but it is at the audio level that a spooky ambiguity seems best achieved.

5   I am unsure if the repetition of gameplay functions primarily to increase the value of new spaces. Perhaps repeat events function as opportunities to re-play towards a more perfect or correct event, or perhaps the lure of repetition is about re-play as deviation, as variation on a theme.

6   Lara raids African, Polynesian and South American sacred sites, London office blocks and Venetian living rooms. Her bizarre global web of blasphemic larceny, and the designation of sites from owned to abandoned, tribal, industrial, magic or occupied, is worthy of further investigation, especially in light of Lara's own supposed racial and class identity (and the weird drooling over her 'aristocratic' roots).

7   This is intended as an exploration of various elements of Lara's construction, not as a prescription of the pleasures involved in gendered reception. There are, of course, additional pleasures and alternative dynamics that could be considered, for instance, the lure of the hermeneutic: the notion that there is a secret truth, a revelation, to be pursued or unveiled, the pleasure of gaining, via a rite of initiation or trial, access to a long sealed chamber or mysterious power. Additionally it would seem worth examining this fascination with revelation in context of emergent media technologies. Perhaps the dislocation of traditional notions of truth, evidence, veracity or history is behind a culturally evident yearning to address a 'loss', via the exposure of commensurate 'authenticities'.

8   Mulvey proposed that the anxiety generated by the image of woman on screen is diverted into either fetishistic or castigating scenarios. I am focusing on the castigated or investigated alternative. A closer examination of fetishism in relation to Lara Croft is justified, but it is beyond the scope of this essay.

9   In analysing porn films, Zizek (2000: 524) describes a shift in agency (from viewer to performer), and suggests that this shift is one of the reasons that porn is so depressing. This notion of a delegation of agency is worth considering in relation to Lara's flagrant objectification (the big breasts and the small clothes). Perhaps, in part, it is discomfort around the agency Lara enjoys on screen that is being responded to or purged via the reactionary tone of much of her extra-game manifestations. Despite all the biographies, web sites and merchandising, and however much some fans may abhor a vacuum, Lara

179

remains empty, a cypher. If the proliferation of detail is a compulsive and compensatory response to her fundamental blankness, she draws it forth, but she is unaltered by it.

10 I have, at times, taken conscious pleasure in driving Lara off cliffs or blowing her up. The question is whether her pain or suffering register in the unconscious, whether her pain (or her 'lack') can figure in psychoanalytic processes such as those described by Mulvey.

11 *Fort-da* refers to the 'go away' game Freud describes in 'Beyond the Pleasure Principle' (1989: 599).

12 In my experience this is reflected in the pronouns friends tend to use when describing their progress (or lack of) through the game. Success is often appropriated by the player ('I'm up to the City of the Dead) while failures and frustrations are described as Lara's responsibility ('she keeps getting eaten', 'she keeps falling off that stupid cliff', etc.).

13 Perhaps it is significant that the feature film *Lara Croft: Tomb Raider* inflates the role of Lara's father. He is central to the plot, despite being dead. Additionally Lara and her father are played by a real life father and daughter, casting that was frequently mentioned in the film's publicity. Of course reading Lara as the 'good female element' expelling or exposing the 'bad female element' recalls Ripley again, especially in *Aliens*. Seemingly, each of the characters reflects our susceptibility to such fantasies, even as the terms of our relationship to each of them remains specific to either medium. And, of course, any number of additional or alternative cycles of mutating fascination may be fuelling our desire to play with Lara Croft.

citations

Clover, Carol (1992) *Men, Women and Chain Saws*. Princeton: Princeton University Press.

Creed, Barbara (1990) 'Alien and the Monstrous-Feminine', in Annette Kuhn (ed.) *Alien Zone; Cultural Theory and Contemporary Science Fiction Cinema*. London and New York: Verso, 128—41.

Deleuze, Gilles (1991) *Masochism: Coldness and Cruelty*. New York: Zone Books.

Freud, Sigmund (1989) 'Beyond the Pleasure Principle', in Peter Gay (ed.) *The Freud Reader*. London: Vintage, 594—625.

Friedberg, Anne (1990) 'A Denial of Difference: Theories of Cinematic Identification', in Ann E. Kaplan (ed.) *Psychoanalysis and Cinema*. London and New York: Routledge. 37—45.

Hills, Elizabeth (1999) 'From 'figurative males' to action heroines: further thoughts on active women in the cinema', *Screen*, 40, 1, Spring, 38—50.

Kristeva, Julia (1982) *Powers of Horror*. Trans. Leon S Roudiez. New York and Oxford: Columbia University Press.

Mulvey, Laura (1990) 'Visual Pleasure and Narrative Cinema', in Patricia Erens (ed.) *Issues in Feminist film Criticism*. Bloomington and Indianapolis: Indiana University Press, 28—40.

Sobchack, Vivian (2000) 'The Scene of the Screen: Envisioning Cinematic and Electronic "Presence"', in Robert Stam & Toby Miller (eds) *Film Theory; An Anthology*. Malden and Oxford: Blackwell, 67—84.

Studlar, Gaylyn (1985) 'Masochism and the Perverse Pleasures of the Cinema', in Bill Nichols (ed.) *Movies and Methods* Vol. II. Berkeley, University of California Press, 602—21.

Zizek, Slavoj (2000) 'Looking Awry', in Robert Stam & Toby Miller (eds) *Film Theory; An Anthology*. Malden and Oxford: Blackwell, 524—8.

chapter twelve

'Oh, Grow Up 007': The Performance of Bond and Boyhood in Film and Videogames

derek a. burill

007 licensed to kill

The circulation of signs, products and representations in the resonant space linking film and videogaming is a rich and multi-layered phenomenon. This is particularly true for the James Bond films and games. The games re-present the films on multiple levels, reproduce a filmic experience through interaction, and teach a tactile and cognitive literacy based upon the actions of a fictional character. Bond, as character and as avatar, represents a distinct methodology in global political relations (and in gaming strategy), a subject position that can be seen, learned, perfected and repeated. Intrinsic to this subject position is a masculinity that appears on some levels to be as fluid as Bond's survival tactics, and on others as invariable as his aim. To kill the nemesis, get the girl and win the game players must inhabit the role of Bond, playing the part as an actor would take on a role, incorporating the character's methodologies along with their own individual traits and tactics. Thus, to play Bond is to perform oneself as Bond, with the stage set by the dynamic history of James Bond as character, actor and, now, avatar.

Beginning in 1995 with the film *GoldenEye*, a steady stream of referent films and tie-in games have appeared at regular intervals. Tie-ins are products based on some referent representation (a standard tactic in videogame production). Watches, for example, are familiar gadgets within the Bond matrix; they double as lasers, electromagnets and complex communications devices. They are, of course, available for purchase (although without the more exotic properties) and are prominently featured on advertisements next to pictures of Brosnan (or is it Bond?). These products, like the Bond BMWs, are released in conjunction with the films and the games. *GoldenEye 007*, the game (Rare/Nintendo, 1997), appeared in the same year as the film *Tomorrow Never Dies*; the game based on the latter was released in 1999 (Black Ops/EA Sports), to coincide with *The World is Not Enough*, the game of which appeared in 2000 (Eurocom/Electronic Arts) along with *007 Racing* (Eutechnyx/Electronic Arts).

In addition to the films and books, games, videocassettes and music also make up an important part of the Bond world. Included in the video release of *The World is Not Enough*, before the start of the film, are a commercial for the entire Bond collection on videocassette and the music video for the title song by the rock group Garbage that features a narrative reminiscent of a Bond film. In the midst of all these products, traversing the network of representations, fictions and tie-ins, is a central thematic, or micro-ideology, that is buttressed, mimicked, reproduced and simulated by each piece of the matrix. This micro-ideology is the 'Bond methodology'. In the game, this strategy is a stealthy, violent sexism, as lethal and seductive as the character's machinations in the books and films.

The ubiquity of the media matrix supporting this Bond methodology creates a schema of slippage and erasure, reminiscent of Baudrillard's 'hyperreality', where signs and referents become mixed and arbitrary, eliding between different levels of simulation. According to Baudrillard, in this 'hyperreality', a theatricalised cultural stage, the concerns typical to a Marxist critique of culture (production, capital, class conflict) become replaced by other concerns. The former logical relation between signs and a living, social reality are replaced by a world dominated by flashing images and signs without referents. In fact, for Baudrillard, the world comes to be comprised solely of free-floating images and signs: 'The real is produced from miniaturized units, from matrices, memory banks and command models – and with these it can be reproduced an indefinite number of times' (Baudrillard 1983: 3). Although the prose is typical of Baudrillard's theoretical histrionics, his concept of hyperreality serves as a useful model for a number of situations: as a hypothetical degree zero; as a warning of what is currently underway (to a certain extent); as that which creates much of the anxiety surrounding simulation (the loss of the real, or, the inability to identify the real); and also as an example of how media/cultural theory can problematise the study of new media by blindly lumping together new media with old. The study of videogames and their relationship with film is clearly a new pursuit, yet at the same time there will be a certain amount of leakage between fields in order to deal with a practice that shares its productive orbit with so many other mediatic satellites. In this sense, the Bond world forms a suitable case study for 'hyperreality'. Within this specific vector, the subject is able to 'try on' Bond through a number of representations, wearing the costume and products in between the distinct media sites, becoming an active participant in the circulation and production of the Bond methodology (and masculinity).

Although my background in performance theory informs my reactions to videogames and interactive software, I also want to clearly situate my critique as historically and materially focused on the three Bond films and games produced within the last ten years. It is a critical account of the cultural construction of a particular strain of masculinity, the theorisation of 'boyhood' in relation to the Bond films and games, under the assumption that the players I am speaking about are mostly young boys. Of course, this subject position is equally accessible by a player of any gender, although it seems clear that, to a certain extent, the games and films hail the spectator/player as male. This pose foregrounds the specific historical moment in which these games and films were produced and the concerns indigenous to the theatre of post-Cold War global politics. By considering the more performative elements of the Bond character induced by the haptic playspace of the games, a performance of masculine, violent 'boyhood' emerges. That said, I have constructed this essay to 'play' as a Bond game might play. In it you will find multiple pathways, some leading to the conclusion of the 'game', some existing as subplots, others offering a micro-narrative of their own. Multiple sites and channels in the essay wind through critical and theoretical passages, and the reader is hopefully teased into an ergodic – or nontrivial, 'readerly' and interactive – relationship with the concepts presented here. This relates directly to the interplay of the many representations of Bond. The real world products – watches, guns, cars – become the props in the performance of the Bond simulation. The films function as a playscript, the games are a type of rehearsal. The historical backdrop, from the former Soviet Union in *GoldenEye*, to Hamburg in *Tomorrow Never Dies*, to Azerbaijan in *The World is Not Enough*, presents a *mise-en-scène* in which weapons, information and energy are bought, sold and fought over by the competing logics of industry, government, politics and ideology.

The stage and its players

Like the films preceding them, *GoldenEye*, *Tomorrow Never Dies* and *The World is Not Enough* all feature plot devices, characters and innuendo endemic to the Bond legacy. At the same time, Bond films tend to change with the times, situating themselves within the current political atmosphere while retaining a fluidity that enables the superspy and the series to survive as entertainment and popular fiction. Scholarship on Bond novels, films and the like tends to support this position. In *Bond and Beyond: The Political Career of a Popular Hero*, Tony Bennett and Janet Woollacott theorise the Bond media machine and its ideological dimensions, identifying three major ideological and cultural 'co-ordinates':

> [Firstly,] representations of the relations between the East and West or, more generally, between capitalist and communist economic and political systems; secondly, representations of the relations between the sexes, particularly in regard to the construction of images of masculinity and femininity; and, thirdly, representations of nation and nationhood. Throughout his career as a popular hero, Bond has been active in each of these areas of ideological and cultural concern. (1987: 18)

Within this very Gramscian ideological analysis, the authors identify Bond as a floating signifier who, as a popular hero, functions as a symbol for the contingent nature of both dominant and subordinate ideologies and the popular reader's equally dynamic and active position in relation to the fiction. Similarly, James Chapman's cultural history of the James Bond films and their relation to British cinema history and film culture shows that the films work under 'twin processes of continuity and change' (Chapman 2000: 248). These 'twin processes' form the basis for the interplay between the films and the games.

From a filmic standpoint, the three 007 films are clearly mainstream narrative cinema, within the action-intrigue genre. Each film features the familiar opening action sequence that structurally links it to the rest of the series. At the outset of *GoldenEye* (the first of the Brosnan films), a man in black is seen running, bungee jumping and breaking into a chemical weapons plant, all without a clear view of his face. The only trace of Bond is a solitary close-up of one blue eye. Moments later, Bond is pictured upside down, lowered silently from the ceiling of a bathroom stall. A solitary Russian guard, sitting on a toilet reading a newspaper, slowly lowers his paper, confronted with Bond and his quip: 'Beg your pardon, forgot to knock.' Knocking the guard out, Bond moves stealthily into the compound. We recognise Brosnan for the first time upside down, slinging a witty comeback, reasserting the Bond character – witty, charming, boyish – while this scene carefully inserts Brosnan into the loop. Yet, presumably, when someone knocks they want to come in. It is strange and compelling that we first see Brosnan in a bathroom stall, alone with another man, upside down. The following shot features Brosnan opening the bathroom door, surveying the scene. Bond needs to sneak in order to come out. This kind of latent, counter-intuitive homoeroticism creates an unresolved sexual tension, configuring Bond's gender and sexuality as polyvalent and shifting. Yet, at the same time, Bond knocks the guard out, violently reasserting his heterosexuality. Consider that homosexuality is clearly represented in earlier films as deviant and dangerous (i.e. Bambi and Thumper and Witt and Kidd in *Diamonds Are Forever* (1971)), while Bond's heteronormativity is constantly being witnessed and proven. Jeremy Black identifies a dialectic between Bond's heteronormative sexuality and other deviant sexualities:

> Bond, himself, and in the films is a visual guarantee of the maleness of the Secret Service, a role he carries forward from the novels without equivocation. His sexuality is central to this, because, in both novels and films, a notion of deviant sexuality fits in with menace. Thus, in the novels, Le Chiffre, like Krest, Slugsby, Horror and Scaramanga, is a heterosexual sadist, while Blofeld is impotent. In the films, Blofeld dresses up as a woman to flee Las Vegas in *Diamonds Are Forever,* while Dr. No has no time for women, and the self-obsessed Zorin does not consummate his relationship with May-Day. (2001: 97)

Bond's sexuality must be both stable and slippery. An assurance of his heteronormativity and masculinity must be performed and maintained through his relation to the 'other', represented by his enemies and foes. At the same time, Bond must retain the ability to change with the times. The dual nature of his sexuality and masculinity mirrors the hegemonic ability to uphold the dominant while subsuming the subversive, incorporating deviance and abnormality into its machinery.

Graphics and visuals in the films and games maintain similar stabilities and fissures. Following the resolution of *GoldenEye*'s initial action sequence, the famous 007 title sequence begins, featuring thematically related graphics and naked women engaging in a variety of activities. In the film, giant hammers and sickles shatter and fall as statues of Lenin topple in slow motion. Lanky and leggy silhouettes of women hammer away at iron stars, writhe in ecstasy (or is it pain?), and give the spectator a virtual lapdance. In *Tomorrow Never Dies*, the women wear skins of glowing digital circuitry, like the neon suits in *Tron* (1982), while at the outset of *The World is Not Enough*, women covered in oil shimmy in front of pumping derricks. All of these sequences objectify the total woman, for no details regarding identity can be discerned from the graphic treatment. Recalling Laura Mulvey's famous essay (1975), their dances fulfil the spectatorial desire of the audience, suturing the male gaze onto the camera, and by extension onto Bond's own eyes. Thus, the spectator is hailed as male while the women are treated as graphic interludes for that gaze, all manufactured by the camera's loving embrace.

Spectating of this sort is manufactured through alternate modes in the video games, as Bond's body simulation, or avatar, remains omnipresent, yet not always visible. Much of the visual pleasure in the games is derived from watching Bond perform his feats of espionage and skill. In the films, however, the camera does not focus on Bond's body as much as on his face. Brosnan is expected to be a 'gentlemen's gentlemen'; perfectly composed, unemotional, calculating, intelligent. But somewhere behind the cool exterior is that boyish charm that wins the girls and vexes the villains. In one scene from *Tomorrow Never Dies*, Bond has donned a pair of cool-blue glasses while strolling through a notorious casino. Because the glasses are X-ray equipped (one of Q's gadgets), Bond can scan the room and see that most of its inhabitants are either armed to the teeth or clad in sexy lingerie. Or both. Regardless, Bond fixates on the women several times and lets a small smile creep over his lips. Like a little boy peeking through a keyhole, Bond watches from a safe vantage point, behind a gadget which hides his (through the glasses) and our (through the camera) spectatorial desires. Oh, grow up, 007.

Playing the part

In the videogame *GoldenEye 007*, the player must navigate Bond through a series of adventures and problems (as in the two other games) based on those seen in the movie. Although these are not identical matches to the film scenes, the game levels usually contain an element or hurdle familiar from the films. Typically, the game level is tailored according to the design of the graphics engine, or to maintain the status of the game within a specific genre (in this case, first-person adventure/shooter). In general, in the 007 games, Bond as avatar and Bond as Ian Fleming's fictional character conjoin to create a subjectivity informed by the character, the actor playing the character and the player playing the character. The discourse surrounding the Bond legend is dynamic and fluid, reacting to the various cultural, national and political reconfigurations of the past fifty years. Real world instabilities are represented in the novels, the films and the games. In the games, these instabilities are countered by using the 'Bond method', or by mimicking Bond's actions in the referent media. The 'Bond method' can be translated as a general level of play with villains, women, technology and the idea of play itself. In terms of real players in the real world, various sociological and psychological studies have shown that the player's concept of self, or the 'social self', can be heavily influenced by their comparison with the virtual character. Because of increased interactivity, this relationship may be more pronounced in videogames, particularly in the case of the Bond games and surrounding media matrix (see McDonald & Kim 2001). In the end, the player can be described as an actor in a virtual theatre that doubles as the space made up of both the film and the game. This is also the space where concerns regarding the potential slippage between media (particularly in terms of violent media) are sounded. Again, let us turn to Baudrillard:

> Today, it is the real which has become the pretext of the model in a world governed by the principle of simulation. And, paradoxically, it is the real which has become our true utopia – but a utopia that is no longer a possibility, a utopia we can do no more than dream about, like a lost object. (1983: 310)

Again, the model of 'lost' reality surfaces, projecting the coup of simulation over an 'objective' reality. Ironically, in the case of the Bond media matrix, the referent was always-already a fiction, as is the case for much of simulation technology. The player/viewer can really go nowhere other than back to the real.

Unlike the Bond of the 1960s and 1970s, the latter Bond (particularly Brosnan) has found himself in a much-transformed world, without the clear-cut ideological, national and political differences created by the Cold War. Of course, throughout the films, Brosnan proves that he is actually fighting terrorism. In reality these are not terrorist organisations, but rogue individuals. In the end, who Bond fights is not so much a matter of what he believes as much as what he is against – anyone threatening free-market capitalism, (Western) humanity and the cocktail hour. These thematics have carried over into all three movies starring Pierce Brosnan in interesting ways that inform and alter the mode of play and subsequent local ideologies fostered by gameplay. This is evinced in the game as well as in how the game must be played. In several of the levels in each game, part of the player's objective includes 'saving the girl' or escorting her out of a difficult situation. Although the female character often carries a gun and will shoot at soldiers and enemies, she is generally unimportant and unnecessary to the player's completion of the level. At the most, if she does not escape with the player, the level objectives are not completed. More important to both the narrative and to play are the avatar's antagonists. The player often pursues one nemesis (or their henchperson) through several levels, completing the game only after solving the 'puzzle' – how to kill the nemesis. Once again, the main point of play is to complete the game with a minimum of personal damage, quickly and efficiently, and – just as Bond would do it in the movies – alone. Illustrated in the films and reproduced in the games, these tactics point to a general disregard for women, as well as to the shady 'necessities' of national security.

The three most recent Bond films pose a relatively new instability in Bond's relations with women, albeit through stereotypical channels and categories. '[GoldenEye's] strategy for incorporating feminist discourses is not to alter Bond's attitude towards women, but rather to alter the attitudes of the women around him to Bond himself' (Chapman 2000: 256). The games follow a much simpler path. As mentioned above, in the games, women hardly matter at all, appearing rarely. But, if they do appear, they appear as (literally) uncontrollable and relatively hapless ingenues that are unessential to the completion of the game, or as a clear external threat, an object that must be destroyed in order to win. Thus, in the games, female characters can be said to represent the masculinist vision of women as other, uncontrollable and unknowable, or as antagonistic threat, waiting to ambush the 'progress' of the (male) protagonist. When the player is in the game, these ideologies are reconstituted along with the action of play, serving to emphasize these attitudes to the player through the repetitive nature of this type of videogame. As Baudrillard might put it, the player may leave the game, but the image world of the film fuses with the action of the game, leaving the player with a referent (now, the films) that appears to function as a base reality for the games, reproduced on the barrage of screens which surrounds the subject. What might make this argument more compelling is the feeling of 'shared reproducibility'; when Bond appears in a film or on television, the player has shared in the production of that aesthetic and method through play. Every player can access Bond, Brosnan and the superspy archetype, performing as an actor, both real and virtual.

You only live once

Many contemporary videogames feature narrative and play structures that operate as a type of 'death machine' – games in which the only logical end is survival or death, and where success can only be achieved through numerous deaths. Of these games, the James Bond series is fairly typical in its use of avatar, narrative, scenario and the like. These particular games, by bombarding the player on multiple fronts, sell a methodology of death and killing that transcends the context of the game. Death becomes the reason to play the game, to both kill and avoid dying. As Black writes, politics serve as the justification behind most of this violence:

> In a wider sense, however, political meanings can be found in the films, and their appeal, in part rests on politics. At the most basic level, this

is the politics of killing and the attendant mayhem. Politics and plot must provide a situation in which it is both legitimate and necessary to kill, a necessity in the plots of both novels and films. There can be no ambivalence about this, because any would threaten to cut approval of Bond's exploits. (2001: 97)

Finally, play becomes a staging of the anxiety of the loss of masculine power. By revisiting boyhood, on the trans-global (and trans-national) killing fields of the game, the player performs a never-ending violence under the guise of an opportunistic patriotism, 'for King and Country'.

There are several distinct levels of death within the games. First, Bond's death is witnessed several times per level. Each time play begins at the first mission, Bond's character starts with a set of 'lives'. These lives can be replenished if the player finds and collects a large, floating, golden '007' symbol. There is usually at least one of these on each mission. But even so, the player can 'die' several times in the first mission and move to the next. Second, these deaths are witnessed from a separate vantage point from that offered in the rest of the action sequences when the player is in control of the avatar. Usually from a point of view above and at a distance, the player watches Bond die, his avatar flashing in and out to signify that play will continue. In an instant, the player is back in the action, watching from the familiar third-person position behind the avatar. When Bond dies for good (when all of the player's 'lives' are used up) the slowly-descending curtain of blood familiar from the opening titles of the films slowly coats the screen, the player's vision rocks back and forth and the view fades away with a trademark, dismal musical flourish. Third, the player knows that the reset button can be hit at anytime, and that with the use of a memory card, play can be 'saved' at any point. Thus, once a level is completed, the level may be saved and the player will never have to complete it again. If the player has died in a saved and completed level, the death is effectively erased – completion of a level equals an overriding immortality-effect. Thus, the performance can be completed in a satisfactory (and exemplary) manner through the calculated use of a recording function. In the game, the utility of death links simulation and reproduction technologies, serving to erase the real constraints of both mortality and 'history'. Add to this that the bodies of those killed by Bond in the game slowly fade away, seconds after they are killed, erasing any evidence of violence and responsibility.

In short, the games become a struggle for the control of stress. During the re-viewing of the films for the purposes of this essay, I was shocked by the level of anxiety I experienced when recalling particular game episodes which caused me considerable 'trouble'. The greater the control, the cooler the composure, the greater the success – like the 'real' 007. As Kevin Robins and Les Levidow point out, playing the games illustrates, 'processes of anxiety and control' (1995: 122).

Video games can thus be understood as a paranoiac environment that induces a sense of paranoia by dissolving any distinction between the doer and the viewer. Driven by the structure of the video game, the player is constantly defending himself, or the entire universe, from destructive forces. The play becomes a compulsive pleasurable repetition of a life-and-death performance. Yet the player's anxiety can never be mastered by that dangerously vicarious play. He engages in a characteristic repetition, often described as 'video game addiction'. (*Ibid.*)

Here, the authors are referring to videogames and the screening of the Gulf War as indicative of the same 'blurring' effect. In a similar fashion, Randy Schroeder identifies a slippage between levels of reality in videogame play. Drawing on Huizinga's notion of the 'playspace', Schroeder designates the leakage from the game into reality as representative of postmodern culture in general.

In a world of immersive simulation the real doesn't leak into the playworld, the playworld leaks into the real, as the simulacrum cancels the original, the referent, the simulated. Play still exists for itself, but so does everything else: existence has become play (a familiar claim of most postmodernists). (1996: 148)

While this may be true, it seems that with the Bond games, the slippage and leakage appears to occur in multiple directions, along multiple pathways. Clearly, the two positions above make similar claims. What I would like to bring to the debate is the notion of 'boyhood', specifically how the Bond films and games produce an immersive world of masculine violence that confounds typical assumptions regarding male violence in the media and the real.

The Bond(age) of boyhood

Will Coleman suggests that the basic assumption shared by his essay and much current sociological theory is that masculinity is 'socially constructed'. Based upon this notion, two strains of theory have arisen, what Coleman dubs the 'structural' and the 'dramaturgical'. The structural conceives of a masculinity where, 'the individual is treated as the outcome of a developmental process at least in part social' (1990: 186). The dramaturgical posits the 'individual as actor', where masculinity is a constant series of theatrical presentations, changing from one moment to the next. While both of these models may be tenable, I would like to focus on the dramaturgical, how it can be used to describe the Bond masculinity, and how it relates to other theories of gender, sexuality and masculinity. When we consider the type of masculinity attributed to Bond, in the films and in the games, we might first think to ourselves how the Bond character has changed over the years and over the change of actors. Although it seems clear that, while each actor has brought 'personal' attributes to the character, Bond has somehow retained an 'identity through-line'. For instance, while Sean Connery is often described as the 'best' Bond – charismatic, charming, athletic – and Roger Moore is considered a lesser, somewhat more comic Bond, Timothy

Dalton met with little critical or public affection. This could be due to the actor, the historical moment or the movies in which Dalton starred. Regardless, each actor, while staying within the boundaries of accepted Bond character traits, established a type of mark each subsequent performer would have to erase, override or incorporate. This points to how masculinity can be thought of as both grounded (in the sense of Bond's fairly consistent production of a certain type of masculinity) and fluid (as interchangeable as the actors in the role, inhabiting a masculinity that exists with or without them). The 'through-line' can be illustrated by Bond's reaction to and treatment of women in the films and games. For, as an effort is made to keep Bond the same, the position of women has changed drastically around him.

Bond, as played by Brosnan, has arguably the most difficult job in dealing with the diversity of women's roles within the films. In addition, the films, while retaining the basic shape and feel of a Bond film, must somehow represent current gender conflicts. The films featuring Brosnan seem to tackle this in two ways. First, they introduce a seemingly wide variety of women who would presumably react to Bond in ways indicative of their character. There is an evil, hypersexualized female henchwoman, a matriarchal boss, a flirtatious yet resistant administrative assistant, various ingenues who can be both active and/ or passive in the action and storyline, an evil ingenue who doubles as a Bond nemesis, numerous sexual objects, and so on. To Bond, this dizzying array of women represents an intellectual (and sometimes physical) challenge in itself, and becomes a type of sub-plot in each film.

This brings me to my second point. Regardless of the variety of types of stereotyped female that appear in the films, or perhaps in spite of it, Bond seems to have regressed to an even more sexist, misogynist position. Thus, while the Bond masculinity in relation to women is clearly a nostalgic throwback to normative gender roles, heteronormativity and the sexism of the 'Martini culture', Brosnan's Bond seems to respond to these 'uppity' women with ever-more articulated 'bad boy' behaviours — constant references to his penis and virility ('one must rise to the occasion'), his seductions of women in positions of power in order to get what he wants (seducing a psychiatrist sent to evaluate him; a doctor authorised to certify his health), and his constant bucking of authority regarding his new boss, the now-female M. In *GoldenEye* Bond's position in relation to the political scene (and to women) is clarified during a tongue-lashing by M: 'I think you're a sexist, misogynist dinosaur, a relic of the Cold War who's boyish charms that are wasted on me obviously appeal to that young woman I sent out to evaluate you.' Yet, as Bond leaves on assignment, M looks at him and admonishes him to 'come back alive', while attempting to quelch a smile. The fact is Bond's boyish charms do work on M. In fact, they work on everyone, except Electra King, who tries to kill him at the end of *The World is Not Enough*. But this kind of slippage is countered by the fact that Electra is suffering from Stockholm Syndrome. By falling in love with her former captor, Renard, Electra is placed in a position of psychological weakness. While she remains relatively free from the charms of Bond, this is only because her restraints have already been secured by another male.

Bond's method of grappling with these new female subjects (and indeed the film's methods) is to go with what has always worked: his charm. What becomes unbelievable is how Bond always seems to get away with it. His 'Bond mots' seems to get more and more egregious – 'I thought Christmas came only once a year' – and his sexual exploits more and more lascivious. Thus, Bond, in response to this (opaquely) complex world, seems determined to 'prove' his manhood through ascending acts of bravado and sexism. This type of proving is usually the realm of rites of passage from adolescence to manhood, but has become in itself a metaphor for the constant process of the production of masculinity. Timothy Beneke claims that 'boys and men defend themselves against a desire to regress and identify with their mothers through institutionalizing a compulsion to prove their manhood, through creating and conquering stress and distress' (1997: 35). In Bond's case, it seems that he acts more like a boy to insure his manhood. Oh, grow up, 007.

Reconsidering Bond's masculinity in light of this hypersexual regression brings us, in part, back to the dramaturgical model. I return to this in order to identify the structures at work in not only the production of masculinity in the films, but in the playing of the games. As I have said, the liminal space created by the referent films and the interactive games requires the habitation of the Bond character, and by extension the Bond masculinity. I have previously referred to this type of masculinity as 'boyhood'. Like the production of masculinity within the subject, the production of the Bond masculinity in the player is 'in the doing'. Through the repetitive inculcation of play and mastery, through the maintenance of 'stress and distress' and through the formation of a referent reality in the films, the subject is formulated by the ubiquity of representations and the interactivity of play. To play Bond is to perform Bond. And now, to play Bond is to perform Bond's masculinity, and the performance of masculinity itself.

David Savran inspects a variety of 'performative' cultural texts – films, dramatic literature, fiction – and a variety of figurative masculinities – Rambo, Iron John, Forrest Gump, Timothy McVeigh – in order to show that 'modern white masculinities are deeply contradictory, eroticizing submission and victimization while trying to retain a certain aggressively virile edge' (1998: 9). This contradiction leads to the position of victimization and self-abjection Savran identifies as 'reflexive sadomasochism'. He points out that, counter-intuitively, 'reflexive sadomasochism ... with its self-contained, narcissistic system of self gratification, would seem particularly adept at reconstructing an independent, autonomous, masculine subject' (1996: 144). In other words, through violence, torture and other forms of self-inflicted and manufactured pain, the masculine subject not only proves his manhood, but relieves the psychic tension of decentered, white, male subjectivity, particularly in the face of the waning political and social power of the lower-middle and middle-class male. Like Robins and Levidow's 'processes of anxiety and control' and Beneke's 'creating and conquering stress and distress', clear similarities exist between playing the games and playing at masculinity. For Savran, masculine subjects may feel a need to stage their own life and death performance because of a presumed victimhood, as a means of managing the perceived threats of the exterior, and as a method of constantly proving manhood. The Bond myth, in a similar fashion, represents a nationalistic and ideological performance, reproducing the crisis and contradiction of a self-reflexive, sadomasochistic masculinity on national levels.

In Bond videogame play, the player must navigate the space of the game, destroy the enemy, save the women, and do it all under control. In a sense, while the process of managing threat, anxiety and stress may be the same in violent videogame play as it is in the sadomasochist male, in the sadomasochist it is realized through the creation of a real and repetitive pain. Boyhood escapes real pain, regressing back to the safety of pre-adulthood, hiding in the trenches and bunkers of the game-space. Boyhood is, essentially, the recuperation of the immortality of youth, a life without end, a masculinity without pain, a fit and muscular body that enables the revenge of the 'cyber-nerds'. Boyhood is pushing reset. By inhabiting the Bond masculinity, as referenced in the films and performed in the games, the male subject might also be attempting to solve the complex, problematic, shifting nature of masculinity through an (imagined) reintegration of the subject. In this case, playing the games, entering into the circulation of signs, represents a desire to return to a time when the social contract had not yet been signed, as well as a desire to become 'wired', to become part of the simulation. Boyhood is a figurative time 'before' adulthood, and like the repetitive experience of videogaming it is a position that can be accessed for a lifetime, a transcendent technological fusion of man and machine.

Bond's surrogate parents, M and Q, are constantly pleading with him to 'grow up.' But Bond won't. Or can't. Regardless, it is expected that he will win in the end using the very boyhood that seems to mark him as irresponsible, untrustworthy, unaccountable. Boyhood, in general, is identified as a time of irresponsibility, where the young male can 'get away with murder'. This once prevalent view has been problematized in the US by a rash of school shootings, one of which (in Santee, California) occurred as I wrote this essay. Clearly, worries regarding the connection between children, videogames, the media and violence are important areas of research for the future. That said, I chose to focus chiefly on male subjects here in order to address problems of a theoretical nature of use in understanding how the simulated configures the real, and how this alters our perception, reception and production of new media and its relationship to gender. Women and videogames, while not the topic of this essay, is an area that also deserves attention if we are to better understand the nature of interactive media, and what these technologies tell us about how gender is produced and reproduced in the real as well as the virtual.

citations

Baudrillard, Jean (1983) *Simulations*. New York: Semiotext(e).(1991) 'Two Essays', *Science-Fiction Studies*, 18, 3, 309–20.

Beneke, Timothy (1997) *Proving Manhood*. Berkeley: University of California Press.

Bennett, Tony & Janet Woollacott (1987) *Bond and Beyond: The Political Career of a Popular Hero*. London: Macmillan.

Black, Jeremy (2001) *The Politics of James Bond: From Fleming's Novels to the Big Screen.* Westport, CT: Praeger.

Chapman, James (2000) *Licence to Thrill: A Cultural History of the James Bond Films.* New York: Columbia University Press.

Coleman, Will (1990) 'Doing Masculinity/Doing Theory', in Jeff Hearn & David Morgan (eds) *Men, Masculinities and Social Theory.* London: Unwin Hyman, 186—99.

McDonald, Daniel G. & Hyeok Kim (2001) 'When I Die, I Feel Small: Electronic Game Characters and the Social Self', *Journal of Broadcasting and Electronic Media,* 45, 2, 241—358.

Mulvey, Laura (1975) 'Narrative Cinema and Visual Pleasure', *Screen,* 16, 3, 6—18.

Robins, Kevin & Les Levidow (1995) 'Socializing the Cyborg Self: The Gulf War and Beyond', in Chris Hables Gray (ed.) *The Cyborg Handbook.* New York: Routledge, 119—25.

Savran, David (1996) 'The Sadomasochist in the Closet: White Masculinity and the Culture of Vicitmization', *differences,* 8, 2, 127—46.

___ (1998) *Taking it Like a Man: White Masculinity, Masochism and Contemporary Culture.* Princeton, NJ: Princeton University Press.

Schroeder, Randy (1996) 'Playspace Invaders: Huizinga, Baudrillard, and Violent Video Games', *Journal of Popular Culture,* 30, 3, 144—52.

chapter thirteen

'I Know Kung Fu!' The Martial Arts in the Age of Digital Reproduction

leon hunt

What is a cyberpunk action hero supposed to do when he's dragged out of a 'computer-generated dreamworld' and thrust into the 'desert of the real', like a gamer rudely separated from their console or PC? The answer, of course, is to download some combat skills and conquer the virtual world with his 'digital self'.[1] This is the trajectory of Neo (Keanu Reeves), the hero of *The Matrix* (1999). As he downloads martial arts skills from a computer program, an array of fighting styles flicker across the monitor: Ju Jitsu, Drunken Boxing, Taekwondo. Suddenly, he sits up and, with a mixture of shock and pleasure, utters the line that prefaces this essay. Neo's implanted 'knowledge' offers a metaphor for two ways in which Asian martial arts have been reconfigured in contemporary culture: arcade, console and PC 'beat-em-up' games, and the transformation of Hollywood stars into martial arts action heroes. I first 'knew' kung fu when I bought a PlayStation specifically to play *Tekken 3* (Namco, 1998) because of my love of kung fu films. Keanu Reeves, Tom Cruise (*Mission: Impossible 2*, 2000) and the cast of *Charlie's Angels* (US, 2000) came to 'know' kung fu through Hong Kong choreographers like Yuen Wo-ping, Hong Kong-style 'wirework'[2] and CGI effects. Recent Hollywood action films have gone to considerable lengths to appropriate the 'look' of Hong Kong films; Hong Kong films have, in turn, drawn on the stylisations of computer games and vice versa; martial arts films and games have both incorporated aspects of Japanese Manga (comics) and *anime* (animation), again in a mutual exchange. Mary Fuller and Henry Jenkins once wondered whether Japan's colonisation of digital space in games represented 'Asia's absorption of (North America's) national imaginary' or a more 'dialogic' relationship marked by an 'intermixing of cultural traditions' (1995: 71–2). The interface between martial arts games and films seems to me to be a three-way dialogue, not simply dependent on East-West binaries: Hollywood ('blockbuster'-spectacle, CGI, *The Matrix*), Japan (*anime*, Manga) and Hong Kong (action aesthetics, kung fu films and stars).

The Matrix explicitly evokes the world of computer games when Morpheus (Lawrence Fishburne) describes 'a world without rules and controls, without borders or boundaries, a world where anything is possible'. But it also references kung fu and *anime* such as *Ghost in the Shell* (1995); producer Joel Silver called it 'full-cel animation, only with people' (quoted in Clarke 1999: 24). The sparring program Neo plugs into is essentially a virtual elaboration of the training mode available in most beat-em-ups. But just as fighting games 'download' kung fu stars and films, so, too, does *The Matrix*. Neo's 'digital self' mimics Bruce Lee (cockily thumbing his nose), borrows the signature stance of legendary hero Wong Fei-hung (arm extended, palm turned upwards in 'invitation') and Jet Li's wire-aided mid-air kicks from *Fist of Legend* (1994). *The Matrix* is especially interesting because, in its comic book way, it is concerned with the 'real' and the 'virtual' and their relationship with a spectacle founded on physical performance. These are important issues for the martial arts genre, in both its filmic and gaming forms, because of their relationship to discourses of 'authenticity'. If digital spectacle is supposedly about 'surpassing the real' (Hayward & Wollen 1993: 1), the kung fu film has a history of investing in the 'real' — the physical authenticity of Bruce Lee and Jackie Chan, the documentary accuracy of the Shaolin forms displayed in films like *The 36th Chamber of Shaolin* (1978). At one level, games have sought to refashion this cinematic authenticity through mimetic fidelity. For a gaming aesthete like Steven Poole, motion-capture can be 'aesthetically impoverishing' because it 'limits the achievable virtual movements and gestures to those that are physically possible in real life' (Poole 2000: 154), but most polygon-based beat-em-ups use the movements of real martial artists as a signifier of authenticity.[3] Motion capture can also add a degree of stylistic authenticity, either by synthesising an existing fighting style or adding 'realistic' touches to more fantastic characters. In *Tekken 3*, the Taekwondo kicks of Hwoa-rang are based on world champion Suira Huang, while Space Ninja Yoshimitsu incorporates some of the signature moves of Pancratium Master, Minoru Suzuki (see Mortlock 1998: 21). Like martial arts films, games such as *Tekken* and *Virtual Fighter* (AM2/Sega, 1996) seek to enhance the 'real', to bend its rules rather than escape it altogether. On the other hand, games offer their own hyperreal authenticity, what Jay David Bolter and Richard Grusin call 'authenticity of experience' (2000: 71), which has, in turn, impacted on the martial arts film.

The Matrix is at the centre of these paradoxes and sends out mixed messages about technological and 'authentic' spectacle, about the real and the digital. According to Manohla Dargis, it created 'a new kind of action hero, one heavily predicated on digital effects' (2000: 23). But publicity also made great capital out of Yuen Wo-ping's input into the fight scenes. Yuen insisted on the cast being trained to perform their own martial arts stunts, a practice carried over into *Charlie's Angels* by Yuen Cheung-yan. *The Matrix* did not just set a new standard for special effects; it also appeared to initiate a trend for 'authenticating' Hollywood stars, as though to counter the 'oft-repeated threat that [the] digital will eventually render the human actor superfluous' (Dargis 2000: 23). In *Charlie's Angels*, we are clearly meant to be impressed by the fruits of the stars' four months' training: 'That *is* Drew [Barrymore], that *is* Cameron [Diaz] and that *is* Lucy [Liu]. They're all doing their own stunts and they're all doing their own thing,' enthuses director McG on the DVD commentary. But where do *The Matrix* and *Tekken* leave stars such as Jackie Chan and Jet Li, the former the star of his own game (*Jackie Chan Stuntmaster* (Radical/Midway, 2000)), the latter given uncomfortable digital treatment in the film *Romeo Must Die* (2000)? What then is the place of the performing body and the 'star' (real or virtual) in new digital technologies?

Bust-a-move: martial arts films and games[4]

According to one players' guide, a skillful *Tekken* bout is 'like watching a good Kung Fu film' (see Mortlock 1998: 18), while, on the other hand, the film adaptation of *Mortal Kombat* (1995) left one underwhelmed critic feeling that its fight scenes were like 'watching someone playing the game badly rather than feeling as if you are in the game itself' (Felperin 1995: 48). What this suggests is that fight games refashion kung fu movies while simultaneously distinguishing themselves by their heightened *immersiveness* (being 'in the game itself').

In terms of adaptations, the martial arts film/game crossover has been almost entirely one-way: from game to film (and TV) rather than the other way around. *Street Fighter 2* (Capcom, 1991) spawned two feature films, the live-action *Street Fighter: The Movie* (1994) starring Jean-Claude Van Damme, and a more faithful *anime* version (Japan, 1994) which retained the 'special moves' from the game. Animated *Street Fighters* have also materialised on television and DVD-only releases (*Street Fighter Alpha/Zero: The Animation* (1999)). Jackie Chan bought the rights to *Street Fighter 2* and included a brief parody of the game in *City Hunter* (1993), while *Future Cops* (1994) also deployed thinly disguised *Street Fighter* characters. The ultraviolent *Mortal Kombat* (Midway, 1992) generated two feature films, an animated TV series and a live-action TV series. While there is presently talk of a series of *Crouching Tiger, Hidden Dragon* games, to date there has been no martial arts equivalent of the *Die Hard* or James Bond games.

It is more useful to think of the kung fu/beat-em-up interface in terms of what Bolter and Grusin call 'remediation', the process whereby a medium 'appropriates the techniques, forms and social significance of other media and attempts to rival or refashion them in the name of the real' (2000: 65). Fight games remediate varying combinations of four media forms: kung fu films, *anime*, manga and wrestling.[5] But this is not simply a linear, successive process, because sometimes media *remediate* each other. Kung fu films, in the first instance, remediate forms such as Beijing Opera (graceful, acrobatic performance) and the storylines, heroic codes and extraordinary feats of *wu xia pian* (martial chivalry) fiction. But in recent years, martial arts films and games have been engaged in a process of mutual remediation. Kung fu films use wirework and SFX to recreate the digital spectacle of hi-tech games, just as those games use motion-capture to simulate real martial arts moves and stunts. In *Dead or Alive 2* (Tecmo, 2000), Kasumi's 'Heaven Cascading Kick' — a staccato tap-dance on her (standing) opponent's head — goes one step further than the wire-enhanced stunts of Hong Kong cinema. On the other hand, Ayane's pirouetting slaps are harder to imagine in a film, but draw on the spinning/twisting dynamics of martial arts choreography. Games also remediate the 'presence' of martial arts stars. *Tekken*'s Lei Wulong is widely taken to be Jackie Chan, even down to his Drunken Master style,[6] but his Shaolin animal styles suggest a broader-based remediation of the kung fu star. His endgame film in *Tekken 3*, for example, alludes to the 'Four Seasons' training sequence from Jet Li's debut film, *Shaolin Temple* (1982).

Bolter and Grusin also provide some ways of thinking about authenticity in the digital age, although their conclusions are somewhat different from those of Walter Benjamin, who places 'authenticity' alongside 'presence' and 'aura' (1979: 851–2), each always eluding technical reproducibility. They suggest, rather, that 'remediation does not destroy the aura of the work of art; instead it always refashions that aura in another media form' (Bolter & Grusin 2000: 75). New media have two seemingly opposed, but in fact closely interlinked goals: *transparent immediacy*, which seeks to render mediation invisible, and *hypermediacy*, which foregrounds it (2000: 272). At one level, these goals are poles apart — one is characterised by invisibility, the other by opacity of mediation (2000: 70–1). But Bolter and Grusin suggest that each also embodies the same desire 'to get past the limits of representation and to achieve the real ... that which would evoke an immediate (and therefore authentic) emotional response' (2000: 53). Transparent immediacy facilitates a feeling of 'presence', while in the case of hypermediacy, the 'experience of the medium is itself an experience of the real' (2000: 71). In other words, authenticity (of experience) does not disappear. Martial arts films have had to respond to this logic, wherein the 'real' has been refashioned by hypermedia. Bruce Lee's films offer a kind of transparent immediacy — 'presence' and 'authenticity' are guaranteed by the invisibility of his cinematic mediation. Jackie Chan is a much more mediated performer, but is able to re-inscribe his 'presence' in other ways. Jet Li is the most visibly mediated of the three, precisely because of the contemporary synergy between films and games; state-of-the-art wirework is almost an analogue approximation of digital spectacle. Games are both more and less 'real' than Bruce Lee and Jackie Chan, offering an authenticity and intensity of experience that transparent immediacy might not be able to match. Choreographer Yuen Wo-ping has expressed a desire to make the audience 'feel the blow' (Bordwell 2000: 244), but the PlayStation's Dual Shock Controller ensures that you can't *not* feel it. Similarly, digital regimes have transformed our perception of speed. Games such as *Bloody Roar 2* (Eighting/Raizing/Hudson, 1999) and *Dead or Alive 2* move at a dizzying velocity. While *The Matrix*'s computerised 'bullet-time' photography abstracts speed, Hong Kong cinema's comparatively lo-tech undercranking captures both the precision and technologically enhanced velocity of motion-captured action. Donnie Yen's 'Shadowless kick' in *Iron Monkey* (1993) is almost identical to Chun-Li's rapid-fire multi-kicks in *Street Fighter Ex 3*.

Martial arts pervade a number of gaming genres, most notably third-person role-playing games like *Oni* (Bungie/GodGames, 2001), where they are part of the central character's combat skills. But the purest distillation of the genre is the beat-em-up, where narrative is largely relegated to extra-textual backstory (endgame films, the often tortuous plots in the games' booklets). The game itself comprises a series of fights within a tournament structure, culminating in a battle with the main boss, usually a malignant patriarch like Bison (*Street Fighter*) or Heihachi Mishima (*Tekken*). Beat-em-ups first appeared in arcades between 1984 and 1985; *Karate Champ* (Data East, 1984) kicked off in the arcades, while *Kung Fu* (Bug Byte, 1984) brought the genre to the PC. Fondly remembered games like *Way of the Exploding Fist* (Melbourne House, 1985) and *Yie Ar Kung Fu* (Konami, 1985) had a limited range of moves, but introduced some of the basics of the genre (such as the best-of-three fight structure). But Steven Poole is not alone in proclaiming *Street Fighter 2* (Capcom, 1991) — a hugely popular refinement of the more modestly successful *Street Fighter* (1987) — the first modern fight game (2000: 45). *SF2* offered more sophisticated gameplay through the innovation of 'combos' (continuous animations produced by elaborate button sequences). It offered selectable characters, organised along lines of cultural, ethnic and stylistic difference — from Japanese and American Karate masters Ryu and Ken to Muay Thai Boxer Sagat and Indian Yoga Master, Dhalsim. It was a more notably cinematic game in its global *mise-en-scène* — 'a Brazilian dock, an Indian temple, a Chinese street market, a Soviet factory, a Las Vegas show palace' (Fuller & Jenkins 1995: 62) — and the visual excesses of its fireball-throwing 'special moves'.

SF2's International Martial Arts Tournament and its global cast of characters suggest that the cinematic model for the beat-em-up was *Enter the Dragon* (1973). Bruce Lee's final completed film revolves around a tournament organised by an Evil Mastermind — 'Final Boss' Han (Shek Kin) is the predecessor of Heihachi and Bison, supported by formidable sub-bosses (Oharra and Bolo). The tournament structure allows narrative to progress *through* a series of fights; the climactic Hall of Mirrors would make an effective game level. The three heroes anticipate the racial-cultural inclusivity of fighting games: Chinese Lee (Bruce Lee), white American smoothie Roper (John Saxon) and African-American Williams (Jim Kelly). Like beat-em-up characters, Lee, Roper and Williams are all backstory; each is given flashback to motivate their entry into the tournament (revenge/honour, gambling debts, problems with racist cops).

But *SF2* has other cinematic referents for its visual spectacle, which conspicuously avoids the B-movie ambience of *Enter the Dragon*. Fireball attacks and other special moves derive equally from the 'Palm Power' and Flying Swords of Chinese *wu xia pian* (martial chivalry film) and the extravagant death moves of Kenshiro, the post-apocalyptic hero of manga/*anime*, *Fist of the North Star*. Chinese martial arts films have long had a *fantastique* tradition dependent on special effects: wires, reverse footage, even animation. 'Palm Power' could propel flying daggers and thunderbolts from the hands of Taoist masters, or characters could use *qi* (internal power) to 'drive a sword flying like a rainbow and behead enemies hundreds of miles away', a technique 'as accurate as any modern day missile system' (Hong Kong Film Archive 1999: 40). As this description suggests, such powers evoke technology as much as mystical expertise. Digital technology first infiltrated the martial arts film in *Zu Warriors of the Magic Mountain* (1982), which employed Western special effects experts for its mythical tale of wizards, blood demons, flying swordsmen and white-haired masters with improbably long, but usefully combat-ready, eyebrows. *Zu* now looks like an interesting hybrid of technologies: western optical effects, wirework and pixillated animation. But digital effects were not fully integrated into Hong Kong martial arts films until recent movies such as *Storm Riders* (1998), which included 550 shots (approximately 40 minutes) using CGI (Hong Kong Film Archive 1999: 50). Digital spectacle was now central to devastating moves such as the 'Whirlwind Kick' and the 'Cloud-Discharging Palm'.

In *Fist of the North Star,* a Manga-derived *anime* TV serial (1984–88), Kenshiro's 'Sacred Martial Art of the Great Bear' attacks pressure points, causing exploding heads and bodies (gory 'fatalities' that anticipate the head, heart and spine-removals of *Mortal Kombat*). Woe betides anyone on the receiving end of 'The Gate of Life with a Thousand Fists of Destruction' or 'North Star's Flowing Dance of Ultimate Emptiness'. Not only do these moves sound as though they should be accompanied by joypad button combinations, but their titles appear as onscreen captions as Kenshiro administers them. As one writer notes, the narrative follows an 'arcade game-style progression' (Swallow 1999: 30), as Kenshiro tackles bigger and more lethal opponents. Like the *fantastique* swordplay films of Hong Kong or Science Fiction *anime*, fight game combos may be 'special effects' pyrotechnics as much as recognisable fighting techniques. In *Street Fighter EX 3* (Capcom, 2000), Zangief's 'Corkscrew Slam' lifts his opponent out of the earth's orbit before descending with a bone-shattering powerslam. *Bloody Roar 2* already encompasses werewolf-style transformations, but Bakuryu's 'Double Inferno Hell' is especially apocalyptic, surrounding his opponent within a circle of flames that incinerates them at the point of two intersecting fiery lines.

The remediation of martial arts stars is the closest fight games have come to film adaptations. Bruce Lee and Jackie Chan have appeared in several games, and, more recently, Jet Li has talked about developing his own game. *Bruce Lee* (US Gold, 1985) was one of the earliest fighting games, a platform game that has Lee fighting his way through a maze to defeat a wizard. Lee has been more vividly represented when his presence is 'unofficial': Fei Long (*Super Street Fighter 2* (Capcom, 1993)), Jann Lee (*Dead or Alive* 2) and, above all, Forest Law (*Tekken 3, Tekken Tag Tournament*). Law has Lee's hairstyle and face, a similar vocal repertoire of shrieks and squawks and seems to have inherited his onscreen wardrobe. He also reproduces several moves from *Enter the* Dragon: a headlock kick, a backflip somersault kick.

Chan has appeared officially in *Jackie Chan's Action Kung Fu* (1988) on the PC, and *Jackie Chan: Kung Fu Master* (1993), an arcade game in Asia only (see Beale & Simons 2000: 19). *Jackie Chan Stuntmaster* is more ambitious, an attempt to transform an all-purpose (if distinctly westernised) 'Jackie Chan film' into a third-person adventure game. Chan was motion-captured for the game and also provides his own voice: 'Don't leave me!' he wails when the game is paused, or, when admonishing villains during a fight, 'I am *very* angry with you'. Most entertainingly, the game features 'out-takes' of the digitised Chan getting his FMV stunts wrong; alas, awkward controls mean the gameplay often resembles these outtakes. In Chan's films, the end-credit out-takes serve both to authenticate Chan — by showing his on-set injuries — and to undercut the invincibility of the action hero (don't try this at home). In *Stuntmaster,* the in-joke both distances Chan from the digital — virtual stunts are risk-free — and further synthesises his vulnerable 'presence'. The game's blocky visual style seems to make few concessions to mimetic realism in its character design, yet motion-capture is evident in the inimitable dynamics of Chan's perpetual motion. He can reach ledges by bouncing off the opposite wall and is literally never still (he fidgets, practices kung fu or sings if the player is slow in operating him). *Stuntmaster* captures some of the good-natured ethos of Chan's films. He will often try to talk henchmen out of fighting him, and the fights are given a comic edge. Like his cinematic counterpart, Jackie uses objects as makeshift weapons: brooms, tables, frying pans and, most pleasing of all, a very large fish.

Like Lee, Chan has also had unofficial game incarnations. *Tekken*'s Lei Wulong performs the Drunken Fist made famous by Chan in *Drunken Master* (1978) and *Drunken Master 2* (1994), while full-motion video sequences connect him to both Chan's *Police Story* series (he is a Hong Kong cop) and more 'classical' kung fu films (Buddhist Temples, flowing silk robes).

Perhaps the most important relationship between the Hong Kong martial arts film and games is in their *affectivity* — their capacity to act directly on the body. In *The Cinematic Body*, Steven Shaviro's 'mimetic, tactile, and corporeal' cinema (1993: 55) leaves out Hong Kong action, yet could easily be describing a great kung fu film or, indeed, any immersive game: an 'ecstasy of expenditure ... and self-abandonment ... the blinding intoxication of contact with the Real' (1993: 54), wherein the body is defined by its 'capacity for being affected' (1993: 59). Most games vary their pace and pleasures, alternating between puzzle-solving, shooting, searching, climbing, jumping. But the beat-em-up offers relentless excitation, constant gratification or its opposite, abject defeat; in *Tekken Tag Tournament*, one's fallen 'digital selves' sink to their knees in humiliation.

For David Bordwell, Hong Kong cinema is the ultimate tactile cinema. Not only does it have the largest performative repertoire of any popular cinema, but its cinematic arsenal carries a multitude of ways of generating a kinaesthetic response; 'the films seem to ask our bodies to recall elemental and universal events like striking, swinging, twisting, leaping, rolling' (2000: 244). Bordwell makes these films sound even more like games in the way they 'offer us the illusion of mastering the action ... the kinetics have stamped the action's rhythm onto our senses' (*Ibid.*).

To make the connection between kung fu films, fighting games and cyber-action like *The Matrix*, it is useful here to refer to Alison Landsberg's notion of 'prosthetic memory', 'memories which do not come from a person's lived experience' (1995: 75). Landsberg cites 1930s empirical/effects research into the sensorial/emotional effects of movies. Phrases such as 'imaginative identification' and 'emotional possession' suggest ways in which media images affect spectators so powerfully that they become 'part of their personal archive of experience' (1995: 179). One might argue that kung fu films' tactile pleasures, *Tekken*'s immersive digital combat and Neo's downloaded skills offer 'prosthetic memories' of mastering martial skills. When Landsberg suggests that mass media 'might be an undertheorised force in the production of identities' (1995: 177), she anticipates Bolter and Grusin's notion of the 'remediated self', the way that 'new media offer new opportunities for self-definition, for now we can identify with the vivid graphics and digitized videos of computer games' (Bolter & Grusin 2000: 231). Her arguments also suggest that identification in games might blur 'real' and 'virtual' memories more than films do. After playing for a lengthy period, I sometimes find myself dreaming in 'PlayStation Vision', as though digital afterimages of action/adventure remain imprinted on the retina. In what ways does this reinforce the memories of my *Tekken*-self, who has won and lost fights in Chinese temples, Aztec ruins and Japanese schoolyards?

Downloading authenticity: the *Tekken* series

Authenticity in fight games can take a number of forms: mimetic realism/motion-capture, immersion/transparency ('feeling' the game), 'cinematic' qualities (Hong Kong-style aerodynamics), recognisable moves and fighting styles, a satisfying 'learning curve'. Poole suggests there is a tension in the genre's aesthetic development between a visual excess facilitated by increasingly powerful consoles, on the one hand, and some nominal realism on the other (2000: 45). Nevertheless, I would suggest that some notion of authenticity remains central to the best-known games.[7]

Three franchises have been especially prominent in the aesthetic evolution of the beat-em-up. *Street Fighter* initiated special moves and combos, *Mortal Kombat* used digitized actors to give greater realism to its fighters, and *Virtual Fighter* was the first fighting game to use polygons to create a 3D look. If each of these games innovated, *Tekken* has arguably consolidated their innovations rather than adding new ones, yet it is one of the most popular and aesthetically evolved fight game series.

Tekken was one of the first games to appear on the Sony PlayStation and the first PS game to sell more than a million copies (see Hill 1998: 152). Namco, the game's publisher, had developed the first polygon-based system board and signed exclusively to design games for Sony (see Parkinson 2000: 11). *Tekken* appeared in arcades in 1994 and moved to the fledgling console in 1995, shortly after the PlayStation's launch. The game's aesthetic development has been driven by technological improvements. *Tekken 2* (arcade 1995, PS 1996) added more characters and modes, 60 frames-per-second animation and improved light sourcing, which added texture and shadow. The original PlayStation could barely accommodate the technical advances in *Tekken 3* (arcade 1997, PS 1998). Namco had developed a more powerful arcade board (the System 12) and only a combination of compression and background reduction could fit the game on the more modest System 11 board (see Parkinson 2000: 13). The game made more extensive use of motion capture and 3D body movement (including side-stepping). *Tekken Tag Tournament* (2000) was one of the first games to test out the more powerful PS2 (or not, as some critics suggested). As its name suggests, the game deployed tag team battles, but otherwise used the PS2 to make the game more aesthetically pleasing, with moving backgrounds and enhanced detail (we can see Ling Xiaoyu blink as she fights and get the full benefit of Law's facial Lee-impersonation). Its PS2 rival *Dead or Alive 2* also used tag fighting (and did it rather better), but emphasised three-dimensional, interactive space rather than the detail and sparkle of *Tekken Tag*'s backgrounds. *DOA2* brings its *mise-en-scène* into the action, with exploding walls, multi-level sets, waterfalls to be kicked *off* and walls to be kicked *through*. In the Dragon Hills set, combatants can be sent hurtling over the side (with the other fighter floating 'weightlessly' down to continue the assault) or sent through a wall into an elaborate temple setting below. For some gaming magazines, *DOA2* was the more innovative game, not least for its extensive countering system; carefully timed use of the counter button could follow blocks with elaborate reversals making the game more tactical than the all-out attack of other fighters. But later reviews found *DOA2* lacking the depth of the more cautious *Tekken Tag*. The latter had a greater range of moves and techniques distributed amongst its 34 plus characters and required one to *learn* these moves as opposed to the instant button-mashing thrills of *DOA2*.

Although *Tekken* has a range of fantasy characters, its main focus is on Japanese, Chinese, Thai and Korean martial arts, as well as the more transnational conventions of wrestling. The literal authenticity of martial arts in fighting games is, by necessity, limited. Lei Wulong's Five Animal Shaolin style is less 'authentic' than the moves documented in 1970s martial arts films, and draws instead on the *idea* of Tiger- or Snake-based attacks. That said, 'real' moves are added to more dynamically fabricated ones: his 'Snake Bite' remediates *qing she chu dong* (snake comes out of his hole), a sequence of coiled fingertip strikes. The real Five Animals system distributes 128 moves across five animal impersonations designed to balance hard/external with soft/internal power (see Wong & Hallander 1988: 5). Dragon, Snake and Crane are comparatively soft and fluid, with sudden explosive attacks mimicking a cobra's head or crane's beak, while Tiger and Leopard are aggressive, powerful forces. The hard and the soft, the external and the internal, describe the difference between meeting force with force and yielding/flowing in order that opposing strength is used against itself. Such principles — fundamental to Chinese martial arts — mean very little in digital space except as aesthetic surface. Their importance in *Tekken*, however, is in distinguishing Lei's fluidity from the more aggressive styles of Jin Kazama, Hwoarang and Paul Phoenix. Ling Xiaoyu, meanwhile, draws extensively on balletic *wu shu*, with graceful sweeps and wide, extravagant stances; like Lei, she is a stance-based fighter and more difficult to learn than the Japanese or Korean boxers.

Some of Lei's multi-part moves are thrilling in their complexity and precision, but I always wonder what I'm thrilled *by* — am I seeing *through* the technology to the (diminished) aura of the motion-captured martial artist? The mutual dynamic of remediation means that the cinematic is the most constant authenticating referent. Where games surpass films, at least in this genre, is in their mastery of space and their technologically enhanced tactility. Many kung fu films have rather impoverished backdrops, and even the most lavish cannot match *Tekken Tag's* *mise-en-scène*: gothic chambers with fire-breathing gargoyles, helicopter launch pads that double as steel-mesh wrestling rings as guards patrol below, Shaolin monks performing 'stamping' exercises in a courtyard of Golden Buddhas.[8] On the other hand, shock-dispensing joypads, fast-cut action replays and inevitable kinaesthetic identification may have set new challenges for film choreography, but the kinetic pleasures of fighting games remain rooted in remediated martial arts action and a cinematic construction of the authentic.

From wire-fu to cyber-fu: did video(games) kill the kung fu star?

Motion capture has helped create 'digital' characters and performances in films such as *Star Wars: Episode 1 — The Phantom Menace* (1999) and *The Mummy* (1999), while games already have their own hyperreal star system; these phenomena combine in *Final Fantasy: The Spirits Within* (2001). Walter Benjamin once argued that the 'cult of the movie star' was symptomatic of the 'shrivelling of the aura with an artificial build-up of the "personality"' (1979: 860); how could he have foreseen the reign of Lara Croft, a star 'built completely from the ground up' (Poole 2000: 151)? By Benjamin's logic, the shrivelling of 'aura' into 'personality' further diminishes into 'design'. Ackbar Abbas suggested that the 'real' was now 'co-produced' by special effects in modern martial arts films like *Once Upon a Time in China* (1991) (1997: 32). Such effects were *not* digital, as they are now in films like *Crouching Tiger, Hidden Dragon* (2000), but can be seen as having been determined by digital regimes. The question is: are performance and technology equal partners in this 'co-production' now that special effects are at least partly digital?

Romeo Must Die was arguably the most contentious of the recent CGI-enhanced martial arts-based films to be influenced by *The Matrix*, and offers a limit-case for CGI-aided martial arts action. *Romeo* was ostensibly a vehicle for a kung fu star, Jet Li, but if CGI offered new possibilities for the cast of *The Matrix*, it was seen by many fans not to enhance but to diminish and 'waste' a performer of Li's talent. The film reflects the game/movie interface through two types of visual excess. The first was referred to as 'Ultra Pain Mode', computer-animated 'X-ray' shots used to represent internal injuries inflicted by Li's character, Han Sing. During the climactic fight, the camera follows the flow of *qi* through someone's shattering spine. In both name and effect, this 'mode' evokes the hyper-mediated violence of fight games, especially those, like *Mortal Kombat*, which fetishize physical damage. Secondly, CGI was used not only to remove wires from shots, but in at least one case, to digitally combine shots. In one scene, Li rotates horizontally in mid-air to kick a collection of heavies, 'reverses' onto a ledge and then jumps down to deliver a couple more kicks. This 'continuous' take was in fact three 'morphed' shots, which already relied on digitally removed wirework. Li had long been the most wired-up of kung fu stars, but the fan response on the Internet suggests that this was a step too far. I suspect that the main source of contention was the impression that Li had been motion-captured, that the kung fu star had been reduced to an animated combo: 'The fighting just plain sucks ...

because it's all made up, with computers and wire-assisted jumps' (Petrigato). But the most overmediated moment in *Romeo* is quickly followed by the blinding return of the real: Jet Li's virtuoso use of a firehose as a rope dart, circling and spinning in a way that only a highly trained physical performer can. It would take more than four months' training to get Keanu or Cameron to do *that*, and, as yet, technology might 'capture' it but never surpass it. In the case of martial arts, at least, it is not just films and games that remediate one another, but, by necessity, technology and the body. The martial artist's body may be extensively (re)mediated, but technology has yet to make it disappear.

notes

1 Steven Poole suggests that fighting computer games update the medieval sublimation of combat into play-form; 'fighting is performed on the player's behalf by a digital "substitute"' (175—6).

2 Chinese martial arts films have a long history of using wires to make characters fly or perform 'weightless' leaps. Primitive wirework can be traced back to Shanghai-produced films such as *The Burning of the Red Lotus Monastery* (1928), but became much more sophisticated in post-1980s Hong Kong films such as *Once Upon a Time in China* (1991).

3 Motion-capture refers to the technique of placing computerised sensors on the bodies of human performers, whose movements can be incorporated into digital characters. Poole's suspicion of the purely mimetic recalls an earlier debate surrounding animation.

4 *Bust-a-Move* was the name of an early computer puzzle game, but interestingly the phrase is now used in the fan culture surrounding Hong Kong action films. Being able to bust-a-move refers to a performer's onscreen martial arts abilities, especially those who 'throw shapes' (intricate stances and styles).

5 Most beat-'em-ups have at least one wrestler, such as the masked Kings in *Tekken* or father-daughter Bass and Tina in *Dead or Alive 2*. Wrestling moves defy, or reinvent, aerodynamics almost as much as kung fu films do, albeit as live spectacle. Fighting arenas are sometimes based on rings or Octagons, while *Dead or Alive 2*'s exploding walls recall the C4-charged ring posts of Japanese 'garbage' wrestling. Wrestling has, of course, generated its own games, remediating stars such as The Rock and The Undertaker. By Christmas 2000, *WWF: Smackdown 2* (Yuke's/THQ) was the biggest selling PlayStation game ever.

6 *Joi-kuen*, or Drunken Fist, is a style of kung fu based on the performance of 'drunkenness': the fighter sways and staggers, but the appearance of helpless intoxication is belied by sudden devastating attacks.

7 Of course, many gamers will not share hardcore kung fu fans' investment in 'authenticity'. However, I suspect that many beat-em-up aficionados will also be fans of kung fu films or have an interest in the martial arts. In terms of consumer choice, this split is perhaps reflected in the tension Poole identifies between virtual spectacle for its own sake (*Street Fighter*, *Bloody Roar*) and mimetic realism (*Tekken*, *Virtua Fighter*, *Dead or Alive*). *Street Fighter*'s 2D *anime* visuals suggest that it is the franchise that invests least in (3D) cinematic mimesis.

8 In a gaming genre that ostensibly offers little variation, elaborate *mise-en-scène* is an important form of product differentiation.

citations

Abbas, Ackbar (1997) *Hong Kong: Culture and the Politics of Disappearance*. Minneapolis: University of Minnesota Press.

Beale, Chris & Ben Simons (2000) 'Retroflex Column: It's Only a Game, Son!', *Screen Power*, 3, 1, 18—20.

Benjamin, Walter (1979) 'The Work of Art in the Age of Mechanical Reproduction', in Gerald Mast & Marshall Cohen (eds) *Film Theory and Criticism*. New York and Oxford: Oxford University Press, 848—70.

Bolter, Jay David & Grusin, Richard (2000) *Remediation: Understanding New Media*. Cambridge, Massachusetts and London: MIT Press.

Bordwell, David (2000) *Planet Hong Kong: Popular Cinema and the Art of Entertainment*. Cambridge, Massachusetts and London: Harvard University Press.

Clarke, Jeremy (1999) 'Schismatrix', *Manga Max*, 8, 22—4.

Dargis, Manohla (2000) 'Ghost in the Machine', *Sight and Sound*, 10, 7, 20—3.

Felperin, Leslie (1995) *'Mortal Kombat,'* *Sight and Sound*, 5, 11, 47—8.

Fuller, Mary & Jenkins, Henry (1995) 'Nintendo and New World Travel Writing: A Dialogue', in Steven G. Jones (ed.) *Cybersociety: Computer-Mediated Communication and Community*. Thousand Oaks, London and New Delhi: Sage, 57—72.

Hayward, Philip & Tana Wollen (eds) (1993) *Future Visions: New Technologies on the Screen*. London: BFI.

Hill, Simon (1998) *Tekken 3 — Prima's Official Strategy Guide*. Rocklin, California: Prima.

Hong Kong Film Archive (1999) *The Making of Martial Arts Films — As Told By Filmmakers and Stars*. Hong Kong: HK Film Archive/Provisional Urban Council.

Landsberg, Alison (1995) 'Prosthetic Memory: *Total Recall* and *Blade Runner*', in Mike Featherstone & Roger Burrows (eds) *Cyberspace/Cyberbodies/Cyberpunk: Cultures of Technological Embodiment*. London, Thousand Oaks and New Delhi: Sage, 175—89.

Lau Shing-hon (ed.) (1981) *A Study of the Hong Kong Swordplay Film 1945—1980*. Hong Kong: Urban Council of Hong Kong.

Masinelli, Todd (2000) 'Jackie Chan Stuntmaster', *Screen Power*, 3, 1, 15—17.

Mortlock, Dean (ed.) (1998) *Playstation Game Strategies Number One — Tekken 3*. Bath: Future Publishing.

Parkinson, Emma (ed.) (2000) *Tekken Tag Tournament: The Official Guide*. Bath: Future Publishing.

Petrigato, 'User Comments', Internet Movie Data Base. Available on-line at: http://us.imdb.com/commentsShow?165929/60

Poole, Steven (2000) *Trigger Happy: The Inner Life of Videogames*. London: Fourth Estate.

Shaviro, Steven (1993) *The Cinematic Body*. Minneapolis and London: University of Minnesota Press.

Swallow, Jim (1999) 'Way of the Fist', *Manga Max*, 4, 28—31.

Watson, Paul & Amos Wong (1999) 'Streetfighting Man', *Manga Max*, 5, 18—22.

Wong, Doc-Fai & Hallander (1988) *Shaolin Five Animals Kung Fu*. Burbank: Unique Publications.

chapter fourteen

Hands-On Horror

tanya krzywinska

'It troubles me that an anonymous oracle knows more of my business than I do.'

— Alice

Figure 15 *American McGee's Alice* (Rogue/EA, 2000)

'Can you survive the horror?' asks the cover of *Resident Evil 2* (Capcom/Virgin Interactive, 1998). The question works at a number of levels to place the game within the rhetoric of the horror film. Yet something greater is needed to survive the specifically interactive nature of the horror game: have you the will power to learn the skills needed to withstand the onslaught of evil monsters and restore equilibrium? In contrast to film, games place a strong emphasis on the act of *doing* that extends beyond the kinetic and emotional responses that are common in cinema. Espen Aarseth proposes the term 'ergodic' to identify forms in which 'nontrivial effort is required to allow the reader to traverse the text' (1997: 1). The task undertaken in this chapter is to explore how this affects the shape and pleasures of horror-based videogames, demonstrating some of their formal differences from cinematic horror. Films based on games — most notably *Resident Evil* (2002) — bear only superficial resemblance to the originals. Despite some references to the games, films such as *Resident Evil* do not adopt aspects of the specific formal nature of their game counterparts (see the introduction to this volume). *Resident Evil 3: Nemesis* (Capcom/Eidos, 1999) and *Clive Barker's Undying* (ELEA/EA, 2001) will be used to show how these horror games organise and manage the game-playing experience to create suspense and tension. The formal structures of the two games will be addressed first, with attention placed on certain key differences from and similarities to the horror film; this material will then be used to indicate the specific types of pleasures offered.

The analysis is framed by my argument that these games are structured at deep and surface levels according to the principles of a 'manichean' moral duality,[1] a factor that the games share with many horror films. This binary structure is embedded within the interactive dimension of the games. Its presence suggests that the pleasures of playing such games hinge on a dynamic experience that oscillates between *doing* and *not doing*. In each game there are periods in which the player is in control of gameplay and at others not, creating a dynamic rhythm between self-determination and pre-determination. This rhythm is present in most games, yet in these particular games it takes on a generically apposite resonance within the context of horror because it ties into and consolidates formally a theme often found in horror in which supernatural forces act on, and regularly threaten, the sphere of human agency. The surface level and deep manichean structure further operates as a containing safety net for the experience of being out of control. My main contention is that the interactive dimension of these particular games is organised to intensify and extend the types of emotional and affective experiences offered by the horror film.

The horror genre has made the transition to videogames for a number of reasons. Horror offers death as spectacle and actively promises transgression; it has the power to promote physical sensation, and the genre appeals to the youth market that is central to the games industry.[2] Many constitutive aspects of the horror film genre inform horror games, primarily in the way they are marketed, their graphic and iconographic styles, their shock tactics, themes and storylines. Like many horror films, many horror-based videogames deploy very conventional and basic notions of good and evil.[3] In both *Undying* and *Resident Evil 3*, the avatar has to restore balance to a world corrupted by evil forces that threaten humanity and rationality. The aim of these games is to defeat the manifestation of such forces, and the games are structured to aid this quest. Both games deploy surface story lines and concomitant aesthetic strategies that reference the good-versus-evil format of many horror films; however, in the games this dualism is more deeply embedded in the infrastructure that shapes the dynamic nature of interactivity. This infrastructure works as a form of 'moral occult'.[4] As used by Peter Brooks, the term refers to the way a transcendent moral order is deployed and articulated in nineteenth-century melodrama, which, he proposes, is defined by the project of making an invisible moral order apparent at a surface level, an idea that can also be applied to many horror films.

Brooks' model is also useful in thinking about the ways *Undying* and *Resident Evil 3* structure their interactive gameplay. All horror-based videogames are resolutely dependent on a hidden 'occulted' or metaphysical dimension that shapes gameplay. This is determined by programming, and its ordering simulates a fixed manichean virtual duality: while players can interact with aspects of the surface dimension and the space of the game, they cannot interfere with the determining sub-strata of the game. (Unless, like Captain Kirk,[5] players are able to interfere with a game's programming.) Whatever players do in most horror-based games, they still have to occupy the position of an avatar of good, not evil. As a predetermined transcendent force, the moral occult is at work in the way these games channel the player through their labyrinths. As a player travels through the spaces of these games, s/he encounters aspects that can either restrict or promote agency. Examples of these include cut-scenes, physical barriers, such as locked doors or barred paths, or the way that helpful power-ups and weapons are littered through the game. The moral occult is also evident in other types of help offered to the player, such as clues as to where to go next, and in the series of rewards given for overcoming obstacles. Throughout the game the effects of a higher power are always in evidence. The element of pre-determination, which lies outside the player's sphere of agency, is therefore linked to the metaphysical dimension in which manicheanism operates. The concept of the moral occult plays a central role in my argument that horror-based videogames are strongly dependent on their capacity to allow players to experience a dynamic between states of *being in control* and *out of control*. The occulted moral structure of a game is linked to the types of pleasures offered. The operation of the game's infrastructure invokes for the player an experience of being subject to a pre-determined, extrinsic, and thereby, Othered force,[6] which is balanced against the promise of player autonomy offered by the game's interactive dimension.

The range and popularity of games based on horror suggests there are aesthetic and marketing advantages in the remediations of cinematic horror in interactive media. Existing horror-based videogames draw on a number of familiar pre-sold horror sub-genres. The *Resident Evil* cycle, *Nightmare Creatures* cycle, *Evil Dead: Hail to the King* (Heavylron/THQ, 2001), *The Typing of the Dead* (Sega/Empire, 2001) (an innovative use of the zombie genre to teach touch-typing: 'type or die', as the slogan goes), and *The House of the Dead* cycle (Sega, 1998, 1999, 2001) each draws heavily on Romero-influenced zombie movies. Vampire-based games are also common, such as *Dracula Resurrection*

(Canal/Multimedia/Dreamcatcher, 2000), *Legacy of Kain: Soul Reaver* (Crystal Dynamics/Eidos, 1999) and *Vampire: The Masquerade* (Nihilistic/Activision, 2000). *Phantasmagoria* (Sierra, 1995), *Silent Hill, Silent Hill 2* (Konami, 1999, 2001) and *Clive Barker's Undying* also employ aspects of the zombie theme, alongside more traditional gothic and Lovecraftian themes. These also have a strong connection to the 'old dark house' format, common in horror films since the 1920s, and enhance this by deploying extra, alternative dimensions within the space of a house or urban environment. The *Alien* games (Acclaim/Probe, 1996; Argonaut/Fox, 2000) use the monster-in-space theme, presold by the films. *The Mummy* (Universal Office/Konami, 2000) takes a slightly different take on the zombie theme, and that too is a direct movie tie-in game. *Tomb Raider: The Last Revelation* (Core/Eidos, 1999) draws on the spectacle of Ancient Egypt for its monsters (the flesh-eating beetles of the game appear in *The Mummy* — both the film and the game). Cyberspace-based gore-fests of shoot-'em-up carnage characterise *Doom 2* (id/GT Interactive, 1994), *Quake* (id, 1996), *Unreal Tournament* (Epic MegaGames & Digital Extremes/GT Interactive, 1999) and *Halo* (Bungie/Microsoft, 2002).

What impact does interactivity have on the rendering of horror genre tropes, strategies and formats? As the name implies, *Clive Barker's Undying* trades on the auteur principle, thereby leaning on a pre-sold brand that includes the *HellRaiser* films (1987–2001) and Barker's novels and comics. *Resident Evil 3*, as with the whole cycle, uses many elements from George Romero's *Living Dead* cycle (1968, 1978, 1985).[7] These two games have very different ways of handling interactivity, however, which impact on their structure and the kind of experience offered to the player. A comparison between the two provides a useful way of understanding how interactivity is used to solicit and manage horror. Both use different forms of restriction to create the type of suspense that underpins the genre and thereby accord with Eve Sedgwick's (1986) claim that gothic horror hinges on the metaphorical and literal trope of burial alive.

The first-person shooter mode of *Undying* affords the player the freedom to look around the 3D virtual space, providing a radical point of departure from the restrictive framing used in film to manage what the viewer sees. The environment of *Undying* is extremely detailed, encouraging the player to spend time taking in architectural details and exploring the vast house and grounds. This investigative mode is aided by the first-person mode and the scope of the 360-degree view that allows players to look where they wish. This freedom to look and explore in *Undying* marks a departure from the way horror films use editing and framing to create tension and claustrophobia. By contrast, the third-person shooter mode of *Resident Evil 3* is closer to film in this respect as the player's ability to look around is more heavily managed by its game engine. *Resident Evil 3* imposes different camera angles onto the perspective of the viewer, withholding visual information and creating a pronounced effect of enclosure. Like a film, *Resident Evil 3* structures space and the player's experience through editing and fixed framing, which is often used to create shock effects. The intrusive effect of pre-rendered camera angles within gameplay reminds the player that control is limited and that the gameplay is highly predetermined. As well as helping to shape the aesthetic experience of the game, this and other aspects of inevitability built into the programming infrastructure operate, like occulted fate, to ordain the path that must be taken.

Because *Undying* does not use editing and fixed framing, it has to use other tactics to contrive suspense and atmosphere. One way this is achieved is directly related to its expansive playing arena. As befits the gothic nature of the house, there are many dark corners and masked spaces that can harbour helpful power-ups and spells or monsters and other dangers. Because the game is in first-person mode, there is increased visual proximity to what lurks within such shadowy places, heightening the sense of contact. This closer proximity to danger builds disquietude and tension, and, because exploring such places is central to the game, it handles horror in a markedly more uncinematic way than *Resident Evil 3*. *Undying* makes direct use of the specific qualities offered by an open environment, actively encouraging an investigative approach. Interactivity, with its emphasis on *doing*, therefore has a significant impact on way the game constructs apprehension and its particular ambience. Further, it shapes the organisation of the story and the experience of gameplay, marking a qualitative difference from the way the horror film organises space. *Resident Evil 3* often allows the avatar the option to run from enemies, and thereby draws more strongly on slasher movie formats, whereas *Undying*, with its shifting environment and vertiginous abysses, renders space itself as threatening, thereby following in the footfalls of the gothic trend of using *mise-en-scène* to create brooding eeriness and make things not what they seem. Here the gameplay space becomes a direct articulation of the intrinsic and extrinsic occult forces at work in the game. Both games make use of horror-based occult themes, and these mirror the predetermined and restrictive occulted nature of the games' own deep structure: 'as above, so below', as the magical axiom goes.

Increased computer power has allowed the storytelling element of games to become more complex, leaving designers to find new ways to allow predetermined storylines to be integrated into gameplay. *Undying* has a convoluted story and, like many games, uses cut-scenes to help it unfold. The cut-scenes provide a significant formal connection with film form as they use cinematic conventions of editing, framing and camera movement to manage the spectator's view and emotional engagement with the text. Although cut-scenes are often referred to as 'cinematic', in many games no 'real' camera, or image *re*-production, is involved. Instead the cuts, the angles and camera movements are generated digitally, either pre-rendered or generated 'on the fly'. The effects of tilts, zooms and tracking shots are manufactured through the authoring software used to produce the games. Referencing cinematic conventions, these narratively loaded scenes are often less 'anchored' by the real environmental factors that influence the way that most live-action is filmed. Unlike most narrative films, the camera positioning used in interactive sequences is linked to the avatar, moving with it through the space of the game (seamlessly in first-person mode and rather less so in third-person modes). The flexibility of digitally produced camera movement in cut-scenes is often more markedly mobile than that found in non-animation-based cinema, permitting greater continuity between the generally rapid speed of movement during most aspects of gameplay and the cut-scene. Further, and this is important to my main argument, the cut-scene wrests control away from the player and reinforces the sense that a metaphysical 'authorial' force is at work, shaping the logic of the game.[8] This evocation of helplessness in the face of an inexorable predetermined force is crucial in maintaining horror-based suspense, in that the game world often operates outside the player's control. Without this sphere of pre-determination, the traditional pleasures of horror are denied us.

The pre-rendered nature of cut-scenes make them appear closer to cinema than other parts of a game, yet they have a very specific function in relation to gameplay and, importantly for this analysis, are part of the way a game creates a dynamic between being in control and being out of control. Within the architecture of a game, the inclusion of a cut-scene allows an important plot point to be marked out. Cut-scenes often function as a means of rewarding players for a mini-victory. They are also used to book-end games, setting up the backstory and framing the motivation of play. At the end of a game a cut-scene often underscores the resolution provided by the final battle. While the cut-scene, alongside other aspects of a game's inherent moral occult, is beyond player control, there are, of course, various ways in which in-game events are determined by the player's actions. *Resident Evil* 3 (like *Silent Hill*) offers points at which the player decides how to proceed. In *Resident Evil 3*, the choices made along the way determine the ending of the game. At these nodal points, *Resident Evil 3* stops the action and presents a list of written options. *Silent Hill* and its sequel integrate choice through action, more effectively structuring it into the real-time flow of the gameplay. In both cases, the storyline offers a variety of potential routes, something not available in conventional film. *Undying* does not deploy multiple endings: the final showdown is presented in traditional linear fashion, culminating, after the death of a 'boss' (the most powerful enemy on a level), in a pre-rendered scene. Smaller decisions and actions help to shape the way the game is experienced, however.

Some cut-scenes have a more direct relationship with gameplay than the telling of the story or the movement of players from one domain to another. They play a key role in confirming the presence of a dimension of the game that is beyond a player's agency. Near the start of *Undying*, for example, a cut-scene intrudes on the action as the player walks down a corridor. This is likely to take the player by surprise because it is not linked to a conversation or to the end of a mini-quest, as is more usual in this and other games. An edit places the camera back down the end of the corridor, which then tracks swiftly towards the avatar, accompanied by the sounds of slamming doors and a supernatural wind. This happens whatever the player does, underscoring the player's sense of the existence of an unseen force – in this case, hostile – at work in the matrix of the game. At the end of the scene the player is trapped at the end of a corridor and cannot escape, unless s/he has gained a particular spell in advance. Here the discontinuity between being in control and out of control, produced by the move in and out of the cut-scene, works to suspenseful effect because it is rapid, unexpected and integral to the gameplay.

211

Figure 16 First-person framing in *Clive Barker's Undying* (ELEA/EA, 2001)

In *Undying* the juxtaposition of the first-person framing of gameplay and that of the cut-scene heightens and assigns the difference that lies between the sphere of agency and the sphere of pre-determination. The camera movement and the first-person framing used in the cut-scene described above, as distinct from the first-person framing anchored to the avatar in the majority of the game, becomes synonymous with the occulted, Othered power lurking in the house and in the infrastructure of the game: the player can do nothing but helplessly watch events unfold. This intrusive strategy accords with the style of horror films that deploy an anthropomorphised, moving camera as representative of a demonic or supernatural threatening force: as with the use of a slightly sea-sick I-cam in many of David Lynch's films, or as used in *The Shining* (1980), *Halloween* (1978) and *Evil Dead II* (1987).[9] In *Undying*, the cut-scenes that use fast tracking I-cam shots operate in contrast to the fairly sedate walking pace at which the player travels through the house, creating a rhythmic differential dynamic that works at a number of levels. This particular use of the cut-scene is one of many strategies used in horror games to warn players that they must be ready to deal with a threatening situation, creating suspense, expectation and refreshing levels of alertness. It further demonstrates the way the games establish a dynamic between self-determination and a manichean-structured pre-determination.

Both *Undying* and *Resident Evil 3* use written sources, such as letters, journals, faxes and books, planted throughout the games to provide clues and forward the storyline. In *Resident Evil 3*, these are quite short and take little time to read, but in the more overtly gothic-based *Undying*, letters and journals are often quite long and involved. They can be re-read at any time, providing clues as to where to go next and playing a chief role in the construction of storyline. The deployment of written texts helps to broaden and consolidate the interactive experience as one significantly different from the way information is imparted in a film. It also allows the games to draw on the potential of written material to fire the imagination and spark personal terrors. The strategic placement of such texts is a further indication that a higher power is at work, which, by aiding the player's quest to defeat evil, is an articulation of a good and helpful embedded force.

Playing even more profoundly on the multimedia capacity of videogames, *Undying* plants clues in the paintings that adorn the walls of the house. One of these can be viewed using a supernatural device to reveal the family portrait in two modes: before and after the infestation of evil. The characters turn from merely a rather odd-looking bunch into a group of supernatural monsters.[10] The central figure is supposed to be good and in need of our avatar's help, but the painting reveals that he is situated at the centre of the monstrous family, and prophesises the nature of the character's eventual demise. This device accords with the manichean structure of the game's moral occult and is a crucial plot point that might be missed if the player does not take time to examine the painting. The painting also underpins the game's adherence to the gothic principle that 'nothing is what it seems'.

The occulted dimension of the painting is also reflected in the game-space itself, in which various radically altered dimensions are harboured (a device that also occurs in other games that reference horror: *Silent Hill*, *Silent Hill 2* and *Legacy of Kain: Soul Reaver*, as well as in the drug-induced scenes in *Max Payne* (Remedy/GodGames, 2001)). In *Undying* the alternative realities are the surface manifestation of the intrusion of evil; they have to be negotiated and overcome if the status quo, rendered as a source of base normality, is to be restored. At one point in the game, however, if a certain doorway is entered, the player is sucked into one of these alternative dimensions in which death is inevitable. Due to its spectacular form, it is a very pleasurable death, however, denied to the player who does not dare to enter.

The presence of altered realities in *Undying* helps to sustain visual and narrative interest and may help to compensate for the absence of what in cinema would be supplied through the use of cross-cutting, a key device used to create tension and signal threat. Sound also plays a crucial role in both media to invoke the emotional impact of horror, and is often linked to the operation of the moral occult. Many videogames deploy sound as a key sign of impending danger, designed to agitate a tingling sense in anticipation of the need to act. The effect can be produced through changes in the type of music being played or through sounds that have their sources directly in the space of the game. These aural cues, present in both *Undying* and *Resident Evil 3*, help to create an increased level of expectation and play a significant role in the creation of atmosphere as well as in emotional and structural dynamics of the games.

Although games may give the player the freedom to look, first-person framing in gamplay is, nonetheless, in cinematic terms, 'restricted'. Often the point-of-

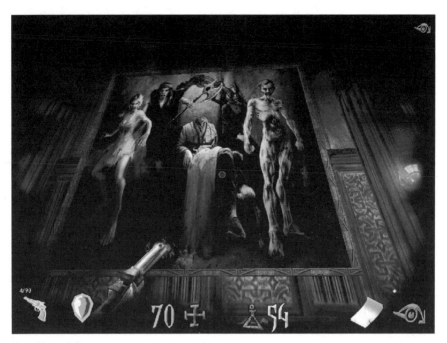

Figure 18 ... and after

view shot in the horror film is synonymous with that of the killer or monster. This is a useful strategy as it keeps the identity of the monster under wraps, as well as setting up complex relationships between the viewer and a monster (see Neale 1984). The first-person strategy in *Undying* is deployed in a very different way from the use of I-cam in the horror film. Unlike its film equivalent, the first-person strategy is not used to create an uncomfortable complicity with the film's monster; instead it facilitates a more benign connection between player and the heroic avatar, working to place both on the side of good, a coincidence of perspectives that is consolidated by the game's first-person mode. Because of this, the game is, in many ways, less complex in terms of the gaze – and its politics – than in many horror films that use a range of enunciative viewpoints (wherein the viewer is marshalled into different and, sometimes, conflicting perspectives and identifications). In *Resident Evil 3*, the connection between player and avatar is diminished by use of a third-person perspective and the game's heavily managed, shifting and pre-rendered framing. Yet even here there is a less complex pattern of viewpoints than commonly found in film, precisely because the shots are oriented around the avatar.

The net difference in effect due to the third- and first-person strategy is apparent in the two games. The third-person strategy tends to distance the player from close contact with the horror. When attacked in *Resident Evil 3*, the player is often not able to effect any actions and can only watch impotently as Nemesis, the arch villain of the game, swings the helpless avatar over his head. By contrast, in *Undying*, the particular form of restriction provided by the

214

first-person mode heightens the illusion that it is the player, sitting in front of the screen, who is being attacked, rather than a virtual abstracted self. When a monster makes a direct hit on the avatar, for example, the framing becomes shaky and the player's aim becomes unstable — the player's visual field and ability to act are directly affected by the blows. The impact of attack in *Resident Evil 3* is rather different. The PlayStation's 'dual-shock' handset registers the effects of the attack through felt vibration administered to the player's hands, but because the avatar's and the player's view points are not correlated there is an odd disjunction between sensation and what is seen; although the player experiences the rumble of the handset, the player sees the avatar as visually distinct from him/herself, like any other character in the game space. The jarring effect of this discontinuity actively encourages the player to become more accomplished in the use of controls, so as to better dodge attacks and be less troubled by the intrusive effects of 'end of life' cut-scenes (albeit that cut-scenes also provide a visual reward in other parts of the game). The reward for increased skill in battle is greater visual continuity therefore enabling an experience of more cinema-like gameplay. The dynamic in play is towards greater control of the game environment, yet control is nonetheless localised and is always qualified by the game's broader infrastructure. Film, however, offers no equivalent. It is unable to exploit the potential of interactive devices to intensify an awareness of the dynamic between *being in control* and *out of control*, and this aspect is key

Figure 19 Third-person perspective in *Resident Evil 3: Nemesis* (Capcom/Eidos, 1999)

to the specific types of suspense and emotion-based pleasures offered by horror games.

The horror film derives much of its power to thrill from the fact that the viewer cannot intervene in the trajectory of events. While viewers might feel an impulse to help beleaguered characters in a horror film, they can never do this directly. The horror film viewer might offer cries of warning to the hapless teenagers who ignore all diegetic warnings and persist in entering into the spook house. The formula is well rehearsed, soliciting groans and verbal advice, yet the pleasure entailed in this process is founded on awareness of the inevitability of the events that will unfold. Characters and action ultimately remain isolated from the sphere of the viewer, regardless of the extent to which he or she might 'identify' with them. When watching a horror film, viewers are always subjected to the flow of events (unless they decide to turn away or cover their eyes — a familiar reaction of some viewers to moments of heightened horror or suspense). In this sense, I concur with Steven Shaviro's argument that horror film suspense trades on a masochistic economy of delicious passivity, visceral affect and expectation (1993: 55). The viewer's experience of a restrictive inability to act on situations is often underlined in the horror film at a thematic level. Zombification, various types of possession and bodily invasion are typical horror film scenarios that represent a loss of autonomy and self-determination (see Krzywinska 2000 for a discussion of these aspects of the horror film). Theme reflects reception here, the viewer — like the beset characters on screen — is also helpless, unable to alter the trajectory of on-screen action. Yet films are less able than games to build into their deep structure a concrete experience of being in control and out of control of on-screen events. None of this means that the film viewer is entirely 'passive' in the reception of the film, however (a rhetorical trap that some games critics tend to fall into). Viewers constantly engage, rationally and irrationally, with the material presented on screen; as Bruce Kawin puts it: 'we interact with the signs in the generation of meaning and ... our attention is selective' (1984: 4). The horror film often plays more overtly with the viewer's inability to affect the action, however, which is the key to some of its pleasures. What, though, of the horror videogame? Does the interactive dimension and the resulting ability of the player to control the action prevent horror games from replicating the terrors and ecstasies of losing control?

It is my contention that the interactive dimension of horror games enables a *more* acute experience of losing control than that achieved by most horror films. This is achieved partly because, at times, the player does have a sense of self-determination; when this is lost the sense of pre-determination is enhanced by the relative difference. As I have shown, game events are often taken out of the player's hands; a stratagem that allows access to pleasures closer to those of the horror film. Control and autonomous action, which are always qualified, does not mean the player is simply in a position of mastery, however. The repeated actions, continual 'dying', the intrusions of the sound field, the cause-and-effect structure, the operations of the 'authored' structure, and the cut-scenes, each work to offer the player a sense that they are being acted upon by the game's deep structure. As with the horror film, it is sharply apparent that the game's virtual world is a closed system: the authored aspect of narration governs the fabric of game and film, channelling the way we negotiate and experience it. As Andrew Darley notes, and I build on this to underpin my argument about the moral occult, there are points in a game at which its pre-programmed nature means that the 'element of control and choice ... is revealed as illusory' (2000: 157). I do not see these moments as 'formulaic' game flaws, as he does. Instead these moments actively work to produce the crucial sense of *being out of control* that is inherent to the experience of horror. Although this is handled in a different and deeper manner to that of the horror film, there is a sense that the virtual world, and its structuring moral occult, is beyond a player's control (even if the player resorts to cheats and walkthroughs, unless the cheat allows a player to defy the game's boundaries in which case the sense of immersion is lost).

There are some significant differences borne of interactivity, however. Games are organised around the traversal of space, to which narrative is often secondary. In a film, narrative is primary and always drives the organisation of space. This distinction provides a further important difference between the two media in terms of the way that 'looking' is treated. Unlike that of the horror film, the operation of the moral occult in videogames is rarely oriented around the punishment of curiosity.[11] As games are deeply dependent on the traversal of space, visual investigation becomes central to the trajectory of a game as well as to the way the story unfolds. Many horror films also deploy an investigative strategy put to the service of narrative, yet it is at one remove from the viewer, and is far more directed than in games, which rarely deploy ellipses to eliminate 'dead' time. In some respects the more open economics of looking in games unravels the predetermined, ideological systems codified in looking patterns in the horror film. Most games, and *Undying* specifically, depend on a player searching areas to find clues, power-ups and other equipment that open the way to the next level. As the game guide to *Evil Dead: Hail to the King* warns, 'Don't be afraid to look around and check out the area. Otherwise, you might miss something important'. In games, therefore, space is something to be actively, physically, investigated if the player is to beat the game. Characters in 'old dark house' type of horror films often performed a similar routine, yet the difference is that in games the player is encouraged to assert an active, rather than passive, mode of looking, that may endanger them but without which progression through the game cannot be achieved.

Through the juxtaposition of being in and out of control, horror-based videogames facilitate the visceral and oscillating pleasures/unpleasures of anxiety and expectation. The interactive dimension heightens this, implicating the player in his or her fate. Failure to progress in games necessitates repetition (being 'stuck', with all its wider mythic and therapeutic meanings). What is 'punished' in videogames is not so much curiosity, as in the horror film, but the failure to make it into the next scene. Through the active mode of investigation facilitated by interactivity, the player may place his/her avatar in peril, yet the trade-off is access to new thrills and the promise of continued gameplay. These are withheld if a player does not pursue active investigation. If a player fails to get through a set task, or fails to explore effectively, the narrative itself is withheld (no story before bedtime), a dimension that is conventionally not available in film. Darley usefully comments on this exploratory aspect of games by suggesting that 'once a game is under way the player is compelled continually and immediately to respond' (2000: 156). Horror-based games are designed to compel the player to investigate and overcome dangerous encounters if they are to uncover the game story and fully 'colonise' the space of the game. While the investigatory mode might appear to be self-determined, it demands a ritualised, mechanical response to events. The moral occult of a game's internal structure pulls the player towards its goal of defeating evil. Along the way, it solicits contradictory desires for intensity, prolonged tension, anxiety, compulsion and resolution. The creation of such an emotionally discrepant scenario fits quite neatly into Julia Kristeva's view that the experience of horror is bound into 'a vortex of summons and repulsion' (1982: 1). In psychoanalytic terms, these contradictory impulses work with the tensions created between the pleasure and reality principles, as well as with the competing drives to life (Eros) and death (Thanatos). Whether we buy into a psychoanalytic reading or not, it is still the case that, at a cognitive level, a number of contradictory psychological processes are likely to be involved. The deployment of extrinsic, Othered forces (akin to Lacan's notion of the 'Big Other') that impinge on the player's freedom to act are rendered within horror's remit to provoke and intensify feelings of powerlessness; offering an important media-specific modulation of the generic paradigm provided by the horror film and affirming the value of looking at horror from a games perspective.

The horror game worlds of both *Undying* and *Resident Evil 3* are enticingly strange and threateningly intrusive. The pleasure of horror, in a general sense, is that it seduces through the arousal of anxiety, yet this is combined with the containment of that anxiety provided by a pre-determined form. In games this safety-net is provided by the forces of 'good', with which the player is aligned, that ensure that evil can, potentially, be defeated. At times play is experienced as fluid, smooth and continuous (the force is with you). This is 'good' interaction, a player's movements perfectly co-ordinate with the demands of the game. At other times frustration and stasis prevail, yet the player nonetheless knows that a way out is always provided. Despite the fact that games are coded as representation, and that they are structured in such a way that good will eventually triumph, the mode of playing has some interesting links to dreamlike, betwixt-and-between states of consciousness. The experience of game playing is often rather like the nightmare scenario of moving yet not moving. Such a contradictory state provides a good analogy for the way games operate: they oscillate between movement and stasis, achievement and non-achievement, self-determination and pre-determination. The dynamic between being in control and then out of control is crucial to the production of the experience of such paradoxical states (which are, ultimately, bound into a paradigm of good versus evil), and they can be linked, in a qualified way, to the experience of the liminal.

The horror genre has a special link with the liminal, through its references to dreams, borders, the unconscious and irrationality. I would argue that games create a direct experience of the liminal, more so than commonly provided by film, precisely because of the contradictory modes encountered during gameplay. Yet while various ambiguities of emotion and category might be experienced, *Undying* and *Resident Evil 3* do consolidate fixed notions of good and evil as discrete transcendent categories. In other words, a moral safety valve is built into the infrastructure of the games that provides narrative structure as well as sanctioning shoot-'em-up mayhem. Ambiguity is also present through the player's interaction with a virtual yet 'realistic' (non)world. This has an impact on the organisation of death in the games. The player dies, yet does not die, which is certainly ambiguous and akin to the liminal, but this too operates within the terms of the manichean structure of the games. Avatars do not die in a decisive sense, because they are in the service of good. Enemies, however, stay dead when properly killed. This difference in death-types links the way the games express a transcendent moral order at both surface and deep levels. Such a dynamic allows death to be pleasurable because the real finality of death is disavowed and it also defends against the lack of an immanent and consummate moral order. Within these games, you have killed and yet not killed, been killed and not, an experience that is ostensibly liminal, yet contained and managed by the dualistic moral order built into the games.

As with certain horror films, some games construct a more relativistic version of traditional moral dualisms (for example *Legacy of Kain: Soul Reaver* and *Vampire: The Masquerade* both are vampire-based games which draw on a sympathy for the vampire that is markedly present in Anne Rice's vampire novels). In such games, the player is not aligned directly with good and the moral status of the avatar is made more complex. Very few games assign moral judgement to the player, with one recent exception: *Black and White* (Lionhead/EA, 2001). As its name suggests, *Black and White* calls on the player to make moral choices. He or she can choose to be an evil punishing god, able to dish out arbitrary violence to the inhabitants of an island, or a benign god. The villagers worship the player either way, as the accompanying game-guide says:

> Remember, you are a god. No one sits in judgement on you. You can do whatever you like. When you enter the world, the ideas of good and evil have not formed. Of course, your actions affect the world helping to define the concepts of good and evil. If you are harsh, brutal and quick to punish, your people will live in fear and, although they will worship you, they will do so out of duty and terror. ... If you are kind and benevolent People will see you as a good, wise god and will worship you with love and thankfulness. However, it is not always wise to be seen as universally soft and helpful. Sometimes raining down righteous fury upon a village is necessary for stamping your authority on unbelievers. (11)

'Faith' points reward actions such as throwing villagers about and sacrificing people at the player's temple. Because the game allows the player to *decide* to become evil, the game departs to an extent from the pre-determined moral positions of most games and horror films. And, unlike most other horror games, interactivity is more fully turned towards soliciting a player's moral engagement. The game is non-generic, yet it does offer the capacity for the player to turn it towards horror; in such cases, however, it is the player, or their creature, that is the agent of evil and chaos. A manichean structure is still in evidence, of course, in the initial decision of whether to play in the role of good or evil.

Potentially, interactivity presents a problem to horror genre dynamics, which often rely on managing what the viewer sees and when he or she sees it. As Poole states: 'For a game to surprise and move the player with its story line, it must necessarily still keep certain plot developments out of the player's control' (2000: 121). Full interactivity would negate the authorial shaping of interaction and, with it, the possibility for a directed storyline, which is crucial to the development of the horror experience in film. It is for this reason that videogames mix interactivity with predetermined boundaries and intrusive interventions that channel the player's engagement with the game. The pleasure/suspense dynamics of horror-based games are, as I have shown, very much dependent on this combination. Both *Undying* and *Resident Evil 3* allow the player to act on events, but only in a manner determined by the game's internal structure. Both games create scenarios in which the erotic economics of masochism can be experienced: the on/off dynamics of interactivity create and heighten this. As such it seems mistaken to call games 'promethean' (Poole 2000: 217): there is no transgression of higher powers; players remain, by and large, dependent on the tips bestowed. At times during gameplay a player is dutifully, sublimely, in their service, and the pay-off is, precisely, the experiential gain of suspense and tension. Yet this is always balanced against the sphere of interaction that promises self-directed agency.

The manichean structure provided by the moral occult built into these games, does, however, work to render these experiences within the context of a 'safe' metaphysical order, in which good, in tandem with perseverance and the 'work' ethic, wins out in the end. Horror games, therefore, do have a strong, conventional, moral ethical framework. Henry Jenkins has suggested that academics need to help games developers build moral structure into games. The argument of this chapter is that most horror games already have a very conventional moral structure, and the manichean organisation of content is reinforced by the games industry's method of regulation, illustrated by *Carmeggedon*'s (Interplay, 1997) run in with the censors. The British Board of Film Classification refused a certificate for the game in its original version because it is based on the player running down pedestrians to gain points. An amended version of the game turned pedestrians into zombies, who threatened the safety of the normal order. The act of running them down, therefore, was translated into a morally acceptable 'save the world' scenario, using horror genre conventions as 'modality markers' to locate the game as fantasy. This is indicative of the way that a conventionalised manichean framework often works to sanction horror themes in general, and by bracketing gameplay with such a blatantly simple moral message that they may bear very little relation to the moral complexities faced in everyday life.

Accordingly, we might question whether such moral frameworks are of importance to players. The good-versus-evil scenario is so ubiquitous and familiar in games and other forms of popular culture that it seems unlikely to have a great deal of impact on the experience of gameplay. Particularly in first- and third-person shooters, the manichean frame functions as a pretext, an excuse, for despatching enemies without guilt or considered thought, rather than involving players in a deep consideration of the morality of their actions. The moral framework regularly becomes secondary to the primary goal of progression through the game. There are games that do play on this, nonetheless, and there might be moments that cause the player to reflect on their actions. While playing *Max Payne*, for example, I was reluctant to shoot a woman in one scene. There had been no women enemies up to that point, and her presence forced me to consider my automatic fire response. As it turned out she shot me, so my hesitation was, in effect, punished by the game, yet it seems likely that this was a strategy deliberately deployed by the game designers based on a player's probable response. In *Half-Life* (Valve/Sierra, 2001), killing employees of the Black Mesa research centre means that a player is 'fired' by their employer and thrown out of the game. In certain other games, a player is disadvantaged if they kill those who have information needed to forward the game. A more active engagement with morality is present in real-time strategy games and Role Playing Games, such as *Baldur's Gate* (Bioware/Interplay, 1998), *Emperor: Battle for Dune* (Westwood/EA, 2001) and *Black and White*, as mentioned above, in each of which the player must make a conscious decision to be either good or evil.

Unlike their film counterparts, and in spite of their often simplified moral framework, horror-based videogames create a complex interaction between bounded choice and determinism that reflects, to an extent, the way in which individuals interact with the social order. Within the safe context of the fantasy arena of videogames, which are modally marked as 'fantasy' rather than reality through their production values and generic intertexts, the determinism of the game accrues for the player a direct and heightened experience of being acted upon. Games are carefully designed and authored to take us to emotional places that would perhaps be avoided if true interactivity were available. The manichean-based safety net actively allows the games to invoke 'dangerous' and liminal experiences. Horror games interface with the way in which technology is often imagined as demonic and Othered, the player is offered the challenge to defeat the technologically-based demon (aided by the 'good' elements of the technology): which, if achieved, can offer a pleasurable sense that the technology has been mastered. The contract drawn up between hands-on interaction and hands-off pre-determinism works, therefore, in part with the emotional and erotic economics of masochism as much as with the drive to act, colonise, and take charge. The switching between the two intensifies the experience of being both in control and out of control, a strategy that is not fully available to the horror film. This is because such switching is grounded in the unique and dynamic interactive nature of gaming media.

I would like to thank Sue Morris, Geoff King, Will Brooker, Harmony Wu and the editors of *Spectator* for their insightful comments on this essay. A version of the essay appears in *Axes to Grind: Re-Imagining the Horrific in Visual Media and Culture*, special issue of *Spectator*, 22, 2, spring 2003, 12–23.

notes

1 The term refers to a model of the universe formulated by a third to fifth-century sect, the Manichees, for whom the cosmos is a site of an endless dualistic battle between good and evil. Many popular texts are structured around a battle between good and evil, good usually winning out in the end (see Krzywinska 2000). The way in which good and evil is defined in a given text is, of course, subject to dominant, and often fundamental, ideological values.

2 The horror genre has played an important role in targeting videogames to young adults (most games fall into the 15 rating bracket). The genre also has an established and very active body of fans, which makes them an ideal grouping for videogames marketing.

3 *Silent Hill 2* (Konami, 2001) is an example of a horror-based game that, in drawing from psychological based horror, makes an attempt to disrupt the conventional good/evil paradigm. This is achieved by building questions about the 'good' status of the avatar.

4 The term was first used by Peter Brooks to describe the way in which melodramas often work to literalise and make visible in a text an ideologically constructed metaphysical order of universe, which is mainly organised in terms of manicheanism: good versus evil. As Brooks puts it 'Balzac and James need melodrama because the deep subject, the locus of their true drama, has come to be what we have called the 'moral occult': the domain of spiritual forces and imperatives that is not clearly visible within reality, but which they believe to be operative there, and which demands to be uncovered, registered, articulated' (Brooks 1995: 20–1).

5 *Star Trek's* Captain Kirk once tampered with the programming of a 'no-win' training simulation, thereby beating an unbeatable scenario.

6 I use the term in a Lacanian sense here. The Other (*L'Autre*) describes the way in which language and other social, extrinsic factors can be experienced as beyond the control of an individual.

7 George Romero was slated to direct the *Resident Evil* film, but pulled out during production.

8 The term is used in a programming context, which is, necessarily, a collective activity.

9 The use of I-cam in the horror film has been explored in terms of suspense, mastery, sadism and masochism by critics such as Steve Neale (1984).

10 One character, Ambrose, is most certainly modelled on author/singer/songwriter Nick Cave, whose work is deeply dependent on Old Testament-style manicheanism. Ambrose is voiced by Clive Barker.

11 For example, Bruce Kawin states that the horror film 'emphasises the dread of knowing, the danger of curiosity' (1984: 8). A very literal rendition of this appears in *Opera* (1988), where the eye is literally and graphically punished.

citations

Aarseth, Espen (1997) *Cybertext: Perspectives on Ergodic Literature.* Baltimore: John Hopkins University Press.

Brooks, Peter (1995) *The Melodramatic Imagination: Balzac, Henry James, Melodrama and the Mode of Excess.* New Haven and London: Yale University Press.

Darley, Andrew (2000) *Visual Digital Culture: Surface Play and Spectacle in New Media Genres.* London and New York: Routledge.

Jenkins, Henry (2001) 'Games as Object of Study', unpublished paper presented at *Games Cultures* conference, Bristol, 29 June.

Kawin, Bruce (1984) 'The Mummy's Pool', in Barry Keith Grant (ed.) *Planks of Reason: Essays on the Horror Film.* Metuchen and London: The Scarecrow Press, 3–20.

Kristeva, Julia (1982) *The Powers of Horror.* Trans. Leon S Roudiez. New York and Oxford: Columbia University Press.

Krzywinska, Tanya (2000) *A Skin For Dancing In: Possession, Witchcraft and Voodoo in Film.* Trowbridge: Flicks Books.

___ (2002) 'Hubble Bubble, Herbs and Grimoires: Magic and Witchcraft in "Buffy the Vampire Slayer"', in David Lavery & Rhonda Wilcox (eds) *Fighting the Forces: Essays on the Meanings of Buffy the Vampire Slayer.* Lanham, Boulder, New York and London: Rowman & Littlefield.

Neale, Steve (1984) '*Halloween*: Suspense, Aggression and the Look', in Barry Keith Grant (ed.) *Planks of Reason: Essays on the Horror Film.* Metuchen, New Jersey and London: Scarecrow Press.

Poole, Steven (2000) *Trigger Happy: The Inner Life of Videogames.* London: Fourth Estate.

Sedgwick, Eve Kosofsky (1986) *The Coherence of Gothic Conventions.* London: Methuen.

Shaviro, Steven (1993) *The Cinematic Body.* Minneapolis and London: University of Minnesota.

Index